Ethnic Americans

Ethnic Americans

A History of Immigration

FOURTH EDITION

Leonard Dinnerstein and David M. Reimers

Columbia University Press   New York

Columbia University Press

Publishers Since 1893

New York   Chichester, West Sussex

Library of Congress Cataloging-in-Publication Data

Dinnerstein, Leonard.

   Ethnic Americans : a history of immigration / Leonard Dinnerstein
and David M. Reimers. — 4th ed.

     p. cm.

   Includes bibliographical references and index.

   ISBN 0–231–11188–6 (cloth). — ISBN 0–231–11189–4 (pbk).

   1. United States—Ethnic relations. 2. Ethnology—United States. 3. United States—
Emigration and immigration. 4. Americanization. 5. Immigrants—United States—
History.   I. Reimers, David M.   II. Title.

E184.A1D48   1999

305.8′00973—DC21   98–42643

Printed in the United States of America

c 10 9 8 7 6 5 4 3 2 1

p 10 9 8 7 6 5 4 3 2

TO

Rita and Levon Kabasakalian

AND

Jack and Dorothy Reimers

Contents

List of Abbreviations

ADL	Anti-Defamation League (B'nai B'rith)
AFL	American Federation of Labor
AHEPA	American Hellenic Educational Progressive Association
AICF	American Immigration Control Foundation
APA	American Protective Association
Balance	Population-Environment Balance
CAPS	Californians for Population Stabilization
CCN	Carrying Capacity Network
DP	Displaced Persons
FAIR	Federation for American Immigration Reform
FBI	Federal Bureau of Investigation
GAPA	Greek American Progressive Association
ILGWU	International Ladies' Garment Workers' Union
INS	Immigration and Naturalization Service
IRCA	Immigration Reform and Control Act
MAYO	Mexican American Youth Organization

Preface

THE ORIGINAL IMPETUS for writing this book was Americans' heightened concern with, and glorification of, ethnicity and ethnic values at the end of the 1960s and early 1970s. Both of us were brought up in the 1930s and 1940s, when one learned that becoming a "good American" meant shedding foreign ties, culture, and religion, and adapting to what now might be called the values and beliefs of white, Anglo-Saxon, Protestant America. By the 1970s, however, ethnicity had become chic. People wore buttons announcing that they were proud to be Polish or Italian; reporters wrote favorably on the virtues and values of ethnic working-class neighborhoods in cities like Baltimore and Pittsburgh; and people of a variety of backgrounds, instead of Anglicizing their names, "ethnicized" them. In such a context we prepared the first edition, confident that Americans were showing renewed interest in the experiences of their immigrant forebears.

Since that time the peoples of European ancestry have mixed with one another in a manner that their grandparents did not dream of, and much of the assertion of ethnicity of the 1970s has proved to be superficial. Yet the interest in immigration is stronger, and scholars of immigration and social history have published a remarkable number of books and articles exploring the nation's immigrant past. The new scholarship has greatly enhanced our understanding of several peoples, and particularly of the women of those cultures. We now know so much more than we did only a few years ago of the Huguenots and Scots of colonial America, of the Irish and Germans throughout the nineteenth and twentieth centuries, of Italians and Jews in a wider variety of American cities and of their unique experiences. There are also a plethora of works on Hispanics and Asians, written by members of those groups, that simply did not exist twenty-five years ago. As a result of this explosion of knowledge, we have attempted to revise this volume, incorporating as much of the recent scholarship as possible while adjusting and enhancing earlier interpretations.

As in the earlier editions, we have focused on those non-English people who came voluntarily to the New World after 1607. By limiting the topic in this fashion we have obviously excluded American Indians and African slaves. Their history is in many respects unique and requires separate treatment. In *Ethnic Americans* we have, of course, discussed blacks who came to the United States voluntarily from Africa and the West Indies. Indeed, more black immigrants have come to the United States in the last fifty years than in the entire period of slavery.

Two years after the publication of the third edition of *Ethnic Americans* in 1988, Congress passed a law that increased yearly immigration allowances by 35 percent; in 1996 Congress made other significant changes. We have incorporated the impact of the provisions of those laws in this text. When the third edition was being written in the middle 1980s, new trends in the history of immigration were becoming visible, and these trends have continued. The last ten years have witnessed the greatest wave of immigration in American history, and it appears that immigration will remain high for at least the foreseeable future. An overwhelming majority, probably 85 to 90 percent, of newcomers hail from Latin America and Asia rather than from Europe. In 1960 the leading country of origin for immigrants in this country was Germany, with nearly one million Germans in the United States. Next was Canada, followed by Poland and the Soviet Union. In 1996 Mexico, the Philippines, China, Cuba, India, and Vietnam headed the list. Just at a time when older European groups have been undergoing rapid change, and in some cases virtually disappearing as separate cultures, whole new ethnic communities have emerged. In the 1990s, final totals for immigration will probably exceed ten million people, more than the sum in any previous ten-year period in American history. Because this volume stresses the twentieth century, we have taken these trends into account.

We offer this fourth edition in the hope that it continues to be not only a brief summary of the immigrant experience but also a reflection of the most recent scholarship and public policies. We want to thank Pat Doherty and Julie Newman for preparing the manuscript.

Leonard Dinnerstein
David M. Reimers

Ethnic Americans

Chapter 1

The Colonial Heritage

NEVER BEFORE—and in no other country—have as many varied ethnic groups congregated and amalgamated as they have in the United States. The original seventeenth-century settlers were overwhelmingly English, and it was they who set the tone for American culture. In spite of its English Protestant orientation, the New World was also characterized by ethnic diversity. After the 1680s millions of others, including Scots-Irish, Germans, Irish, Scots, French, Dutch, Italians, Russians, Poles, Scandinavians, Greeks, Chinese, Japanese, Africans, and Latin Americans, eventually emigrated to America. Today most Americans are unable to trace any pure lineage. How many among us can say that we are 100 percent French or Dutch or English or German or any of the other strains that built America?

The English were the first Europeans to colonize successfully in the New World. The Dutch, French, and Spanish claimed large empires of land and established settlements earlier, but they were unable to induce significant numbers of their countrymen to leave their homes. On the other hand, the British, zealous in their pursuit of gold and silver, recognized that productive inhabitants increased the wealth of the nation. Even after the restoration of Charles II in 1660, when the English for a time were discouraged from leaving home, England established policies to encourage others to settle in her colonies. Whereas the French and Spanish ruled their overseas domains closely from Paris and Madrid, respectively, and expected colonists to adhere to the Roman Catholic faith, England rarely interfered with the American settlements, except for the regulation of trade. The English colonists, almost always short of labor and desirous of populating the wilderness as a buffer zone against the Indians, French, and Spaniards, shared the mother country's enthusiasm for immigrants. As a result of such attitudes and policies, the greatest population movement in history began. Eventually, over 40 million people left Europe in search of the reputed golden opportunities in the New World.

During the colonial period, the vast majority of immigrants was European Protestants, who eventually blended in with other newcomers. Between 1680 and 1760 dramatic growth occurred in the British mainland colonies as the population soared from approximately 250,000 to over 2 million. Chief among these newcomers were 250,000 Scots-Irish (Presbyterian Scots who settled in Ulster County, Ireland, early in the seventeenth century and whose descendants started emigration to the American colonies in the eighteenth century); over 125,000 Germans were the second most significant European minority. About 2,000 Huguenots (Protestants who were evicted from France after the revocation of the Edict of Nantes in 1685 withdrew their privileges of worship there) made a much greater impact than their number might suggest in places like Boston, New York, and South Carolina. Untold numbers of Scots, Dutch, and Swedes rounded out the European population of the colonies. Here and there were small enclaves of Roman Catholics and—in the port cities of Savannah, Charleston, Philadelphia, New York, and Newport—scatterings of Jews.

Despite the generally tolerant attitude of the English government toward the newcomers, the English colonists, who were the dominant group in each area, were not always as gracious as officials in the mother country. Though they too had come for economic opportunity and freedom to worship God as they thought appropriate, they made no pretense of being tolerant of anyone who differed significantly from themselves. Hence the arrival of the Scots-Irish (whom colonists referred to as the "Irish"), the Germans, and others aroused opposition. Americans of every generation have been frightened that newcomers would subvert established customs and undermine the traditions of society, and the dominant group in colonial America was no exception. In 1698 South Carolina passed a law giving bounties to newcomers but exempting the Scots-Irish and Roman Catholics. At about the same time, Maryland temporarily suspended the importation of Scots-Irish servants, and Virginia prohibited the sale of more than 20 of them on any one river. In 1729 Pennsylvania placed a 20-shilling duty, to be paid by the colonist to whom the servant was indentured, on each imported servant. "The common fear," one Pennsylvania official said at the time, "is that if they [the Scots-Irish] thus continue to come they will make themselves proprietors of the Province."

Similar concerns have been repeated generation after generation—only instead of the Scots-Irish being the "villains," groups of Americans at different times and in various regions have substituted Italians, Chinese, Jews, African Americans, Poles, Puerto Ricans, Irish, Mexicans, and other ethnics. The paradox, which began in colonial America, is this: whereas on the one hand we have welcomed strangers to work and live among us, on the other hand we have scorned and abused immigrants or minority groups who have deviated from the dominant culture.

Nevertheless, Americans throughout the twentieth century have actively recruited European, Asian, and Latin American people and emphasized the opportunities available to, rather than the hardships endured by, newcomers. Many colonies sought immigrants, and along with ship companies they sent agents (newlanders) to Europe to promote their attractions. The newlanders often dressed in fancy attire and wore pocket watches with heavy gold chains to attest to the wealth found in the New World. They carried tales of maids who became ladies, tenants who became landlords, and apprentices who became artisans only a few years after reaching the colonies. But "the best advertisement for the colonies," one historian has written, "was clearly the success of the pioneers. Messages they sent back home inevitably had the effect of removing the last psychological barrier from the minds of many already inclined to leave." "It is as Good Country as any Man needs to Dwell in," one Scots-Irishman wrote home in 1767, "and it is much better than I expected it to be in every way." Going to America thus came to mean, as one scholar put it, not launching into the vast unknown, "but moving to a country where one's friends and relatives had a home."

But life in the colonies was rarely as wonderful as emigrants had anticipated. The wilderness had to be cleared and existence could be boring, barbaric, and demoralizing. Outside of the few towns there were no fairs, no markets, and hardly any people with whom to exchange pleasantries. In these places people saw only a harsh workaday world that had to be faced from sunup through sunset. In 1734 an emigrant from Belfast noted in his journal, "We were oppressed with fears on divers accounts, especially of being massacred by the Indians, or bitten by snakes, or torn by wild beasts, or being lost and perishing in the woods."

These experiences often came after a journey full of untoward hardships. A German-speaking Swiss reported after living one year in America:

Whoever wishes to go to the New World
Should be sure to take a sack of money
And also a strong stomach
So he can withstand the demands of the ship.

He was referring to the trials of passage to America. Part of immigrants' meager funds had to pay for passage to ports of embarkation, and once there, travelers had to guarantee that the ships would sail to the final destinations on the agreed dates. Extra days ashore meant added expenses for food and lodging. Finally, they faced weeks and sometimes months of dismal living conditions on overcrowded and disease-ridden vessels. Shipowners regarded their passengers as freight on which they hoped to maximize profits. The space between decks seldom exceeded five feet, and the immigrants, regardless of sex or marital relation, slept two or three to a berth; each rarely had an area of more than two feet by six feet to call their own. Voyages lasted six weeks to six months. Stormy days forced passengers below deck, but portholes for light and ventilation were practically nonexistent. Overcrowding, disease, pestilence, brutal shipmasters, and shortages of food and water added to the tribulations of the ocean crossing. Many children under 7 sickened and died, and older folk too were lucky to reach the New World. In 1752 on a ship from the Netherlands to Pennsylvania, only 21 out of 340 passengers disembarked; the others had starved to death. On another voyage from Belfast in 1741, 6 of the 46 who died "were consumed by the sixty survivors." On a third ship, many drank salt water and their own urine; and on another those who complained of hunger "were put in irons, lashed to the shrouds and flogged." No wonder that one immigrant German schoolteacher wrote, "The glimpse of land revives the passengers, especially those who are half dead of illness. Their spirits, however weak they had become, leap up, triumph, and rejoice within them. Such people are now willing to bear all ills patiently, if only they can disembark soon and step on land."

Despite these hardships, hundreds of thousands reached their destinations. Many of those who came had lived in poverty in their old homes and were penniless. Shipping agents accepted indigents who signed indentures agreeing to work in the New World for a period of three to seven years to pay for their passage. The immigrants who came in this fashion were often "sold" on board ship, and not infrequently members of the same family wound up with different "masters." Some parents had to "sell their children as if they were cattle," and if parents or spouses died, the remaining members of the family had to serve extra time to pay for the deceased's passage. Unaccompanied children or those whose parents had died during the journey were usually indentured until the age of 21.

Before the 1660s most colonists came directly from England. They laid the foundation and set the direction for the future development of American society. The settlement at Jamestown in 1607 resulted from the visions of some London-based fortune hunters. By 1622 famines, pestilence, and Indian troubles had practically destroyed the colony, and the English crown assumed possession.

The first English colonists in Virginia had difficulty surviving. They struggled against disease, poor work habits, and hostile Indians. Eventually both Virginia and Maryland found their salvation in growing tobacco. Indentured servants, and later slaves from Africa, provided field labor. At the end of their terms, freed servants received some money, tools, new clothes, and sometimes land. The harsh living conditions took their toll, and not everyone survived the indenture. Although men predominated, women and children were also indentured. Indentured widows had their choice of marriage partners if they survived their husbands. One historian noted that in addition to their household duties, "rural Englishwomen weeded, pulled hemp, and used hoes to cultivate corn and sickles to harvest wheat and rye." In the seventeenth century more than half of all immigrants to the English colonies came in this manner. Indentured servitude continued until about 1820.

Pilgrims and Puritans who went to New England avoided the plague of a faltering European economy. Their move to the New World, however, also afforded them the opportunity to implant their own cultural values. No other groups, no matter how large, were ever as significant in the development of the United States as the Pilgrims and Puritans. Their ideologies emphasized the importance of the Protestant faith, diligent application to work, and individual accomplishment. They often paid homage to those who attained great wealth. They cherished the Anglo-Saxon legal heritage and revered the written compact. They brought the English language to the New World, along with a strong sense of the role of families. Men dominated their families and were political leaders. But women too had roles in society: they ran the households and reared the children. All of these aspects of their culture were firmly implanted in American soil, and became the foundations for American society. Every succeeding immigrant group that came to the English colonies, and later to the United States, had to absorb these aspects of the dominant culture to be accepted as Americans.

After Charles I succeeded his father, James I, on the English throne in 1625, domestic concerns prevented him from giving much attention to the colonies. Nevertheless, he granted an area of land north of Virginia to George Calvert, Lord Baltimore, which was christened Maryland. Calvert, a Roman Catholic, hoped the colony would be financially profitable and serve as a haven for his coreligionists. He died before actually receiving the grant from the king, and the deed went to his son, Cecilius, who embarked on a voyage to the New World in 1634. From the beginning there were large numbers of Protestants in Maryland, and to protect Catholics in case of eventual discrimination, Lord Baltimore urged passage of the Toleration Act in 1649; it granted freedom of religion to all who believed in the divinity of Jesus Christ. Five years later, however, under the domination of a Protestant legislature, the act was repealed and Catholics were denied legal protection. The repeal signified quite strikingly how the colonists, and in later centuries other Protestants, regarded the Roman Catholic faith.

From 1649 until 1661 Oliver Cromwell governed England as a protectorate, but upon his death Charles II, son of the beheaded monarch, reinstituted the monarchy and claimed the throne as his birthright. During his reign (1661–1685) England discouraged emigration. The mercantile theory, which held sway for the next century, dictated that the wealth of nations lay in their inhabitants and their production, and that loss of population meant, in effect, loss of riches. The English colonists therefore had to seek other sources of population. In 1662 the Royal African Slave Company received a monopoly from the crown and began importing African slaves in increasing numbers. By 1680, however, William Penn received a grant of land from King Charles II and went to Europe to recruit settlers directly.

At first William Penn made his colony a haven for his fellow Quakers. About 25,000 English and Welsh members of the Society of Friends settled in the colony's Delaware Valley from 1675 to 1725; Congregationalists and Anglicans arrived too. But the Quakers set the tone for society in that half century. Like the Puritans, they were a deeply religious people persecuted in England for their religious beliefs. Quakers rejected the doctrine of predestination and held an enlightened view of humankind. They opposed taking oaths, fighting wars, and establishing a rigid religious hierarchy, and they were generally tolerant of other religions and immigrants. Although Penn condemned Jews for rejecting the New Testament, he urged them to "see the error of their ways and accept the divinity of Jesus." His intolerance of Jews, however, did not affect other Quaker concerns. Their humanitarianism led them to attack the institution of slavery and recognize the need to improve women's rights.

Penn printed hundreds of pamphlets in English, German, French, and Dutch, describing the wonders of Pennsylvania. Europeans were told over and over again that it was a land where crops never failed, where game roamed aplenty, where abundant supplies of wood stood ready for use in building houses, barns, and furniture, where religious freedom was guaranteed to all, and where no political restrictions harassed dissenters. Moreover, the colony promised universal male suffrage, a humane penal code, and no compulsory military service. As one historian later wrote, "Pennsylvania was in truth a land of milk and honey." No wonder that in the colonial era more immigrants sailed for Philadelphia than for all other ports combined.

People came to the New World for a combination of economic, religious, and political reasons: some came to escape persecution in states where tyrannical princes had different faiths; others came because crop failures, famines, or never-ending wars made prospects for the future seem bleak. The relaxation of emigration restrictions in Switzerland and the German states in the eighteenth century also stimulated them, as did glowing letters from friends and relatives who had already gone to the English colonies.

The majority of Germans were Lutherans or members of Reformed churches. Germans formed churches even in back country several hundred miles from Philadelphia. By 1760 there were 18 German communities; by 1780 the number had reached 30. Yet Germans were by no means limited to these two denominations. The radical pietistic sects also took hold in America, and made up about one fourth of the German congregations at the time of the American Revolution. Many members had experienced persecution in Europe and were eager to find the freedom to follow what they believed to be the true faith. Among them were Moravians, Mennonites, Swenkfelders, and Amish. These deeply religious immigrants tended to settle and even migrate together as distinct enclaves.

Pennsylvania received the largest number of Germans, but they spread out across most of the colonies. The English government was eager to recruit Germans to develop its land and to build ships along New York's Hudson River. By promising to pay their way to America, Queen Anne induced several thousand to head for New York. The program, however, lacked funds and was poorly planned, so shipbuilding efforts failed. But some Germans stayed on near Rhinebeck, New York, while others left for better opportunities elsewhere.

Germans also struggled to make a living in the back country of the southern colonies. In the early 1740s Moravians abandoned their Georgia settlement and began moving to Pennsylvania, the center of the largest German community in the New World. In the end colonial Germans prospered. Their concern for their property was proverbial; it was often said that a German took better care of his cows than of his children. After settling on good land the Germans built sturdy houses and barns and tilled their farms with diligence and enthusiasm. One historian has written that they "produced in their children not only the *habits* of labor but a *love* of it." They fed their stock well, exercised frugality in diet and dress, and were known for their thrift, industry, punctuality, and sense of justice.

But the colonial Germans had little desire to blend with the rest of the population. They kept to themselves, continued speaking German, attended their own churches, and rarely took the opportunity to become British citizens. They maintained their own culture and feared that the use of English and contact with other groups would completely anglicize their children. Because of their aloofness they antagonized the dominant English group in the colonies, especially in Pennsylvania, which viewed them as dangerous elements. Even Benjamin Franklin, an urbane and decent man, disliked the Germans who poured into Pennsylvania in the eighteenth century, and he demanded: "Why should the *Palatine Boors* be suffered to swarm into our Settlements, and by herding together, establish their Language and Manners, to the Exclusion of ours? Why should *Pennsylvania*, founded by the *English*, become a Colony of *Aliens*, who will shortly be so numerous as to Germanize us instead of our Anglifying them?"

The Scots-Irish, like the Germans, were Protestants who left their homes for religious and economic reasons. In the late seventeenth century, English mercantile laws had prohibited the exportation of Irish woolens except to England and Wales, and this nearly crippled Ulster's profitable foreign trade. Then successive increases in rents, termination of farm leases, poor harvests, curtailed supplies of flax to linen manufacturers, increased food costs, and restrictions precluding Presbyterians from holding political offices piled woe upon woe. Furthermore, the English Parliament decreed that the children of all Protestants not married in the Church of England must be declared bastards. The absurdity of this ruling also resulted in "'many persons of undoubted reputation' [being] prosecuted in the bishops courts as fornicators for cohabitating with their own wives." But not until 1717, when the fourth successive year of droughts ruined crops, did the Scots-Irish begin serious preparations for migration to the New World. The first group to leave their homeland may have been motivated by religious as well as economic conditions, but thereafter, glowing shipping advertisements, letters from friends and relatives in the colonies, and poor economic conditions in Ireland sparked further movement. Intensive and protracted Scots-Irish emigration to the American colonies correlated with the ebb and flow of prosperity in the linen industry in Ireland.

The original Scots-Irish settlers went to Worcester, Massachusetts, and Londonderry, New Hampshire, where they met a chilly reception. New Englanders regarded them as "uncleanly, unwholesome and disgusting." Pennsylvania, on the other hand, because of its tolerance, received them readily. Perhaps even more important, the ships carrying flaxseed went to Philadelphia, and so the Scots-Irish went there too. Most arrived as indentured servants, but once their periods of service ended they moved to the frontier, and their settlements predominated in central Pennsylvania and portions of Maryland, Virginia, and the Carolinas. Unlike the Germans, the Scots-Irish were forever on the move.

Although they were a colonial minority, the Scots-Irish left a mark on American society that remains to this day. Wherever they went, the church and the schoolhouse followed. Devoutly religious and with an intense desire for learning, they stressed the importance of an educated ministry and the dissemination of knowledge. Their stern morality pervaded the American scene. The Presbyterians frowned on dancing, card playing, the theater, breaking the Sabbath by any diversion, and engaging in frivolous pastimes. On the other hand, not all were as dour as this might suggest. One scholar tells us that many among them "also danced, fiddled, sang, reveled, raced horses, gambled, got drunk and fought, celebrated St. Patrick's Day and shot off guns on New Year's Eve."

A number of other ethnic groups also populated the English colonies, and in some areas their culture and values predominated. Because they constituted a smaller percentage of the total population than did the English, Scots-Irish, and Germans, their influence and their continued existence as separate groups were not as lasting; but almost all made their mark in colonial America.

The Huguenots, French Protestants who settled in virtually every region of the colonies but who concentrated in the port cities, stand out as a people that relinquished its heritage quickly. They included a high proportion of professionals, merchants, and craftsmen and a small number of indentured servants. Most of the Huguenots, who constituted the first major wave of newcomers from the European mainland after 1685, took non-Huguenot spouses, which ensured their group's disintegration as a separate people. As a result they quickly blended in with the most prominent colonists and not only occupied several important political offices but also became extraordinarily wealthy. Many of their contemporaries envied them, and the phrase "rich as a Huguenot" often contained a tinge of bitterness.

The Dutch, in New York and New Jersey, and the Scots, mostly in New Jersey and the South, are more representative of immigrants to America who held on to their cultures and values for several generations. They considered their heritage too important an aspect of their lives to relinquish it easily. Dutch influence lived on in New York's Hudson Valley and the eastern parts of Long Island, as well as in significant areas of New Jersey, long after the British had conquered New Netherland and renamed it New York. Worship in the Dutch language continued in some parts of New York and New Jersey until the 1820s and farmers continued using Dutch dialogue in some of their ethnic enclaves into the twentieth century. Education was quite important to the Dutch, and their children were taught not only the three Rs but also enough religion to make them God-fearing Christians. Instruction was in the Dutch language until approximately the middle of the eighteenth century. Girls were not given as sophisticated an education as boys, but they did learn to read and write and were taught needlework at home. They also were given particularly careful tutoring in the Bible and religious studies because inculcating religion in the children was considered the mother's responsibility.

Unlike English law, Dutch law gave women certain property and inheritance rights. Partners in a Dutch marriage held property equally, and widows and children split inheritances. Gradually English customs crept into Dutch practices and the women found themselves receiving less of their husbands' estates. This change, like others within the eighteenth-century Dutch community, marks the gradual loss of Dutch culture.

Like most other ethnics, then and in subsequent centuries, the Dutch were exceedingly clannish and sought to isolate themselves from other colonists. In fact, many observers regarded them as aloof, but that did not seem to

10   The Colonial Heritage

bother them or cause them to alter their ways. The Dutch relaxed by skiing, sleighing, and horse racing; they were known to enjoy drinking, and many of the women found pleasure in smoking tobacco. Economically they were quite successful.

The Scots were another group that not only kept to themselves but also welcomed newcomers from various regions of the old country and absorbed them into the ethnic community. They made their mark in the colonies in the organization of commerce, the development of mining, and advances in medical science. They were merchants and proprietors in a variety of businesses and, like the Dutch, valued education for their offspring. Most were overwhelmingly attached to the evangelical Presbyterian church, and family networks among Scottish settlers were an important source of religious unity.

One of their primary areas of settlement in British America began in the 1680s, when approximately 600 Scots moved into east Jersey. By 1750 one fifth of the population of New Jersey was made up of Scottish settlers and their descendants; by the middle of the eighteenth century, these people "turned central Jersey and the whole corridor from New York to Philadelphia into the center of Scottish Middle Colony life."

Although they were not as large in numbers as the Scots-Irish from Ulster and the Germans, one scholar reminds us that

> In several particulars, the experience of Scottish settlers can serve as a model for that of many colonial ethnic groups. With a few striking exceptions—such as the Huguenots, who were notorious for submerging their national identity and attaching themselves to other Protestant communities—the confrontation with alien cultures in the New World helped to unify settlers from diverse and seemingly unconnected regional backgrounds under a common national banner. They often achieved that consolidation around a particular religious identity, such as Scottish Presbyterian, Dutch or German Reformed, or, in the next century, Irish Catholic. That process often created ethnic entities that seemed more Scottish, or more German, or even more English, than their European counterparts.

What this scholar really was saying, and what is common today in some parts of the United States, was that in colonial America religious and ethnic identities were often intertwined. One was not merely French, Dutch, or Scottish, but French Huguenot, Dutch Reformed, or Scottish Presbyterian. Colonists thought of one another in terms of these double identities and denounced one another more often in religious than in national terms. The governor of New York, for example, in 1686 complained that the colony contained too many Dutch Calvinists and French Calvinists, Dutch Lutherans, and "Singing Quakers, Ranting Quakers; Sabbatarians; Antisabbatarians; some Anabaptists, some Independents, some Jews. . . ."

On the other hand, in the American Southwest, from Texas to California, Mexican immigrants and influence dominated. This region did not become part of the United States until the nineteenth century, and when it did Hispanic culture became part of America's diversity. As the English, Dutch, and French settled the Atlantic coastal region that eventually became the United States, Spaniards were exploring and settling the Southwest. Spanish colonization was quite different from that of the English, Dutch, or French. In the first place, it was not characterized by the family migration of men, women, and children that was the pattern in New England, the middle colonies, and to a lesser extent in the southern colonies. Priests and soldiers followed the first Spanish explorers. It was the mission's task to convert the Indians, and it was the role of the *presidio* to defend the frontier.

The economy and society also differed. In both California and Texas, the Spanish introduced ranching along with farming; these became the mainstays of the economy. Towns were few and far between. Spanish society was ruled at the top by male government officials, friars, and the military. Because of the shortage of women many Spanish men intermarried with Indians. The women lived proscribed lives, though on the frontier they had more say in running ranches and farms.

Finally, the Southwest was sparsely settled compared to the Atlantic seaboard English colonies. Spain induced a few of its citizens to sail for New Spain. The Spanish government also turned to the Canary Islands for settlers; in 1731, 56 immigrants from the Canary Islands arrived to found a colony along the San Antonio River. Yet these efforts were not particularly successful, and by the time the United States became independent only a few thousand Hispanics, along with a variety of Indian peoples, lived in the Southwest.

Louisiana was another region explored and settled by non-English but that only became part of the United States in the nineteenth century. In this case it was France, not Spain, that took the lead. The French sent a few colonists in the late seventeenth century, mainly for military purposes. In the eighteenth century prisoners were sent to labor in Louisiana along with indentured servants. Most of the new settlers were men, and the colony held little attraction for women or families. It was poor, unhealthy, and dangerous. France also imported slave laborers to develop the colony. One group of French speakers were Acadians who had been driven out of Canada by the British. Some had gone first to France or the middle English colonies before arriving in Louisiana.

After 1750 about two to three thousand Acadians migrated to Louisiana, mostly as families. They were viewed as desirable immigrants, for the French were looking for permanent settlers and men to support the military. They formed tight-knit agricultural communities that, once established, helped others to settle, and became the foundation for the Cajun culture of Louisiana.

Spain took over Louisiana in 1763 but did little to change the essential French character of the colony, though Louisiana achieved more stable rule. The Spanish Crown did send soldiers and encouraged the settlement of Canary Islanders in Louisiana. The first arrived in 1778, largely as family units. Others followed, and the total of Canary Islanders to disembark at New Orleans numbered two thousand. But the voyage over took many lives, and disease claimed many more during the early years, as did hurricanes. Some Canary Islanders spread into the countryside to become farmers, but a small number remained in New Orleans. They never achieved the impact that Acadians had on Louisiana. On the eve of the American purchase of Louisiana in 1803, the colony had a total of about 40,000 people, half of whom were slaves.

While the colonists noticed the arrival of large numbers of non-English newcomers, many people from England continued to migrate to the New World in the eighteenth century. Emigration from Great Britain increased after 1760 and remained heavy until the American Revolution. How many arrived in the eighteenth century is not known, but scholars have estimated that 30,000 English people emigrated between 1760 and 1775 alone. Most of them settled in the 13 colonies that became the United States.

Historian Bernard Bailyn has studied the records of those leaving Great Britain in the early 1770s. The English immigrants of those years were usually young, single males who settled mainly in New York, Pennsylvania, North Carolina, Maryland, and Virginia. Like so many seventeenth-century English immigrants, they frequently came as indentured servants. While some were poor, the largest group, skilled artisans, were responding to the labor shortage in the colonies. Carpenters, farmers, bricklayers, shoemakers, tailors, and all skilled workers were needed in America. As Bailyn tells us, "The forces of attraction were powerful, generated by the magnet of a labor-short American economy, which grew swiftly in certain regions and in certain kinds of activities."

Another source for colonial workers was convicts. Instead of imprisoning criminals, the British commuted their sentences to banishment to the colonies for periods of 7 to 14 years. It has been estimated that 50,000 such convicts found themselves in the colonies rather than in jail between 1718 and 1775. Some were no doubt hardened criminals, but many were tradesmen who had fallen on hard times and had run afoul of the law. Minor crimes at that time carried heavy sentences. The colonies were not always receptive to convicts, but local governments could not halt this traffic. Besides, the convicts' labor was needed, and they were put to work in the New World.

While convicts were viewed with suspicion at times, no group was as hated in the British colonies as the Roman Catholics. Carrying with them their European traditions, some of which harked back to the Reformation, the Protestant settlers had tolerance for almost no deviants, but "the prospect of the arrival of Roman Catholics of any nationality" particularly, one scholar tells us, "curdled the blood of most provincials." Roman Catholics constituted less than one percent of all of the colonists and half of them were in Maryland, but their numbers had nothing to do with Protestant fears. Those who hated Catholicism exaggerated its potential influence. Most Pennsylvanians, for example, imagined swarms of Irish and German Catholics in their midst even though statistics belied such apprehensions. One Pennsylvanian disinherited a daughter because she married a Roman Catholic.

Catholics lived freely in the middle colonies, but in times of social crisis, an inordinate amount of fear swept the towns in which they dwelled; their presence was deemed harmful to community harmony. This was especially true in the middle of the eighteenth century during the French and Indian War. In December 1760, the Catholic church in Lancaster, Pennsylvania, was completely destroyed by enraged Protestants, and Catholics were penalized in the colony in other ways as well. They were disarmed, prohibited from serving in the militia, and forced to pay double taxes. "And those residing in the colony were registered so that their every movement could be scrutinized."

In the Revolutionary era this hostility toward Catholics knew no bounds. Even as intelligent a man as John Adams, our second president, could write to his wife after visiting a Catholic church in Philadelphia:

This Afternoon's Entertainment was to me most awful and affecting. The poor Wretches, fingering their Beads, chanting Latin, not a Word of which they understood; their Pater Nosters and Ave Maria's. Their holy Water—their Crossing themselves perpetually—their Bowing to the Name of Jesus, whenever they hear it—their Bowing and Kneelings, and Genuflections before the Altar. The Dress of the Priest was rich with Lace—his Pulpit was Velvet and Gold. The Altar Piece was very rich— little Images and Crucifixes about—Wax Candles lighten up. But how shall I describe the Picture of our Saviour in a Frame of Marble over the Altar at full Length upon the Cross, in the Agonies, and the Blood dropping and streaming from his Wounds. . . .

Here is every Thing which can lay hold of the Eye, Ear, and Imagination. Every Thing which can charm and bewitch the simple and ignorant. I wonder how Luther ever broke the spell.

Hostility toward Catholics may have been the most virulent prejudice, but there was little affection between and among most groups. Jews and Catholics did not always enjoy the right to vote in colonial America; Jews in particular were proscribed from becoming physicians and attorneys in some places. Quakers and Jews did not have the legal right to testify in criminal court cases in New York City until after the American Revolution. Many colonies had an established church—Congregational in New England and usually Anglican elsewhere—and residents were taxed to support it.

To be sure, ethnic tensions and disputes in colonial America were rarely as intense as those in the late nineteenth and twentieth centuries, but they did exist. The English squabbled with the Germans, with the Palatines, and with the Swiss. Tensions between English and Scots, in fact, stood near the center of New Jersey's land riots of the 1740s. Also, French Huguenots saw their churches burned in South Carolina, and one observer characterized the Dutch in this fashion: "Their notions were mean and contracted; their manners blunt and austere; and their habits sordid and parsimonious."

But community mores in most of the colonies generally were favorable to intercultural marriage as long as the non-English or non-Protestant member accepted the dominant religion of the spouse. As a result the commercially successful Huguenots and Jews, to name but two of the groups, often made alliances with the "best families" in the colonies and then raised their children as Anglicans or, later, Episcopalians. Consequently both the Huguenot and the Jewish communities practically disappeared. In the United States today the only remnants of Huguenots are their historical and genealogical societies in places like South Carolina; New Rochelle, New York; and Rhode Island. As for the colonial Jewish population, it was absorbed into the dominant culture. Today, a majority of American Jews trace their ancestries either to the great migrations from Eastern Europe in the late nineteenth and early twentieth centuries or to the movement from the German states in the 1840s and 1850s.

In contrast, numerically larger colonial minorities like the Scots-Irish and the Germans preserved and maintained their traditional ways well into the nineteenth century. Germans in places like Pennsylvania and the Carolinas continued speaking their own language, the Dutch maintained schools for their children in New York until after the Revolution, and a good deal of sectional controversy that has generally been attributed to geographical locale may in fact have had its roots in ethnic differences. The Scots-Irish on the frontier in Pennsylvania may have been angered as much by Quaker control in the Keystone State as by lack of military protection. The Regulator movement in the Carolinas, which pitted Scots-Irish in the West against English descendants in the East, may also have had ethnic overtones.

As the colonial period ended, a rather distinctive ethnic picture could be seen. In New England an overwhelmingly English heritage predominated; aside from some Scottish, Huguenot, and Scots-Irish elements, few other minorities could be found. In the southern colonies was a large black population of slaves who coexisted not only with the English but also with strains of all the groups such as the Germans, Scots-Irish, Scots, and Huguenots. However, it was in the middle colonies that diversity was so pronounced. Cities such as New York and Philadelphia counted all sorts of people within their environs, while the rural areas of these states, and New Jersey as well, seemed more Scottish, or Dutch, or Scots-Irish, or German. In time, ethnic diversity was spread to the rest of the United States as millions of immigrants poured in from all over the globe. In the Southwest, not annexed until the mid-nineteenth century, Hispanic culture dominated. But the population of that large region, from Texas to California, numbered only a few thousand compared to over two million people of European stock in the English colonies in 1776.

By 1790 people of English ancestry still formed the majority in most of the states of the new United States, but Germans constituted fully a third of Pennsylvania's population and the Scots and Scots-Irish totaled almost 37 percent of the remainder of the people in the Keystone State. One analysis of ethnic groups in the new nation at the end of the eighteenth century still found English majorities in New York, New Jersey, and Maryland, but noted how strongly represented other groups were in those states' mixture of people. Nonetheless, the white minorities eventually blended with the dominant American-English culture, and although there were varieties of Protestant churches, their children and grandchildren learned to tolerate differences within Protestantism.

The pattern of minority life developed in the English colonies in the seventeenth century set the standard for future European minorities in this country. The English colonists and later Americans of the majority group appreciated the labor that the newcomers could provide, but expected them to absorb existing customs while shedding their own as quickly as possible. Minority group members were despised for their ignorance of English, their attachment to cultures and faiths prevalent in the Old World, and their lack of knowledge of the American way.

The passage of time, community pressures, and heroic endeavors have always worked against the maintenance of minority cultures in this country.

The war for independence from England and the formation of a new American government had a nationalizing effect on the formerly separate colonies and their inhabitants. Many of the immigrants and their children were now quite proud to regard themselves as Americans, not as transplanted Europeans. Some ethnic groups—notably the Germans who lived between the Delaware and Susquehanna rivers in Pennsylvania, and the Broad and Saluda rivers in South Carolina—resisted Americanization longer than others, but sooner or later most of them assimilated. The Napoleonic Wars, which began in the 1790s and lasted through 1815, slowed the pace of emigration from Europe, and this hiatus quickened the Americanizing process among immigrant stock* in the United States.

---

*"Immigrant stock" refers to people who came from abroad and their American-born children.

Chapter 2

A Wave of Immigrants, 1789–1890s

IN THE 210 years following the end of the American Revolution the great-est migrations of people in the history of the world occurred. Sparked by the Industrial Revolution, which forced peasants off the land and into the cities, the movement also gained momentum from many other factors in European social history, including the doubling of population between 1750 and 1850. At the same time, intensified religious persecutions and relaxation of emi-gration restrictions in various European nations combined with a trans-portation revolution to facilitate the movement of those who wanted to travel. Meanwhile, receptive countries in southern Africa, Oceania, and North and South America sought people to exploit resources. Finally, two devastating world wars uprooted millions. More than 60 million people left their native homes from 1820 to 1940. Some went from one European or Asian country to another, but others sought riches in Africa, Asia, and South America. More than 15 million went to Canada, Argentina, and Brazil. About two thirds of the migrants, who were primarily European but in-cluded considerable numbers of Asians and Latin Americans, chose the United States as their destination. Their arrival would be one of the most significant factors shaping the destiny of this country.

After a lull in immigration at mid-twentieth century, major patterns of migration appeared again. While western Europeans no longer were on the move, peoples from southern Europe went to labor in northern Europe, and refugees from communism fled to western Europe. From the former colonies of Great Britain, France, and the Netherlands immigrants headed for the mother countries. America's immigrants in the second half of the twentieth century have largely been from Asia, the Caribbean, and Latin America. Just as America has become more diverse through immigration, so have Canada and Australia. Other Asians have sought jobs in the Middle East or in Latin America, and refugees have fled countries such as Cambodia, Vietnam, and Laos. In Africa too refugees have left, desperately trying to find a haven in another land.

In the years between 1820 and 1930 America received more than 37 mil-lion immigrants, mostly from Europe. An analysis of time periods reveals that those coming from northern and western Europe predominated through the 1880s, whereas southern and eastern Europeans overshadowed the others after 1896. As table 2.1 shows, the great change began after 1880.

Not all of these people can be treated in one chapter, of course. Hence discussion of the different groups has been divided into three roughly chronological periods. The so-called old immigrants, those of northern and western Europe, are considered in this chapter along with some Mexicans, the French Canadians, and the Chinese, most of whom came in the nineteenth century. The next chapter deals with both the "new" immigrants from southern and eastern Europe and the Japanese, whose major emigration occurred roughly between 1880 and 1920. Later chapters deal with the Hispanic migrants from Mexico and the Caribbean, whose presence is, for the most part, a twentieth-century phenomenon; the refugees coming as a result of Hitler's persecutions, World War II, and the Cold War; and Asians and Latin Americans who have become eligible for admission to the United States because of congressional action since 1965.

Although foreigners came to the United States throughout the nineteenth century, statistics reveal that before 1880 the bulk of them arrived in two major periods: from 1845 to 1854, when more than 3 million people landed at American ports; and from 1865 to 1875, when the numbers reached almost 3.5 million. In the first period the Irish and Germans exceeded all others; in the second the English and Scandinavians figured heavily along with the first two; and after 1880 all these groups were joined, and then swamped, by southern and eastern European emigrants who pushed American immigration totals to new heights. Asians and Latin Americans, on the other hand, predominated after 1970.

Most immigrants came essentially because of poor economic conditions in their native lands and prospects for a better life in the United States. Local concerns and variations, the pace of industrialization on the Continent, the disruptions of World War I, and the restrictive immigration quotas of the 1920s had much to do with the timing of the emigrants' departures. In Great Britain the industrial change began in the eighteenth century, and the British clearly dominated American immigration statistics until the 1820s; in the German states the transformation of the social order was most profound in the second third of the nineteenth century; hence the Germans began to move after 1830; and in Scandinavia the decade of the 1880s, with its economic upheavals, proved most significant for migration. Nevertheless, the peaks and troughs in foreign arrivals after 1819 correspond roughly with fluctuations in the business cycles in the United States. Good years such as 1854, 1873, 1892, 1907, and 1921 were high points for immigration, but they were followed by industrial depressions that resulted in correspondingly low totals for new entrants.

Table 2.1 Immigration to America, 1820–1930

Decade	Germany	Ireland	England, Scotland, Wales	Scandinavia	Italy	Austro-Hungary	Russia and Baltic States	Totals
1820	968	3,614	2,410	23	30		14	8,385
1821–1830	6,761	50,724	25,079	260	409		75	143,439
1831–1840	152,454	207,654	75,810	2,264	2,253		277	599,125
1841–1850	434,626	780,719	267,044	13,122	1,970		551	1,713,251
1851–1860	951,657	914,119	423,929	24,680	9,231		457	2,598,214
1861–1870	827,468	435,697	607,076	126,392	11,725	7,800	2,515	2,314,824
1871–1880	718,182	436,871	548,043	242,934	55,795	72,969	39,287	2,812,191
1881–1890	1,452,970	655,540	807,357	655,494	307,309	362,719	213,282	5,246,613
1891–1900	505,152	388,416	271,538	371,512	651,783	574,069	505,281	3,687,564
1901–1910	341,498	339,065	525,950	505,324	2,045,877	2,145,266	1,597,308	8,795,386
1911–1920	143,945	146,199	341,408	203,452	1,209,524	901,656	921,957	5,735,811
1921–1930	412,202	220,564	330,168	198,210	455,315	214,806	89,423	4,107,209
Totals	5,947,883	4,579,182	4,225,812	2,343,667	4,751,311	4,279,285	3,370,427	

SOURCE: Immigration and Naturalization Service, Annual Reports.

People do not cross continents and oceans without considerable thought, nor do they uproot themselves from family, friends, and familiar terrain without significant strain. The motivation to emigrate must be overwhelming before the fateful step is taken. In the nineteenth century, as in the seventeenth and eighteenth, poverty was the chief spur to movement. One eminent historian has written, "The most powerful factor impelling emigration was an extraordinary increase in population, preceding the ability of agriculture to feed it or of industry to give it jobs." The industrial and agricultural revolutions wrought such profound changes in Europe that large numbers of people were forced by circumstances beyond their control to relinquish ancestral dwellings and move to where they could find jobs. Yet a variety of other impelling reasons cannot be ignored. Religious intolerance, demeaning social gradations, political upheavals—all these pushed people across the Atlantic, and the ubiquitous "American letters" describing the Garden of Eden in the New World pulled countless thousands to America. Nevertheless, it must still be acknowledged that the economic factor was the most compelling for the majority of emigrants.

From 1790 to 1820 fewer than 500,000 immigrants came to the United States. The new Constitution of 1787 said virtually nothing about immigration, and after passing a few laws in the 1790s, the federal government generally allowed states to regulate immigration until 1875. Germans and Scots-Irish continued to arrive after 1790, including a few German soldiers who had fought in the Revolutionary War. But other groups were more prominent. During the upheavals of the French Revolution and the slave rebellion in Haiti, which began in 1791, thousands of French-speaking refugees arrived from France and Haiti. Most of the French exiles settled in coastal cities such as Philadelphia, Baltimore, New York, and Charleston. Occasional groups of political refugees, like the 25,000 or so French-speaking immigrants who fled their Caribbean plantations in the 1790s in the wake of slave uprisings, might be given safe havens. But these newcomers, usually middle or upper class, brought a courtliness or sophistication that allowed them to mingle with the elite in American society. As a result they assimilated rather quickly and suffered much less from minority status than did those of lesser education, wealth, or position. Many, however, returned to France after 1800, and those remaining made only a minor impact upon American society.

English radicals, fleeing political oppression in Great Britain, also entered the United States during the 1790s, as did members of the United Irishmen. The United Irishmen were part of a movement to end English domination of Ireland, and when their movement failed in the late 1790s, some fled to America. Federalists worried about these immigrants with radical ideas, and some Jeffersonian Republicans believed that French refugees did not have a proper appreciation of American republicanism. As a result, Congress gave President John Adams power to deport persons deemed dangerous, even in time of peace. Adams did not use this authority. However, a sedition act was used against Irish-born Congressman Matthew Lyons for libeling President Adams in the press. The crisis and conflict over immigration resulting from the French Revolution ended in 1800, however. In 1790 Congress passed the first naturalization act; it granted whites the right to become citizens after only two years' residence in the United States. Legislators subsequently altered the period of years required for citizenship, but in 1800, after the election of Thomas Jefferson to the presidency, Congress set the time at five years, where it has remained ever since. The Napoleonic wars after 1800 and the War of 1812 between the United States and England reduced the opportunities for emigration from Europe.

The low levels of immigration and the nationalistic spirit engendered by the American Revolution combined to weaken the old ethnic communities. This process of Americanization seemed a prelude to the end of diverse cultures in the United States. The Welsh, Dutch, German, and French languages were already being replaced by English, and the process of acculturation continued. The Dutch Reformed Church, finding the younger generation did not understand Dutch, switched its bibles, hymn books, and prayer books to English. At one time New York and Philadelphia each had several German newspapers; by 1815 they had none.

The Irish were the first group of impoverished Europeans to leave their homeland in the nineteenth century. The Irish Poor Law of 1838, the enclosure movement on the land, and finally the great famine at the end of the 1840s, when blight ravaged the potato crops and brought untold misery and starvation to millions, combined to increase emigration. A French observer who had visited both America and Ireland before the Great Hunger said the condition of the Irish was worse than that of black slaves, and concluded: "There is no doubt that the most miserable of English paupers is better fed and clothed than the most prosperous of Irish laborers." As hundreds of thousands starved to death during the famine, one of the few lucrative trades left in Tipperary was the sale of coffin mountings and hinges. One man lamented, "Every day furnished victims, and the living hear, and endeavor to drive from their minds, as soon as they can, the horrifying particulars that are related. I have this day, returning to my house, witnessed more than one person lying in our district at this moment unburied. I have known of bodies here remaining in the mountainous parts, neglected for more than eight days." Many of the destitute went to England and some to South America, but more than a million came to the United States. The majority of these people remained in the port cities of New York and Boston, where they landed, because they were too poor to move any farther; but others traveled west. As conditions improved in Ireland in the middle of the 1850s, emigration subsided, but another potato rot in 1863 and still another famine in the 1880s swelled the Irish emigration statistics. Almost 4 million Irish came to the United States in the nineteenth century. Their impact in this country has far exceeded both their numbers and their percentage of the population.

Within nineteenth-century immigrant groups, only among the Irish did women predominate. The famine and the shortage of land left many of them with dim prospects for marriage. Many decided not to marry or to postpone marriage, and to support themselves. They went to the cities, frequently finding jobs as domestic servants. But why stop in Dublin, many asked, when stories of America made emigration sound like such a better choice? So they headed for New York and Boston and other cities, where they readily found jobs in domestic service.

For contemporary Americans such work has a low status, but this was not necessarily the case for Irish women. In contrast with grim prospects at home or jobs in sweat shops, domestic service offered food and a clean place to live. Thus the Irish women became the ubiquitous "Bridget," the domestic worker employed by each middle-class family. Some of these women eventually married and left their jobs, but others remained single. Many opened bank accounts and provided passage money to bring their brothers and sisters to the United States.

Along with the Irish came the Germans. But unlike the Irish, they continued to be the largest ethnic group arriving in all but three of the years between 1854 and 1894. Before the end of the century more than 5 million Germans reached the United States; in the twentieth century another 2 million came. The exodus, at first primarily from the rural and agricultural southern and western regions of Germany, fits the general pattern of immigration. Crop failures, high rents, high prices, and the changeover to an industrial economy stimulated the move. Conditions were not as bad as in impoverished Ireland, but they were bad enough. One observer told of the "poor wretches" on the road to Strasbourg: "There they go slowly along; their miserable tumbrils—drawn by such starved dropping beasts, that your only wonder is, how can they possibly reach Havre alive." Relatives and friends who went first to America wrote glowing letters, for the most part, and this in turn stimulated further waves. Rich farmers who saw a bleak future in Germany, poor ones who had no future, peasants and paupers whom the state paid to leave, a handful of disappointed revolutionaries after 1848, and an assortment of artisans and professionals came in the 1840s and 1850s.

In late 1854 reports circulated in the German states of large numbers of shipwrecks and cholera epidemics at sea that resulted in death rates as high as 50 percent. At about the same time, nativist agitation in the United States reached a peak and the American economy turned downward. These factors slowed immigration in the late 1850s. Then came the Civil War, which deterred people already beset with their own troubles from emigrating.

Between 1866 and 1873, however, a combination of American prosperity and European depression once again increased German emigration totals. Congressional passage of the 1862 Homestead Act granting free land to settlers, the convulsions in the German states owing to Bismarck's wars in the 1860s, the high conscription rate, and low wages at home also prompted German emigration. When the United States suffered a severe depression between 1873 and 1879, immigration figures were correspondingly depressed. But when the American economy improved, anxious Europeans once again descended on American shores. Germans who believed that prosperity would never be theirs at home left in record numbers; in 1882 more than 250,000 passed through the immigration stations here. The American depressions of the late 1880s and 1893–1894 cut emigration sharply, but by then an improved industrial economy in Germany provided greater opportunities than in the past, and fewer Germans felt compelled to seek their fortunes in the New World.

Scandinavians—the largest northwestern European group, after the British, Germans, and Irish, to populate America in the nineteenth century—increased their numbers in the United States markedly after the Civil War. The first group of nineteenth-century Scandinavians arrived in the autumn of 1825, when about 50 Norwegians settled in Kendall, New York, about 30 miles southwest of Rochester. In 1841 a Swedish colony developed in Pine Lake, Wisconsin. During the next decades, Scandinavians continued to come, but never in the numbers that either the Irish or the Germans did. For example, Scandinavian immigration totaled only 2,830 in 1846 and not much more in 1865. After 1868, however, annual immigration from Norway, Sweden, Denmark, and Finland passed the 10,000 mark. Jacob Riis, social reformer and friend of Theodore Roosevelt, for example, left Denmark for America in 1870. Like so many other immigrants, he arrived with little but "a pair of strong hands, and stubbornness enough to do for two; [and] also a strong belief that in a free country, free from the dominion of custom, of caste, as well as of men, things would somehow come right in the end." Other Danes and Scandinavians obviously agreed, for annual immigration from Scandinavia did not fall below 10,000 until the disruptions caused by World War I. In the 1920s, when other Europeans resumed their exodus, the Scandinavians joined them.

As in the case of the Irish and the Germans, Scandinavian immigration can be correlated to a large extent with economic conditions at home and in the United States. Sweden enjoyed a period of good crop production between 1850 and 1864; the years between 1865 and 1868, however, culminated in a great famine that coincided with particularly bountiful times in the United States. During those years, the numbers of emigrants increased sharply, doubling from 1865 to 1866 and tripling from 9,000 in 1867 to 27,000 in 1868. The exodus from Norway of a large percentage of the nation's entire population at that time can be explained almost wholly by the industrial transformation and the consequent disruptions at home. Norwegian migration can be grouped into three significant periods: from 1866 to 1873, when 111,000 people came; from 1879 to 1893, when the figures went over 250,000; and from 1900 to 1910, when the numbers totaled about 200,000.

Industrialism came earlier in Denmark than in either Norway or Sweden, and the rural upheaval sent people into the cities and towns. But there were simply not enough jobs for those willing to work, and many artisans and skilled laborers sought opportunities in America. Wisconsin was the first state to attract Danes in any substantial number, but subsequently large contingents could be found in Iowa and Illinois as well. Before 1868 families generally emigrated from Denmark as units, but thereafter unmarried, young adult male immigrants exceeded married ones by an almost 3:1 margin. A plurality of these Danes were farmhands, but there was also a sprinkling of small landholders, craftsmen, and unskilled factory laborers. By 1920 United States census figures recorded 190,000 Danish-born.

Although economic factors overshadowed all others for the Scandinavians, it would be misleading to overlook social difficulties as motivating forces, except in the case of the Danes, who had no serious political or religious problems. In Sweden and Norway church and state were aligned, and both dissenters and nonconformists were penalized. There was no universal suffrage, and tightened conscription laws bothered many young men and their families; one scholar noted a particularly high proportion of emigrants among those eligible for military service in Sweden in the 1880s. Swedes in particular also abhorred the hierarchy of titles and the rigidly defined class system. After living in the United States, one Swede wrote home that his "cap [is not] worn out from lifting it in the presence of gentlemen. There is no class distinction between high and low, rich and poor, no make-believe, no 'title-sickness,' or artificial ceremonies. . . . Everybody lives in peace and prosperity."

Another compelling, perhaps decisive, reason was something called "American fever." After Europeans left their homelands, they wrote to their compatriots and described the wonders of America, or the "land of Canaan." Nowhere did these letters have a greater impact than in the Scandinavian countries. They were passed carefully from family to family, published intact in the local newspapers, and discussed avidly from pulpits on Sundays. The influx of favorable mail inspired whole villages with the fervent desire to emigrate to America. Not all the letters from the United States glowed with praise, however, and many complained of the adjustment to the New World. But as one emigrant succinctly put it, "Norway cannot be compared to America any more than a desert can be compared to a garden in full bloom."

The Irish, the Germans, and the Scandinavians constituted the main group of non-English European immigrants before the 1890s, but others also chose to emigrate to the New World. Between 1815 and 1850 the predominantly rural Welsh endured severe agricultural discontent as the nation began industrializing. A depression hit Wales after 1815. The winter of 1814 had been the coldest in memory; and in 1816, "the year without summer," Wales began to feel the effect of a population explosion. By mid-century the region's inhabitants, like those in the rest of Europe, had doubled in number. The high birth rate, the increase in illegitimate births, and the pauperization of the peasants compounded the discontent. By comparison, the United States, to which an individual could sail for £2 or £3 from Liverpool in 1836, seemed to be a pot of gold at the end of the rainbow. The availability of land, the growth of American industry—especially in iron making and mining, where many Welshmen could use their skills—and the increasing number of "American letters" tempted those most inclined to seek a better life.

Dutch religious dissenters also considered American economic opportunities inviting. Beginning in the 1840s they founded colonies in Michigan, Wisconsin, Iowa, and what would later be South Dakota. Their departures from Europe corresponded with the potato blights and economic depression in Holland. By 1902 more than 135,000 Dutch, most of whom had arrived in the 1880s and 1890s, lived in the United States.

Several other groups, including the French from France, French Canadians, Chinese, and German Russians, also made significant impressions on the United States. Overpopulation at home and the diminishing size of agricultural plots that had been divided and subdivided for generations finally induced French Canadians to start emigrating in the 1830s, although most left Canada between 1860 and 1900. The approximately 300,000 emigrants settled for the most part in the mill villages and factory towns of New England, although scattered communities developed in New York and the upper Midwest.

The discovery of gold in California in 1849 had a great impact on the Chinese. News of the strike reached China by way of American merchant ships, but only the people of Toishan, a depressed agricultural province about 150 miles northwest of Hong Kong, responded. Toishan's agricultural output could feed its population for only about one third of the year, and floods and typhoons frequently devastated the community. As a result, many Toishanese moved into commercial activities and came in contact with West-erners in Hong Kong and Canton, the two major cities closest to their province. They were therefore receptive to the opportunity for enrichment in the United States, and a number of the more adventurous males made the long journey. Only a few women accompanied them. Perhaps half of these young men left their wives and families behind, and a good number returned home after a period of years in the United States working in the mines or on the railroads. It was not acceptable for single women to emigrate. Some who did were virtually seized from their families or sold to merchants who brought them to America to become prostitutes. In 1870 61 percent of the 3,536 Chinese women in California had their occupation listed as prostitute. Other immigrant women ended up as prostitutes, but these Chinese women prompted some charges that the Chinese were immoral and unworthy of becoming Americans.

After the initial discovery of gold, about half of the Chinese settling in the United States came from Toishan, and a large percentage of the others came from areas surrounding that province. Lack of contact with Americans probably deterred other Chinese from going to the United States, and after 1882, when Chinese laborers were banned, few entered. The ban on Chinese immigrants did not include merchants and they and their wives continued to emigrate, though in small numbers. In 1930, 80 percent of the Chinese in America were men, largely living in bachelor societies, and about half of the women resided in San Francisco. These women were mostly confined to their prescribed roles in families.

The United States added Spanish speakers to its population when it acquired Florida in 1819 and many more following the Mexican-American War. The Treaty of Guadalupe Hidalgo (1848) permitted the nation to annex most of the Southwest. About 75,000 Mexicans living in this region were granted the right to become American citizens. Many did so, but a switch in loyalty did not prevent them from being overwhelmed by European Americans following the discovery of gold in California. Mexicans endured the loss of their lands, sometimes fraudulently; the loss of power; and an end to the pastoral life of Mexican California. The shabby treatment did not deter others from Mexico from emigrating to the United States. Like Europeans and Chinese, they came to work in the gold fields, along with other immigrants from Peru and Chile. Still other Mexicans, mostly men, came to work as cowboys or in agriculture. They were the forerunners of a greater migration from Mexico that occurred after 1910.

German Russians, Germans who had settled in western Russia several generations earlier and who had been allowed not only to maintain their cultural heritage but also to be free from military service, began arriving in the United States in the 1870s after the Russian government abrogated earlier agreements and tried to incorporate these people into the nation's broader society. Most of these Germans traveled to what later became North and South Dakota, but others could be found in Montana, Kansas, and Nebraska. Almost all were Lutherans, Mennonites, and Hutterites, and some of their colonies today are more in tune with the values of yesteryear than they are with those of contemporary American society.

The physical and economic growth of the United States in the nineteenth century made it mandatory for Americans to turn to the new settlers for cheap labor to plow fields, build canals and railroads, dig mines, and run machinery in fledgling factories. Without the newcomers the vast riches of the nation could not have been exploited quickly. Major efforts and inducements were made to lure Europeans, French Canadians, Chinese, and, later, Latin Americans to the United States. Their strong backs and steadfast enterprise were necessary to turn American dreams into American accomplishments. At the forefront of these efforts were the state and territorial governments, the railroads, and the various emigrant-aid societies, which were buttressed by federal legislation.

Just as the Atlantic seaboard states had made efforts in the colonial period to attract settlers, so in the nineteenth century practically every state and territory of the American West, plus several others, sought to entice select groups of Europeans to their area. More people meant more schools and post offices, larger federal appropriations for internal improvements, larger markets for goods, faster economic development, "and the speedy arrival of the eagerly desired railroad."

In 1845 Michigan became the first state to provide for the appointment of an immigration agent to recruit settlers at the New York docks, and Wisconsin followed suit seven years later. After the Civil War, though, the competition among states for Europeans intensified, and efforts to attract them expanded on a vast scale. At least 33 states and territorial governments eventually set up immigration bureaus, advertised in European and American foreign-language newspapers, sent agents to northern and western Europe, and published their brochures, guidebooks, and maps in English, Welsh, German, Dutch, French, Norwegian, and Swedish. Each state elaborated upon its virtues, "the likes of which," one historian has written, "had never been known—except to other states seeking immigration." Minnesota, proud of its "beautiful lakes, forests, prairies and salubrious climate"—and quiet about its subzero winters—offered two prizes for the best essays on the state as a place for European immigrants and then published them in seven languages. Kansas specifically exempted the Mennonites from militia service, and thousands of them moved there from central and eastern Europe in the 1870s.

In 1870 the recruitment movement came to a head when several midwestern governors organized a national immigration convention at Indianapolis. Delegates from 22 states and the District of Columbia discussed how the federal government could be more helpful in encouraging foreigners to settle in the United States, and they petitioned Congress to establish a national immigration bureau. The heyday for the state bureaus ended with the depression of 1873, but several continued into the 1880s and 1890s. On the eve of World War I, Louisiana officials still distributed enticing brochures in several foreign languages to those disembarking at New Orleans, and the legislatures of Michigan, Wisconsin, and South Dakota continued to make appropriations to induce foreigners to settle in their states.

The railroads worked as hard as the states to attract immigrants and, in fact, in the words of historian Carl Wittke, were "probably the most important promotional agencies at work for some years around the turn of the century." After 1854, but especially in the 1870s and 1880s, most of the transcontinental railroads actively promoted immigration to the areas where they owned lands. The more people who settled in any given location, the more business and profits for the trains. Crops and merchandise would have to be moved. With additional markets and sources of labor, industrialists and governmental aid would surely follow. Like the states, the railroads subsidized agents in Europe, advertised and printed brochures in many languages, and played up the virtues of their respective territories. In addition, some gave free or reduced passage to prospective settlers, established immigrant receiving houses near their terminals, and built churches and schools for fledgling communities.

The first railroad to seek foreigners aggressively, the Illinois Central, inaugurated its program in 1854. The line sent special agents to the German states and the Scandinavian countries, and these men attended fairs and church services, arranged meetings, advertised in the local press, and promised fabulous inducements to prospective settlers. Not only did they help secure ocean passage, but they also provided free railroad transportation to Illinois for prospective land purchasers and their families. If the immigrants then bought land from the company, the Illinois Central allowed for long-term payments at 6 percent interest, gave discounts to the farmers for shipping their future crops on the line, and agreed to pay all land taxes until land-buying payments were completed. Immigrants preferred buying railroad lands to homesteading free governmental acreage because of these inducements, and because the railroads often offered choicer properties.

The Illinois Central had almost completed its efforts in 1870 when most other railroads were inaugurating their land and development bureaus. Some functioned as agents for states: the Burlington line, for example, represented

Iowa; and the Northern Pacific line acted as Oregon's East Coast representative. Railroad companies also published monthly newsletters in various northern and western European languages, and the Northern Pacific even set up its own newspapers in Germany, Switzerland, and England. From 1882 to 1883 alone, the company printed 635,590 copies of its publications in English, Swedish, Norwegian, Danish, Dutch, and German and also distributed a monthly newsletter for immigrants, *Northwest*. The Burlington's efforts resulted in the sale of nearly 3 million acres in Iowa and Nebraska, and the Northern Pacific is credited with having more than doubled the population of Minnesota, the Dakotas, Montana, and the Pacific Northwest between 1880 and 1900.

Working together with the railroads and state agencies to encourage immigration were the various emigrant-aid societies. But unlike the state agencies and railroads, these semiphilanthropic organizations were more interested in assisting departing Europeans and easing their travails in a foreign land by providing interpreters, clean boardinghouses, and employment bureaus in the United States than in encouraging them to come to America in the first place. This aid was clearly necessary, for as one Swedish emigration agent explained, "most of the emigrants are entirely ignorant about how to come to America."

Numerous steamship lines also promoted vigorously their own interests by seeking out immigrants. By 1882, 48 steamship companies traversed the Atlantic, each competing furiously with the others for the immigrant traffic. Fares were relatively cheap. One could go from England to the United States, for instance, for about $12 to $15, from Copenhagen to New York for about $30, and from Odessa to Dakota Territory for $75. In many cases minor children accompanied their parents at no extra cost. Publicity and services attracted customers. The Red Star, Anchor, and Hamburg-American lines, among others, established more than 6,500 agencies in the United States to sell prepaid tickets. As early as the 1850s the Irish were sending more than a million dollars a year—about half in prepaid tickets—to their relatives and friends at home, and other immigrant groups were no less diligent. Estimates are that in the 1880s most of the Scandinavians emigrating to the United States came on prepaid tickets or purchased them with money specifically sent for that purpose. Although there are no exact statistics available, historians assume that 25 to 70 percent of all immigrants in the late nineteenth and early twentieth centuries received either prepaid tickets from the United States or money designated to facilitate the journey.

Although the companies vied for the immigrant traffic, few felt compelled to make the voyage comfortable for steerage passengers. Before the 1850s immigrants came in sailing vessels similar to those the colonists had arrived in a century or two earlier. The average journey across the Atlantic took about 44 days; voyages of four to six months were not uncommon. Like their forebears, many of those arriving in the nineteenth century, especially on English packets, which had been built for carrying cargo and not people, suffered inhumane treatment. Overcrowding, filth, stench, and poor ventilation were standard on almost all vessels, and tales of starvation and brutal assaults stand out in the accounts of the crossings. In 1846 a Dane who sailed to New York on a German ship wrote home, "Steerage became a regular brothel. We had four prostitutes and five thieves." Dysentery, cholera, typhoid fever, lice, and a disease known as "the itch" also presented problems. Those housed in the ship's bowels slept and ate on wooden bunks, which looked like dog kennels. One mid-century ship from Ireland possessed only 36 berths for 260 people; another had only 32 for 276. After one Irish ship had docked in New Orleans, customs officials found passengers and pigs lying together in "filth and feculent matter." One observer wrote that "it was a daily occurrence to see starving women and children fight for the food which was brought to the dogs and the pigs that were kept on the deck of the ship." An emigrants' guide in 1851 likened the fate of steerage travelers to that of prisoners on the African slavers; and as a surgeon who had served on six emigrant ships wrote, "The torments of hell might in some degree resemble the suffering of emigrants, but crime was punished in hell, whereas in an emigrant ship it flourished without check or retribution."

With the advent of steamships, however, conditions and amenities improved. The average crossing lasted fourteen days in 1867 and only five days in 1897. On the steamers all passengers had their own berths, women slept separately from men, and the galley provided three meals a day. Overcrowding and foul odors still existed, and the turbulence of the North Atlantic still forced many passengers to their knees to pray for divine assistance; but temporary inconveniences for two weeks or less could be endured. Moreover, between 1855 and 1875 both European and American governments established stringent rules to improve conditions for emigrants and restrict abuses by shipmasters.

Immigrant traffic followed commercial routes. Because of the Canadian timber trade and because British officials concluded that the fastest way to send mail to Canada was via Boston, a number of vessels, mostly British ships carrying the Irish, went to Massachusetts. Trade along the Mississippi River made New Orleans the major southern port; consequently it received the bulk of immigrants landing in the South. Since the journey to Louisiana took an extra two or three weeks and the climate in the lower South was muggy, most Europeans shunned that route. New York, the nation's major commercial center, also served as its chief immigration depot. After 1816 it accommodated more than 70 percent of the newcomers, and its reception centers at Castle Garden (on the southern tip of Manhattan) and later at Ellis Island became world famous.

Regulation of foreigners entering British America had been a function of the individual colonies and later, by tradition, of the states. Beginning in 1819 the federal government required the collection of vital statistics but otherwise allowed immigrants to enter unfettered until 1875, when it imposed additional regulations.

New York State, where most of the newcomers landed, passed a series of laws, beginning in 1824, requiring ship captains to post bonds indemnifying the state for any expenses incurred in connection with paupers disembarking there. Later the state required a $1 head tax on every steerage passenger to finance an immigrant hospital. In 1847 New York established the State Board of Commissioners of Immigration. The commissioners were granted the power to collect vital statistics, board and inspect incoming ships, establish and manage an immigrant hospital, and quarantine those who had communicable diseases. The commissioners, who served without pay, made every effort to assist the newly arrived foreigners. In 1855 they set up Castle Garden, a model reception center, through which everyone disembarking in New York had to pass. In this way the foreigners were counted, and their ages, occupations, religions, and the value of property they brought with them were recorded. Immigrants arriving at the center had to bathe with soap and water. Afterward they could purchase items like bread, milk, and coffee and use the extensive kitchen facilities to prepare their own food. Although officials encouraged everyone to leave the depot within hours of arrival, those who wished to remain could sleep overnight in the galleries. Beds were not provided, but a few thousand could be lodged. Immigration officials had already inspected and licensed numerous New York City boardinghouses and posted lists of suitable accommodations. Before this time many "greenhorns," as the immigrants were called, had been fleeced by boardinghouse agents and cheated by phony ticket sellers and other swindlers. To counteract this, Castle Garden also provided money exchanges and railroad and canal ticket booths for those going inland and disseminated information about the United States and employment opportunities throughout the country.

Castle Garden remained the nation's chief immigrant depot for more than 35 years. In 1876 the United States Supreme Court forbade New York State to collect bonds from ship captains on the ground that they were equivalent to head taxes, and for the next six years the state financed the reception center out of its general funds. In 1882 Congress levied a 50-cent head tax on newcomers and defrayed New York's expenses out of the monies collected.

The federal government finally took charge of immigration in 1890. Ellis Island then replaced the abandoned Castle Garden as the gateway to America for millions of Europeans. On the West Coast, Angel Island in San Francisco Bay received newcomers from China and other nations that bordered the Pacific Ocean.

Once through Castle Garden or Ellis Island, foreigners dispersed quickly (see table 2.2). Those too poor to go anywhere else remained in New York. Others, determined to reach the wooded regions and fertile prairies of the Midwest, obtained the necessary railroad or canal tickets and proceeded on their journeys. A favorite route began with a boat ride up the Hudson River to Albany and across the Erie Canal to Buffalo, then continued by water, rail, or wagon to the ultimate destination. Most of the nineteenth-century newcomers from Germany and Scandinavia wanted their own farms; the Homestead Act, invitations from the states and the railroads, and letters from relatives drew them to the north central plains, where land was either free or cheap. (As late as 1879 some Wisconsin land sold for 50 cents an acre.)

Those too poor to finance any trip—like many of the Irish—accepted offers from canal and railroad builders to be taken to various construction projects throughout the nation. As a result, pockets of Irish could be found in every region of the country. Most, however, remained in port cities or their environs, although by the end of the nineteenth century Irish colonies existed in San Francisco and New Orleans. The majority of Irish immigrants were in Massachusetts, New York, Pennsylvania, and Illinois.

As already noted, Germans constituted the most numerous of the nineteenth-century immigrants. Originally they hoped to plant a new Germany in America. Missouri in the 1830s, Texas in the 1840s, and Wisconsin in the 1850s were the states that they had hoped to make their own, but American expansion and ideology quickly frustrated such visions. Americans were unwilling to allow any group to carve out its own exclusive territory in the United States, and subsequent waves of immigrants showed no respect or tolerance for the wishes of those Germans who wanted to insulate their settlements. Germans toiled as farmers in rural areas and as both skilled and unskilled laborers in urban communities. Nearly half of them settled in Illinois, Michigan, Missouri, Iowa, and Wisconsin, but Texas published its laws in the German language in 1843, and Germans constituted one fifth of the white population there four years later. Many of the counties of west Texas owe their beginnings to German immigrants, and by 1900 about one third of the state's white population had German parents or grandparents. Germans also dominated the foreign-born statistics and lent a particular flavor to cities like St. Louis, Cincinnati, and Milwaukee. In New York City they outnumbered all other foreigners except the Irish in 1870. One observer described New

Table 2.2   The Urban Immigrant, 1870

Irish, German, and English Populations in American Cities

Name of City	Total Population	Irish	Germans	English
1. New York, N.Y.	942,292	202,000	151,203	24,408
2. Philadelphia, Pa.	674,022	96,698	50,746	22,034
3. Brooklyn, N.Y.	376,099	73,985	36,769	18,832
4. St. Louis, Mo.	310,864	32,239	59,040	5,366
5. Chicago, Ill.	298,977	40,000	52,316	10,026
6. Baltimore, Md.	267,354	15,223	35,276	2,138
7. Boston, Mass.	250,526	56,900	5,606	6,000
8. Cincinnati, Ohio	216,239	18,624	49,446	3,524
9. New Orleans, La.	191,418	14,693	15,224	2,005
10. San Francisco, Calif.	149,473	25,864	13,602	5,166
11. Buffalo, N.Y.	117,714	11,264	22,249	3,558
12. Washington, D.C.	109,200	6,948	4,131	1,231
13. Newark, N.J.	105,059	12,481	15,873	4,040
14. Louisville, Ky.	100,753	7,626	14,380	930
15. Cleveland, Ohio	92,829	9,964	15,855	4,530
16. Pittsburgh, Pa.	86,076	13,119	8,703	2,838
17. Jersey City, N.J.	82,546	17,665	7,151	4,005
18. Detroit, Mich.	79,577	6,970	12,647	3,282
19. Milwaukee, Wis.	71,440	3,784	22,600	1,395
20. Albany, N.Y.	69,422	13,276	5,168	1,572
21. Providence, R.I.	68,904	12,085	596	2,426
22. Rochester, N.Y.	62,386	6,078	7,730	2,530
23. Allegheny, Pa.	53,180	4,034	7,665	1,112
24. Richmond, Va.	51,038	1,239	1,621	289
25. New Haven, Conn.	50,840	9,601	2,423	1,087
26. Charleston, S.C.	48,956	2,180	1,826	234
27. Indianapolis, Ind.	48,244	3,321	5,286	697
28. Troy, N.Y.	46,465	10,877	1,174	1,575
29. Syracuse, N.Y.	43,051	172	5,062	1,345
30. Worcester, Mass.	41,105	389	325	893
31. Lowell, Mass.	40,928	103	34	1,697
32. Memphis, Tenn.	40,226	2,987	1,768	589
33. Cambridge, Mass.	39,634	7,180	482	1,043
34. Hartford, Conn.	37,180	7,438	1,458	787

(continued)

Table 2.2 (*continued*)

Irish, German, and English Populations in American Cities

Name of City	Total Population	Irish	Germans	English
35. Scranton, Pa.	35,092	6,491	3,056	1,444
36. Reading, Pa.	33,930	547	2,648	305
37. Paterson, N.J.	33,600	5,124	1,429	3,347
38. Kansas City, Mo.	32,260	2,869	1,884	709
39. Mobile, Ala.	32,034	2,000	843	386
40. Toledo, Ohio	31,584	3,032	5,341	694
41. Portland, Me.	31,413	3,900	82	557
42. Columbus, Ohio	31,274	1,845	3,982	504
43. Wilmington, Del.	30,841	3,503	684	613
44. Dayton, Ohio	30,473	1,326	4,962	394
45. Lawrence, Mass.	28,921	7,457	467	2,456
46. Utica, N.Y.	28,804	3,496	2,822	1,352
47. Charlestown, Mass.	28,323	4,803	216	488
48. Savannah, Ga.	28,235	2,197	787	251
49. Lynn, Mass.	28,233	3,232	17	330
50. Fall River, Mass.	26,766	5,572	37	4,042

SOURCE: U.S. Census. 1870.

York's German section in the 1850s: "Life in *Kleindeutschland* is almost the same as in the Old Country. . . . There is not a single business which is not run by Germans. Not only the shoemakers, tailors, barbers, physicians, grocers, and innkeepers are German, but the pastors and priests as well. . . . The resident of *Kleindeutschland* need not even know English in order to make a living." One chronicler made the same observation about people in and around Fort Wayne, Indiana. Until World War I it was possible for German immigrants, and for their children, to live a German-American life—attending German-language parochial or public schools, dozing through long German sermons from the pulpit, reading Fort Wayne German newspapers, purchasing grocery, hardware, and agricultural supplies from German stores that prudently employed German-speaking clerks, attending German band and choral performances, sharing a "grawler" of locally brewed German beer and locally packed German sausages with fellow workers at one of the 170 friendly ethnic saloons, and ultimately to take final rest in an exclusive German Lutheran, Catholic, or Jewish cemetery.

Scandinavians, a third group whose presence in nineteenth-century America is frequently noted, went mostly to the wheat-growing regions of Illinois, Wisconsin, Iowa, Minnesota, the Dakotas, Kansas, and Nebraska. The rich and fertile soil, the open spaces, and the harsh winter climate reminded them of their European homes, and with each successive wave of settlement there was the added attraction of living near friends and relatives from the old country. The solicitations from the actively recruiting states and railroads steered them into the Midwest, and the boom times of the early 1880s kept them there. Minnesota's population, buttressed by heavy migration from Germany and Scandinavia, soared from 8,425 in 1860 to 101,109 in 1870 and to 1,301,826 in 1890. Wisconsin, Iowa, Illinois, and the Dakotas showed similar rises. But the bitter winter of 1886–1887 and the successive years of failing wheat crops slowed the pace. Beginning in the early 1890s Scandinavians responded to the industrial opportunities in the Northeast and the Middle Atlantic states as well as in the lumber camps and sawmills of the Pacific Northwest. The influx of Scandinavians and others into the state of Washington, for example, reached such proportions that the state population jumped from 75,000 in 1880 to over 1 million in 1910. Every census after 1910 shows more than 60 percent of the Swedish-born and their children living in urban areas. In 1917 Chicago had the largest number of Swedes and Norwegians in the world next to Stockholm and Oslo, respectively, and 13 years later the federal census found a sizable Norwegian population comfortably established in a middle-class neighborhood of Brooklyn, New York.

Other nineteenth-century newcomers went to both urban and rural areas. The French Canadians had established small communities in Winooski, Vermont and Woonsocket, Rhode Island, as early as 1814 and 1815, respectively, and before 1850 in Madawaska and Burlington, Vermont. By the end of the nineteenth century they constituted a major minority in New England and much smaller ones in the cities of northern New York, Michigan, Illinois, and Wisconsin. Welsh people who came to America headed for the mining camps in Pennsylvania and Ohio. The Dutch, who went to the wooded and lake regions of southwestern Michigan, northern Illinois, and southern Wisconsin, also had settlements in Iowa, New York, Wyoming, and Arizona. Czechs, on the other hand, went mostly to the prairie lands in Wisconsin, Nebraska, and Texas. Some of the mountain states in the West attracted English, Scottish, and Welsh settlers, and the Mormons in Utah were particularly successful in converting some Dutch and Scandinavian peoples who then went on to places like Ogden and Salt Lake City. Immigrants from the British Isles, Germany, and the Russian Empire found the coal mines of the foothills of the Kiamichi Mountains in southeastern Oklahoma compelling because of the relatively high wages they could earn there.

Even the South—where officials and some businessmen desired northern and western Europeans to fill the labor ranks (white Southerners commonly considered blacks unsuitable for any work other than farm and domestic service) but the population in general did not want intruders—received contingents of foreigners. Swedes went to Thornsby, Arkansas; Danes farmed in Mississippi. Italians worked in Louisiana, Mississippi, and Tennessee; the Irish bolstered the populations of several southern cities; a Slavic community developed near Petersburg, Virginia; and some Chinese planted themselves in Mississippi. In the 1900 census of Alabama, Italians were the most numerous foreigners in Mobile County, the Irish stood out from all the rest in Bibb County, and Germans ranked at the top of Europeans living in Colbert, Montgomery, and Culliman counties.

Wherever they went and whoever they were, the immigrants lived and worked under conditions that were far from idyllic. Male workers were always needed in the dangerous construction of the canals and railroads, and strapping Irishmen won a reputation for talent and skill in these construction industries. Irish laborers built the Illinois Central Railroad before the company employed German hands. The Union Pacific used Mexicans, Germans, Chinese, and Irish to get its lines going. In rural areas, prairie fires, blizzards, the pestilence of grasshoppers, and the ravages of storms or long spells of dry weather were not unknown. Food was often scarce. Many Danes in Nebraska wore wooden shoes rather than leather ones; among many of the pioneers, who depended upon the homespun garments that their women made for them, underwear was also considered a luxury that hardier settlers did without. A German in Indiana wrote home in 1842, "We have reduced our requirements for luxuries very sharply: We drink coffee on Sundays only, go barefoot all summer and make our own clothes because we keep sheep and can also make flax."

Life in rural America was exceedingly difficult for women. Farm lands had to be cleared and crops planted and harvested. Women were expected to help with these tasks in addition to rearing children and running the household. Unmarried women carried a major farming burden. Because doctors were rare, women also helped one another in sickness and childbirth. Although immigrants set up ethnic organizations, the church being the most important, to aid in settlement and survival, primitive transportation made communication with friends and family difficult during the harsh winter months. Because of their isolation, rural families were apt to cling to traditional practices and values, in which the women played such a vital role. They spoke in their native language to the children, prepared ethnic foods, and in general conveyed a sense of the Old World culture. It is no doubt true that women in immigrant families were the main keepers of ethnic cultures because of their central role in family life, and in rural America it was possible to resist the process of Americanization more easily than in the cities.

Mass immigration also resulted in new social problems for urban dwellers, especially in congested cities like New York City and Chicago. Many immigrants were either unemployed or underemployed, and disease and poverty were common. Inexperienced immigrants found coping difficult.

Immigrants generally found work easily in the United States, but often in unskilled jobs. In cities like New York, Boston, and Chicago immigrants composed the bulk of the unskilled laborers, porters, street cleaners, bartenders, waiters, draymen, cabmen, carmen, livery workers, and domestics. The Irish could be found as stevedores on docks at every major port in the country. In New England they replaced young American women in the mills and later stepped aside for the French Canadians. Germans in New York held menial positions but also qualified as tailors and skilled craftsmen in furniture, cabinet making, and bookbinding firms; in Cincinnati they were dominant in the stove and musical instrument industries. Those Norwegians who did not farm worked in the iron mines and lumber camps in Michigan, in the sawmills and fisheries in the Pacific Northwest, and at other industrial tasks in places as diverse as Tacoma, Cleveland, and Brooklyn.

Irish women constituted two thirds of the domestics in Boston as early as 1860. Many Scandinavian women also migrated alone and became domestic servants. Swedish women, no less than Swedish men, found limited economic opportunities at home, and it became common for young daughters to seek outside employment. But as with Irish women, employment in their home country offered them little chance for advancement. From the 1870s to World War I, single women constituted nearly 30 percent of Swedish immigrants. They quickly found that domestic service was a better job in America than in Sweden. One historian examining the letters of these young women wrote that in America, unlike Sweden, a domestic was "treated like a human being." Newcomers tended to find jobs near other Swedes with whom they could associate during their leisure hours. Many woman looked upon domestic service not as a loss in status but as an improvement over conditions they had left at home.

Most immigrant men expected their wives to stay home, raise the children, and care for the household, for immigrant families often included five or more children. Women also served as midwives to bring their neighbors', friends', and relatives' children into the world. Unmarried women were usually sent to work to contribute to the family income. They found jobs in the nation's growing number of garment shops, in the printing business, as domestics, and as dressmakers. After women married they usually remained at home, but on occasion some still sought outside employment. Others added to their domestic responsibilities, and contributed to the family coffers, by taking in lodgers. One historian described the situation among Irish anthracite miners in Pennsylvania: "in addition to a married couple and their children, households often included other relatives, or a number of boarders, or in some cases a second family. These households were almost ethnically exclusive."

Widows and those whose husbands had deserted them needed to support their children. Socially acceptable work for which they had the necessary skill, such as sewing at home, was not lucrative. Not even the labor of their children, who went to work at an early age, could provide enough income. Thus in much of the United States a strikingly large number of households headed by women lived in a precarious state. Scandinavian, Irish, and German women had no qualms about serving as domestics, but French Canadians shunned personal service for factory work. The mainstay of the late nineteenth-century New England textile mills, French-Canadian families, insisted that all their members be employed at the same establishment. They put little premium on education and thought that children as well as adults should contribute to the family coffers. One overseer in a textile mill recalled telling a French-Canadian family that the law prohibited the hiring of children under the age of ten, "and the next day they were all ten." In the West the Chinese were forced to accept the menial jobs that whites shunned in mines, in domestic service, and on farms. Chinese also opened restaurants and laundries, and they made up half of California's agricultural workers by 1884.

Some immigrants were excluded from unions; others, unfamiliar with American labor practices and the advantages of unions, worked as scabs and strikebreakers. Chinese laborers showed little regard for the white man's union; when white miners struck in 1875, the Union Pacific brought 125 Chinese to mine in Rock Springs, Wyoming. Ten years later a similar problem resulted in the further importation of Chinese workers, who refused to join the Knights of Labor. This no doubt precipitated the September 1885 massacre in Rock Springs, where whites killed 28 Chinese laborers, wounded 15 others, and chased several hundred out of town.

The conditions under which Americans and immigrants labored were often appalling. Since American wages were much higher than those in Europe and Asia, emigrants did not realize that there could be economic hardships in the United States, due to a correspondingly high cost of living. In Sweden farmhands earned $33.50 a year, plus room and board. It is no wonder, therefore, that a salary of $40 a month in the Pennsylvania coal mines, $1.25 to $2.00 a day on a railroad construction gang, or $200 a year as an American farmhand would be appealing. Not until they reached the United

States and had to cope with the realities of urban squalor or rural depression did the emigrants realize that the American laborer did not lead a princely existence.

During the boom times in the Midwest after the Civil War, farm income was relatively high. Wheat sold for $1.50 a bushel, and hard work seemed to ensure prosperity. But in the 1890s wheat prices fell on the world market to 50 cents a bushel. Countless farmers were ruined. There is no doubt that the failure of wheat crops in places like Kansas, Nebraska, Minnesota, and the Dakotas contributed to the decline in migration to those areas in the late 1880s and early 1890s.

Employees in industrial enterprises fared just as badly as those on the farm. In the nineteenth century there was a chronic labor shortage even though at times cities like Boston had more people than jobs. But the pay in most occupations failed to sustain even a modest standard of living. In 1851 *The New York Times* and the New York *Tribune* published estimated budgets for a family of five. The first came to about $600 a year, the second to $539. Yet the wage scales reveal that most employees' yearly incomes fell far short of these figures. A skilled tailor might earn $6 to $9 a week but did not work a 52-week year. Cabinetmakers earned $5 a week, and common laborers took home $20 to $30 a month. A journeyman dressmaker earned $1.25 to $1.50 for a 14- to 16- hour day. In Boston, in 1830, when the annual cost of living was $440, the average working person earned $230; in 1864, when the cost of living rose to $810, the average unskilled laborer made only $465. Real wages increased in the decades after the Civil War, but many immigrant families received only a few hundred dollars a year and had to struggle to maintain a modest standard of living.

Such low wages and yearly incomes make clear why so many immigrants, as well as many native-born Americans, lived in humble and often squalid dwellings. The typical Norwegian in the upper Midwest built a log cabin 12 feet by 12 or 14 feet, with a height of 7 to 14 feet, for himself and his family. The early Dutch pioneers of Michigan lived under bedsheets framed on hemlock branches, with cooking pots outside. When they earned enough to build a more commodious abode, several families shared a one-room log cabin. The German Russians in North Dakota put together homes representative of many others on the Great Plains. Inexpensively built, they had interior walls plastered with a straw- or prairie-grass clay mud and limewashed. Few of the homes had wooden floors since lumber was too expensive and the original occupants did not expect to remain long.

Urban enclaves also left much to be desired. In small cities like Fall River and Holyoke, Massachusetts, French Canadians crowded into dark, dank, rat-infested tenements that one chronicler pronounced "worse than the old slave quarters." Housing in most of the major urban centers was also appalling. In Boston the Irish resided in "crammed hovels . . . without furniture and with patches of dirty straw," in damp cellars that flowed with raw sewage after heavy rains, or in reconverted factory lofts with leaking roofs, broken windows, and no running water. Historian Oscar Handlin, who vividly chronicled their experiences, tells us that in winter the Boston Irish often remained in bed all day to protect themselves from the cold or "huddled together like brutes, without regard to sex, or age, or sense of decency." Similar hovels existed in New York as well. In the middle of the century 18,000 people lived in cellars without light, air, or drainage, and even those residing above them had to use outdoor, and often malfunctioning, privies—winter and summer. Overcrowding was proverbial; half a million people lived in 16,000 dilapidated tenements. The Irish often grouped five or six families in a single flat. Three quarters of the city had no sewers; garbage and horse droppings littered ghetto streets.

The appalling overcrowding of immigrants and lack of proper sanitation led to continual bouts with disease. Slum dwellers suffered from consumption, cancer, pneumonia, diarrhea, and bronchitis. They were also victims of periodic epidemics of typhoid, typhus, and cholera, which spread through the neighborhoods like fires in a parched forest. Cities having the largest immigrant populations—New York, St. Louis, Cincinnati, and New Orleans—suffered the most from such outbreaks. In 1851 a cholera epidemic hit Chicago, and in one three-block section where 332 Scandinavians (mostly Norwegians) lived, *everyone* died from the disease. Hospitals and lunatic asylums housed disproportionately high numbers of newcomers. In 1850s New York City, 85 percent of the foreign-born admitted to Bellevue Hospital were Irish; so were most of those admitted to Blackwell's Island, the city's asylum.

In rural areas too settlers, poorly versed in the need for proper sanitation, preventative measures, and the benefits of quarantines during bouts with contagious diseases, often fell prey to the ravages of epidemics. In 1898 a wave of diphtheria spread through McIntosh County, North Dakota, yet the German Russians insisted that every member of the family attend all of the funerals of neighbors who perished. As a result all the adults and children in the community either had the disease or had been exposed to it. One cabinetmaker there, who worked day and night building coffins, had to construct three for his own children, ages 12, 10, and 3, who died within a week of one another.

Poverty was another common affliction for the immigrants. Rural folk would sometimes benefit from the generosity of their neighbors, but in the larger cities many of the poor turned to almshouses. Those forced to accept charity also had to tolerate the sanctimonious declaration that they were merely "the indolent, the aged, and infirm who can earn their subsistence nowhere, [but must] become a burden, and often because of their vices, a nuisance to the community." The foreign-born outnumbered the native-born in the poorhouses of the nation in 1850; in some states, like New York, the ratio was greater than 2:1. The problem worsened with the arrival of new immigrants.

Among the most serious difficulties newcomers encountered was American intolerance for ethnic differences. Each immigrant group experienced hostility in countless ways. The best jobs were closed to them, and employers posted signs saying NO IRISH NEED APPLY or some variation on that theme. Institutions dealing with the foreign-born—almshouses, hospital dispensaries, employment bureaus—treated their clients with "a ridiculous, often brutal disdain." Hardly any minority escaped the barbs of the prejudiced. The Germans received abuse from several sides. Temperance advocates did not like their making merry, drinking beer, and ignoring the Puritan Sabbath. Conservatives distrusted radical and reform-minded German exiles from the abortive revolutions of 1848 who supported the abolition of slavery, women's rights, and other liberal causes in America.

Economics in part explains ethnic intolerance. The increase in immigration, especially of many poverty-stricken refugees from Ireland, aroused American fears of having too many poor people. And large numbers of unskilled laborers, it was argued, would depress wages and the American standard of living. Americans also deplored what they considered the immigrants' striking personal deficiencies. A Massachusetts Bureau of Labor Statistics report in the 1880s censured the French Canadians for their lack of "moral character, their lack of respect for American institutions, their failure to become naturalized, and their opposition to education."

Before the Civil War the most important source of conflict between native-born and immigrant was religion. More precisely, the key battles were fought over American objections to Irish Catholics. The underlying issue revolved around the American belief that Roman Catholicism and American institutions, which were based on Protestant concepts, were incompatible. In this view, if Catholics "took over" America, the pope in Rome would rule and religious and political liberty would be destroyed. Samuel F.B. Morse, inventor of the telegraph, believed that there was a Catholic plot to destroy the United States. He held that the Church was sending Jesuit-controlled immigrants to America. Writing in 1835, he asked his countrymen not to be any longer "deceived by the pensioned Jesuits, who have surrounded your press, are now using it all over the country to stifle the cries of danger, and lull your fears by attributing your alarm to a false cause. . . . To your posts! . . . Fly to protect the vulnerable places of your Constitution and Laws. Place your guards; you will need them, and quickly too.—And first, shut your gates."

Morse was not the only impassioned enemy of Catholicism. Militant Protestants wrote sensational exposés of the Church. The most famous of the anti-Catholic diatribes was Maria Monk's *Awful Disclosures of the Hotel Dieu Nunnery of Montreal*, published in 1836. This gothic horror tale was frequently reprinted and sold several hundred thousand copies. According to her inflammatory story, the author was compelled to live in sin with priests in the nunnery and witnessed the execution of nuns for refusing to submit to the men's carnal lusts. She even insisted that babies were strangled and buried in the basement of the Hotel Dieu Nunnery. Such yarns created inevitable controversy. On the one hand, Monk's work was cited by anti-Catholics as proof of their worst fears, and on the other hand, indignant Catholics and skeptical Protestants denounced the book as a fraud. Investigations turned up no evidence to support her charges, and Maria Monk was personally discredited as a prostitute. Nevertheless, many believed her story, and the book continued to inflame the passions of the anti-Catholic crusade. Her success encouraged others to publish similar hair-raising studies, and she herself added to the literature by writing *Further Disclosures*, also about the Hotel Dieu.

These accounts fanned the passions of the day and contributed to violence. In August of 1834 an angry mob burned the Ursuline Convent outside of Boston. Nativist violence occurred in other places in antebellum America, including a riot in Philadelphia in the summer of 1844. Most conflicts did not lead to violence but involved controversies over control of church property, religious teaching in the schools, and the general issues of separation of church and state.

Not satisfied with exposés and agitation, the nativists turned to state and national politics for weapons against the detested Catholics. A few nativist political organizations and parties existed prior to 1850, but the major nativist party flourished during the 1850s. Called the Know-Nothings, this large secret organization suffered from a number of sectional disagreements and eventually fell apart as a national movement. At its peak it was held together by a suspicion of the Roman Catholic Church. In 1854 the party scored victories at the polls, won control of several state governments, and sent dozens of congressmen to Washington. The Know-Nothings were strongest in the Northeast and the border states. Once in office the nativists proposed a number of bills to restrict the franchise and to make naturalization a longer process. They also established legislative committees to investigate alleged misconduct in Catholic institutions. Many Know-Nothings who took Maria Monk seriously were convinced that nuns were virtual prisoners in convents, and they petitioned state governments to free these women.

The proposals and investigations produced few results, and did not lead to immigration restriction. The movement failed in part because the party was fragmented, in part because discussions concerning the morality and extension of slavery consumed American political attention in the late 1850s. But most important, despite fears about Catholics and their imagined habits and other alleged evils of immigration, was the fact that Americans welcomed immigrants because they were needed to help the nation expand and develop economically.

Yet even without native hostility, foreigners and their children preferred living in ethnic enclaves and often resisted moving into the mainstream. In some Norwegian communities a "yankee was almost an alien" and a visitor to Scandinavia, Wisconsin in 1879–1880 noted: "On the streets, in stores, one heard only Norwegian. The church was a replica of those at home; the minister wore the vestments of the State Church; the hymnbooks were the same as those used in Norway." A more recent commentator wrote that although his grandparents lived in the United States for more than sixty years, "There's no evidence that they had more than glancing contact with anyone who was not Norwegian."

Several groups, including Irish Catholics, Germans, and Scandinavians, established parochial schools to preserve traditions and thwart assimilation. The French Canadians feared that losing their language would mean losing their faith, which to them meant absolute loss of identity. For the Irish, language presented hardly any problem, but their church claimed their staunchest allegiance. To them nothing seemed as important as keeping the faith. Many sermons and religious tracts of the Irish Catholics, historian Hasia Diner tells us, "linked common schooling with Protestantism, atheism, sexual depravity, and social unrest." In the upper Midwest, among other places, Germans and Scandinavians maintained Lutheran parochial institutions of learning. In 1917 Minnesota alone had over 350 elementary and secondary schools; 270 different German-language texts were in use. Fewer than one third of all the parochial schools in Minnesota on the eve of World War I taught their children in the English language. Most of the rest utilized German, but there were also public schools conducted in Polish, French, Norwegian, Danish, Dutch, and Czech.

Schooling and language were closely tied to religion, and many religious groups split over the appropriate course of behavior and action. Most curricula opted for the maintenance of established values. Among Catholics, liberal cardinals like James Gibbons of Baltimore and John Ireland of St. Paul argued for a gospel of success and accommodation with the members of the dominant society. They favored assimilation, opposed parochial schools, and frowned on Catholic insularity. But the more conservative theologians of the Northeast, like Bishop Bernard McQuaid of Rochester, Archbishop Michael Corrigan of New York City, and William Cardinal O'Connor of Boston, did not agree with their more liberal counterparts. "Clinging to medieval visions of church and society," prize-winning historian Kerby Miller tells us, "the conservatives revered tradition, order, and authority both religious and secular." They feared socialism and progressive change and aligned themselves "with the most reactionary elements of native society. Likewise their refusal to attribute social and spiritual ills to any source other than 'Anglo-Saxonism' (their synonym for Protestantism and materialism) impelled conservatives to segregate their flocks behind rigid ideological and institutional barriers."

Protestants suffered from similar woes. One chronicler of newcomers to South Dakota noted, "The central role of the church as a conservative force that defended cultural continuity with the past cannot be overstated. It was the key to cultural maintenance and local identity in all immigrant communities." Constant admonitions from Scandinavian clergymen that "language saves faith" and knowledge of English promoted loss of heritage permeated the region.

Germans especially clung to their religious traditions and fought bitterly any attempt to interfere with their cultural heritage. In 1889, when Wisconsin and Illinois passed laws requiring some of the education of school-age children to be conducted in English, both Lutheran and Catholic Germans denounced the new measures. Their united opposition led to Republican electoral defeats in both states and the subsequent repeal of the offensive acts. The strong stand Germans took against compulsory education in English reinforced prevailing views about their clannishness. What is more, they did little to alter this impression, making great efforts to maintain the Old World culture. In Nashville, Tennessee, observers noted that the newcomers "used the German language as a weapon to ward off Americanization and assimilation and used every social milieu—the home, the press, and the church—in the fight to preserve the German language and German customs among their children and grandchildren." Historian Andrew Yox, who wrote about newcomers in the North, reiterated almost the same point.

The German immigrants who came to America in the mid-nineteenth century established a counterculture they called *Deutschtum*. In medium-sized cities like Buffalo, Cincinnati, and Milwaukee, the German quarter consisted of Gothic steeples, rows of small frame cottages, open-air markets, and the ubiquitous saloon. Unlike the sedate neighborhoods of the Anglo-Americans, the German district rustled with sounds. Beer gardens, brass bands, shops, dance halls, and "slumber-breaking" bells, installed in the steeples to rouse the artisans for work, teamed up to deprive the Yankees of their once-quiet weekends. The German community was younger, more tolerant with regard to beer and dancing, and more populated than the native American sectors. With respect to other immigrant enclaves, the German colony was larger and more developed. In major cities, *Deutschtum* consisted not only of stores and saloons, but banks, hospitals, orchestra halls, and elite social clubs.

Efforts were made to keep everything German; women in particular were admonished "that they must seek to preserve the German spirit in their children." A Texas grandmother, who had come to this country as a 10-year-old girl in 1846, published her memoirs, *Was Grossmutter Erzählt* (1915), in her native tongue and reminded readers that "German family life stands for the preservation of an ideal culture, which can only continue to exert its influence if respected from generation to generation." Most German Americans obviously felt the same way, for at the beginning of the twentieth century it was rare for midwestern Germans to choose mates from other ethnic groups, and on the eve of World War I, 70 percent of the Lutheran churches in St. Louis conducted their services in German. In some German-Russian areas of North Dakota, moreover, church services and Sunday schools in the German language continued into the early 1950s.

The intense concern for preserving the culture of the *Vaterland* also led to vigorous organizational activities. German Americans maintained newspapers, fraternal organizations, gymnastic and cultural societies, choral and athletic groups, and benevolent organizations. Newspapers not only preserved cultural identity but also explained the American scene, helped promote settlement, urged readers to become citizens, and related quantities of information about the homeland to homesick emigrants. By 1900, over 750 German-language newspapers existed in the United States, 64 of them in North and South Dakota alone. In fact, in 1905 the *Dakota Freie Press* had more subscribers than any English-language newspaper in South Dakota. German daily and weekly papers also dotted the landscape in all of the major American cities.

Germans also enjoyed their ethnic theater, their beer, their convivial picnics, their pleasure-filled Sundays, and their melodious music. While parks all over America had bandstands filled by German oompah bands, their *Liederkranz* (singing societies) and *Sangerbunde* (regional and national associations of song groups) made an even more significant national impact. The *Liederkranz* groups were among the most popular cultural societies in the nation between the end of the Civil War and the advent of World War I.

Composed of all-male choruses (some cities had female auxiliaries), they promoted not only choral songs but also classical music, opera, and philharmonic concepts. These singing societies were a major force on the cultural scene in cities like Chicago, Buffalo, Philadelphia, Pittsburgh, Cincinnati, and many other cities. In Louisville, Kentucky, "the Liederkranz was the most prestigious of all the musical organizations," while in Wheeling, West Virginia, there were eleven different German singing societies from 1855 until their demise in 1961 and, we are told, "for many of Wheeling's German citizens the singing societies were a way of life."

The coming of World War I marked the decline of the German American culture. Other Americans demanded 100 percent loyalty and renounced everything and everyone that smacked of "the Hun." Though many resented these pressures, German Americans made a strong effort to conform to the dominant customs and thereby weakened their own heritage.

Scandinavians, who were mostly Lutheran, were more devout and strait-laced than the Germans. No one caricatured them as jolly or frolicsome. Their faith, a stern one that frowned on drinking, dancing, and levity, also provided a complete philosophy of life stressing piety along with the work ethic. This influence was so pervasive and persistent that in 1934 fully two thirds of all the Protestant church members in Minnesota, Wisconsin, and the Dakotas still belonged to the Lutheran church.

The security derived from family, ethnic neighborhood, school, church, society, and newspapers hastened the day when immigrant children or grandchildren could stand securely on their own and move into the mainstream of American life. Having been nurtured in relative security, they had the strength to meet new challenges of becoming Americanized head-on. They knew, however, that the customs that provided a secure ground for their parents or grandparents would not suffice for them in the United States. Girls and women, more sheltered from the outside world than boys and men, took their cues from fathers and husbands, changing their ways to the extent that the head of the household dictated. Yet disclaimers must be made. To be sure, in the German and Scandinavian households traditional values and lifestyles prevailed. In most of these homes women were respected and appreciated for what they were—"good, laborious, submissive, and silent housewives." But among some of the German Russians in the Dakotas, women were somehow thought to be of considerably less value to a family unit; one popular saying among them went

When women die, it is not a tragedy
But when horses die, it is a disaster.

Among the Irish, however, women dominated family life. Perhaps because "the tone of male-female relations within Irish families was indeed characterized by intense animosity," as historian Hasia Diner tells us, as well as "a high rate of domestic violence and discord, [and] the frequent desertion of the male breadwinner," wives and mothers emerged as the strong and stable forces in the family. And because so much violence and disorder occurred in Irish families, a larger percentage of Irish females than those of any other immigrant group sought work outside of the home and delayed or refrained from marriage. Political activist Elizabeth Gurley Flynn recalled: "A domestic life and possibly a large family had no attraction for me. My mother's aversion to both had undoubtedly affected me profoundly. She was strong for her girls 'being somebody' and 'having a life of their own.'"

And of those who did marry, Irish women more than any other ethnic females except blacks appeared in census rolls as heads of family. For example, in 1870 in Philadelphia 16.9 percent of Irish women headed families, compared to only 5.9 percent headed by German females. (Only black families had a higher percentage of female heads in Philadelphia that year.) The tradition of strong, assertive Irish women provided excellent role models for their daughters, many of whom later became successful as nurses and teachers. Jobs existed for Irish women who wanted to teach, for they spoke English. The public schools did not wish to spend much money educating the growing number of immigrant children pouring into their schools, and Irish women provided them with a supply of low-wage teachers. They soon made up about one fourth of the teachers in many cities.

Irish women and their daughters also found career opportunities in education, especially in the expanding parochial school systems. Although the Catholic Church called for a school in every parish, it was unable to fulfill its goal. Still, the parochial school system expanded at the end of the nineteenth century, and women constituted the bulk of instructional staff; they even ran some of the schools. Irish women also became nurses and worked in a variety of religious charities. In some of these institutions they held supervisory positions.

Thus, as we summarize the lives, experiences, and adventures of these immigrants, we reiterate that the complexities, the inequities, and the incongruities of so many immigrants' lives combined with the dynamics of American society to foster a new type of individual in the United States. Almost always rooted in and committed to their ethnic heritage, and often desperate to preserve their native cultures intact, these newcomers frequently discovered that the realities of life in both urban and rural America eventually intruded on the values they wished to continue. To a certain extent, of course, modicums of the culture were preserved. But each successive generation viewed itself as more American and less ethnic. And the advent of World War I in 1917 proved a mighty blow to ethnic life in the United States.

Chapter 3

A New Wave of Immigrants, 1890s–1920s

AS THE NINETEENTH CENTURY progressed, industrialization spread southward and eastward in Europe. Uprooted peoples left their farms and villages, moved into towns and cities, crossed national boundaries, and traversed the oceans. In this worldwide movement millions of uprooted Europeans dispersed. Warsaw, Berlin, Vienna, Naples, and London were as much inundated by newcomers as were New York, Chicago, and Philadelphia. Germany, France, Brazil, Argentina, and Great Britain received hundreds of thousands of immigrants. However, the United States, with its higher standard of living and reputation for being a land of golden opportunity, attracted the largest number. Between the early 1880s, when southern and eastern Europeans began impacting American immigration statistics, and 1930, when the combination of restrictive legislation and a major depression established barriers, the United States received a total of 27 million immigrants.

After 1890 newcomers from northern and western Europe continued coming to American shores, but they had less impact. Of the 788,992 immigrants of 1882, for example, the nineteenth century's peak year for immigration, 250,630 were from Germany, whereas only 32,159 were from Italy, 27,935 from the Austro-Hungarian Empire, and 16,918 from Russia and the Baltic countries. In 1907, the peak year for early twentieth-century migration, of the 1,285,349 recorded entrants only 37,807 came from Germany, whereas 298,124 came from Italy, 338,452 from the Austro-Hungarian Empire, and 258,943 from Russia and the Baltic States.

Just as the Germans, Irish, and Scandinavians had before them, southern and eastern Europeans were escaping from economic strangulation and despair. Southern Italians, especially, fled horrendous conditions, including unemployment, high birth rates, overpopulation, and cholera and malaria epidemics. Many Italian peasants lived in houses of skew (straw) or even in rock caves and abandoned Greek tombs. Often, one-room shacks housed people and livestock together. An agricultural laborer earned 8 to 32 cents a day in Sicily but rarely worked an entire year. Furthermore, while the population in Italy increased by 25 percent from 1871 to 1905, the economy slackened. Wheat, citrus fruits, and wine, commodities that were the mainsprings of the

Italian rural economy, declined drastically in price on the world market. The resulting poverty made some Italian arrivals in the United States declare afterward, "we would have eaten each other had we stayed."

Some northern Italians had left the country earlier in the nineteenth century. After national unification in 1859, though, relaxed emigration restrictions and expanded steamship advertising combined with a depressed economy to induce southern as well as northern Italian men and boys, and a few women, to seek their fortunes in the New World. Many went to Brazil and Argentina, but depressions in those countries in the 1890s encouraged emigrants to opt for the United States even though it too experienced severe economic woes. The comparative prosperity and opportunities here, which were communicated in letters and reported by returning immigrants, finally resulted in a deluge of emigrants, many of whom left Italy through Naples. Between 1876 and 1930 more than 5 million Italians sailed for the United States. Table 3.1 indicates the peak years for Italian arrivals.

Jews ranked second to Italians among the immigrants. In the late nineteenth and early twentieth centuries over 2 million of them left eastern Europe, more than 70 percent coming from Russia. Over 90 percent of the Jews headed for the United States, the remainder going to cities in central and western Europe, Canada, and Latin America. While others were victimized by a changing agricultural economy, the Russian Jews were aliens in the land of their birth. Russian laws, with few exceptions, restricted them to life in enclosed settlements (mostly in eastern Poland and western Russia), curtailed their educational and occupational opportunities, and conscripted Jewish youths for years of military service. Things were made still worse by violence. The assassination of Czar Alexander II in 1881 set off a wave of government-condoned pogroms—brutal beatings, killings, and lootings—which lasted for about 30 years. Jews never knew where or when the terror would strike next. A particularly devastating pogrom in the city of Kishinieff in 1903 involved 2,750 families; 47 people were killed and 424 were wounded, many Jewish homes were burned, and Jewish shops were pillaged. The massacre received worldwide attention and vastly increased the number of Jews emigrating from Russia. As a consequence of these east European migrations, the Jewish population in the United States soared from about 250,000 (mostly of German descent) in 1877 to more than 4 million in 1927.

The Slavic groups—which included Russians, Ruthenians (Ukrainians), Slovaks, Slovenes, Poles, Croatians, Serbs, and Bulgarians—together accounted for about 4 million of the new arrivals in the United States. Each of these ethnic groups had a distinctive language, set of customs, and historical experience, but most dispersed themselves throughout the country and

Table 3.1   Italian Immigration in Peak
Years, 1905–1920

Year	Number
1905	316,797
1906	358,569
1907	298,124
1909	280,351
1912	267,637
1913	376,776
1920	349,042

SOURCE: Immigration and Naturalization Service, *Annual Reports*

either set up separate enclaves or blended in with other Slavic groups. Many were mistakenly identified in the census tracts or lumped together as Slavs and otherwise ignored.

The Poles, the largest of the Slavic groups, were counted separately after 1899, and as a result we know that after the Italians and the Jews, they were the third largest element among early twentieth-century immigrants. Well over a million Poles arrived before World War I; their coming can be attributed to the acute poverty in territory controlled by Russia and the suppression of Polish culture and nationalism in the sections of Poland under Austrian domination. The Poles, like practically all other Europeans, were influenced by letters from compatriots who had already settled in the United States. Many of these were published in newspapers, while others circulated widely in the villages.

Several other groups came to the United States for similar reasons. Among them were about 1 million Magyars from Hungary, perhaps 400,000 Greeks, 233,000 Portuguese, 105,000 Czechs, 70,000 or 80,000 Armenians, and thousands of Syrians escaping from Turkish tyranny; about 90,000 Japanese came from Asia and Hawaii. World War I temporarily interrupted the major flow, but in the 1920s another 800,000 Italians, 160,000 Scots (more than the entire colonial migration from Scotland), almost 500,000 legally accounted-for Mexicans (many more crossed the border illegally), and over 400,000 Germans streamed into this country.

One of the most overlooked groups was the Basques, who settled in the Great Basin (the area roughly between Salt Lake City and the Sierra Nevada

Mountains in eastern California, which includes most of Nevada, southeastern Oregon, and southwestern Idaho) at the end of the nineteenth and the beginning of the twentieth centuries. Their homeland, Basque country on the Iberian peninsula in Europe, had been taken over partially by France in 1789 but mainly by Spain in 1839. Since generation after generation of Basques produced larger families than the local economy could absorb, grown children frequently emigrated. There were and are Basques in many Latin American countries, and the Basques also populated California during the Spanish and Mexican periods. Today Boise, Idaho contains the largest Basque contingent outside the Iberian peninsula. Other Basque colonies are in eastern Oregon, California, Nevada, Wyoming, and Colorado. Since the Basques are Caucasians, they have not been enumerated separately in either immigration figures or census returns. Including members of the second and third generations, there are more than 20,000 Basques in the West today.

In recent decades many Koreans, Asian Indians, and Filipinos have immigrated to the United States in large numbers, but they were not the first of their groups to arrive. Several thousand Koreans went to Hawaii around the turn of the century. They had been recruited to work in the sugar cane fields. Most were males who came to make money and return home, but some came as families; both men and women labored in cane fields. A thousand or so went from Hawaii to the United States, where they usually settled in California. About 80 percent of these Californians were men who became agricultural workers. Asian Indians, numbering 6,500, also came to work in agriculture. Their main location was the Imperial Valley of California. Often called "Hindoos," these overwhelmingly male immigrants from Punjab were Sikhs. In the United States about half married Mexican women. When Congress barred the immigration of Korean and Asian Indian workers, Hawaiian cane growers turned to Filipino men to replace them. Filipinos also came to the West Coast, where they too labored in agriculture, in Alaskan canneries, or as domestic servants. Few brought their families, and like many Chinese, Koreans, and Asian Indians, they lived chiefly in bachelor societies.

Caribbean immigrants, who often went to other places in the Caribbean and Latin America in search of work, also began coming to the United States. Bahamians headed for Florida to pick crops, and after 1900, they tended to settle in Miami where they worked as construction laborers and as service personnel in the expanding tourist industry. A larger group of black immigrants went to New York City. They were mostly English speakers, but some from Haiti and Martinique spoke French, and formed their own communities and published their own newspapers. Cuban immigrants at first arrived as political exiles during the nineteenth century. These were middle-class immigrants, but others came in the late nineteenth and early twentieth centuries to work in the cigar making industries of Key West and Tampa, Florida.

Arabs also arrived after 1880. These immigrants from Syria or Lebanon, like others, left because of economic reasons. During World War I living conditions in the Middle East were particularly harsh. But in addition, the people had heard from Protestant missionaries about the wonders of America. The early waves arriving before World War I were mostly Christians. Most settled in New York City; others peddled throughout the United States. As a result, small Arab communities eventually developed in places such as Detroit, Washington, D.C., and Iowa. Other Lebanese immigrants worked in factories in New York City, Maine, and Michigan.

Except for the Irish, the majority of European and Middle Eastern immigrants consisted of young adult males. Among European immigrants, 78 percent of the Italians, 95 percent of the Greeks, and about half of the Jews were male. From Asia, Japanese immigrants, like the Chinese before them, were overwhelmingly male. Although many men sent for their wives and children, others hoped to make their fame and fortune and return to their native countries. Few made fortunes, but many returned.

Intelligent estimates of how many foreigners returned to their native countries range from a high of nearly 90 percent for the Balkan peoples to a low of 5 percent for the Jews. We do know that in the period between 1908 and 1914, immigration officials recorded 6,703,357 arrivals and 2,063,767 departures. During these years, more than half the Hungarians, Italians, Croatians, and Slovenes returned to Europe. For the most part returnees included a high percentage of single men. A number of Italian men migrated annually to Italy in the fall, returning to the United States the next spring. Availability of jobs determined their movement. During the winter months, many Italians in railroad, construction, and mining work saw no point in remaining unemployed in the United States. From 1908 through 1916, 1,215,998 Italians left. This back-and-forth migration virtually ceased by the mid-1920s after the quota system went into effect.

Eighty percent of the new immigrants settled in the northeastern quadrant of the United States, roughly delineated by Washington in the southeast, St. Louis in the southwest, the Mississippi River, Canada, and the Atlantic Ocean. Two thirds of the immigrants could be found in New York, New England, Pennsylvania, and New Jersey; sizable numbers also gravitated toward states like Illinois and Ohio. Relatively few went to the South.

Major cities, especially New York and Chicago, proved particularly attractive because of the jobs available, their location as major transportation depots, and the presence of compatriots who could help the immigrants adjust to the New World. A majority of the Jews and many Italians remained in New York City. Other groups also found city life desirable. According to the census records of 1910, about three quarters of the population of New York City, Chicago, Detroit, Cleveland, and Boston consisted of immigrants and their children. Foreign enclaves also dominated cities like Philadelphia, St. Louis, Milwaukee, Buffalo, Baltimore, Pittsburgh, and Providence. In 1916, 72 percent of San Francisco's population spoke a foreign language in addition to English.

Although some habitats naturally had more to offer than others, no *area* of the United States escaped the immigrants' attention or proved totally unsuitable to all groups. Thus one could find—then as now—Italians in Louisiana, Michigan, and Colorado; Hungarians and Greeks in Florida; Slavs in Virginia; Mexicans in Illinois; Irish in Montana; Armenians in Massachusetts and California; Basques in Idaho and Oregon; Serbs and Croatians in Nevada; German Russians in North Dakota; and Jews in Arizona and New Mexico. Foreigners, including the English, Russians, Lithuanians, Poles, Magyars, and Italians, outnumbered the native-born throughout the Oklahoma coalfields by a margin of 2:1 in 1890. One Oklahoman noted, "You name it and they were all workin' together here. And they got along just fine too." Certainly these immigrants constituted minorities in the states where they lived, but it is significant that so many places in the United States afforded opportunities to the venturesome.

The immigrants came with high hopes, and although in some places they got on well, in general they were unprepared for the coolness with which so many Americans received them. Like those who had come earlier, the new immigrants were often stereotyped as representatives of some kind of lower species. None of the newer groups escaped contempt. Greeks were physically attacked in Omaha, Nebraska and forced out of Mountain View, Idaho. A New Englander, observing some Poles weeding rows of onions, commented: "Animals, they work under the sun and in the dirt; with stolid, stupid faces." On the West Coast, San Franciscans created an international incident by segregating the fewer than 100 Japanese students in the city's schools.

Italians, who outnumbered all other twentieth-century European immigrants, were one of the most despised groups. Old-stock Americans called them "wops," "dagos," and "guineas" and referred to them as the "Chinese of Europe" and "just as bad as the Negroes." In the South some Italians were forced to attend all-black schools, and in both the North and the South they were victimized by brutality. In 1875 *The New York Times* thought it "perhaps hopeless to think of civilizing [Italians] or keeping them in order, except by the arm of the law." Other newspapers proclaimed that Italians were criminal by nature, and a supposedly intelligent and sympathetic observer wrote that Italians "are as a race simpleminded and often grossly ignorant." University of Wisconsin sociologist E.A. Ross, one of the Progressive Era's most outspoken bigots, explained that crime in Italy had declined significantly since the migrations began "because all the criminals are here." Americans were fortified in their beliefs about southern Italians because many northern Italians, who had arrived here decades earlier, also regarded their compatriots from the south as "an army of barbarians encamped among us."

Jews experienced similar problems. In colonial America they had not been allowed to vote, and the restriction lasted, in some states, well into the nineteenth century. Not until New Hampshire removed its barriers in 1877 did American Jews have the franchise in every state. Even where there were no Jews, prejudice and misconceptions abounded. On stage Jews almost always appeared as scoundrels. To have portrayed male Jews in a sympathetic or admirable vein, one scholar tells us, "would have been in defiance of the centuries-old tradition that in the drama the Jew must be the villain or the object of derision."

When the east European Jews arrived, they were often scorned, even by German Jews. The Germans, who had arrived in the mid-nineteenth century, did not want Russian, Galician, and Rumanian Jews in their midst. German Jews had achieved considerable success in the United States and had absorbed the nation's values; many had even refurbished their religious practices, bringing them more into line with Protestantism. The stampede of east European Jews, with their long beards, peculiar clothing, and staunch devotion to an orthodox faith that seemed strange to many Americans, threatened members of the established Jewish community. They envisioned, correctly, an increase in anti-Semitic feeling, which would affect their hard-won respectability. Their views were most specifically stated in an 1894 issue of the *Hebrew Standard*: "The thoroughly acclimated American Jew . . . has no religious, social or intellectual sympathies with the east European Jew. He is closer to the Christian sentiment around him than to the Judaism of these miserable darkened Hebrews." But the American Jews could do nothing to stem the east European tide, nor could they stop other Americans from lumping all Jews together. Once they recognized these facts, they reversed their position and did what they could to help the newcomers adjust to life in America.

Although the German Jews eventually reconciled themselves to having their coreligionists from eastern Europe in the United States, other Americans did not. Beginning in the 1870s, latent or often privately uttered anti-

Semitism emerged into the open and struck first at those Jews who were the most Americanized. The New York Bar Association blackballed a Jew who applied for membership in 1877; a City College of New York fraternity did the same thing a year later; and a major resort hotel in Saratoga Springs, New York, barred a longtime guest, Joseph Seligman, one of New York City's leading bankers. Thereafter, clubs, resorts, and private schools increasingly turned away Jewish patrons. Hostility toward Jews knew no geographical bounds. In the 1890s, Jewish merchants in the South had their stores wrecked and were harassed by threats to leave town. In a New Jersey mill town several days of rioting resulted after a local firm hired fourteen Jews. By the Progressive Era, open discrimination prevailed in housing and employment. Hotels displayed signs proclaiming NO JEWS ALLOWED, and job advertisements specified CHRISTIANS ONLY.

No amount of prejudice or hostility toward the newcomers, however, prevented employers from putting the greenhorns to work. The industrial sections of the country needed cheap labor and foreigners provided the necessary hands. Older immigrants and native-born workers would not tolerate conditions the immigrants had to accept, and so toward the end of the nineteenth century Slavs and Italians replaced British, Irish, and Germans in Pennsylvania coal mines; Portuguese, Greeks, Syrians, Armenians, and Italians worked alongside French Canadians in the New England textile mills; east European Jews and southern Italians took over the jobs formerly held by the Irish and Germans in New York City's garment factories; and the Japanese on the West Coast did the agricultural and menial tasks that had formerly been the province of the Chinese. The United States was certainly not paradise for the foreigners. However, one immigrant residing in Chicago probably summarized the majority feeling when he wrote to his mother in Europe: "Nowhere there is heaven, everywhere misery, in America no good, but still better than in the [old] country."

Because immigrants felt more comfortable working and living among friends and relatives, ethnic groups concentrated in particular industries and occupations. The Slavic groups located in the mining and industrial regions of western Pennsylvania, Ohio, Illinois, Michigan, and New York. They also provided the bulk of the labor in Chicago's slaughterhouses and Pennsylvania's steel mills, where they were considered desirable because of "their habit of silent submission, their amenability to discipline and their willingness to work long hours and overtime without a murmur"—or, as the Pittsburgh *Leader* bluntly put it, because the east European immigrant made "a better slave than the American." About one third of the Poles also went into farming in the Northeast and the Midwest. They did truck gardening on Long Island, cultivated tobacco, onions, and asparagus in the Connecticut Valley, and planted corn and wheat in the north central Midwest.

Greeks avoided farming but went into industry or operated small businesses of their own. One survey at the beginning of the twentieth century found that about 30,000 to 40,000 of the 150,000 Greeks in the United States were laborers in factories or in railroad construction gangs. But others peddled fruit and vegetables or maintained shoeshine and ice-cream parlors, flower shops, restaurants, or confectioneries. The association of Greeks with candy and food was proverbial. Chicago became the center of their sweets trade, and in 1904 a Greek newspaperman observed that "practically every busy corner in Chicago is occupied by a Greek candy store." After World War II Greeks still maintained 350 to 450 confectionery shops and 8 to 10 candy manufacturers in the Windy City. Most Americans still connect the Greeks with restaurants, and for good reason. Almost every major American city boasts fine Greek eating establishments, a tradition that goes back more than half a century. After World War I, for example, estimates were that Greeks owned 564 restaurants in San Francisco alone.

Italians settled everywhere and entered almost every occupation, or so it seems at first glance. They built subways in New York, manufactured cigars in Florida, and made wine in California. In Chicago they manned the stockyards, and in San Francisco they caught fish. They constituted a large segment of New England's textile workers and were second only to the Jews in New York's garment trades. They provided gang labor on railroads and construction projects and worked underground in the bituminous coal fields of Illinois, Kansas, and Oklahoma, the iron mines of Michigan and Minnesota, and the copper and silver mines of Colorado, Arizona, and Montana. In 1894 they constituted all but one of New York City's 474 foreign-born bootblacks; in 1897, 75 percent of the city's construction workers. They moved into public sanitation departments in New York, Chicago, and Philadelphia. In 1911 a federal commission found that they accounted for the largest number of common laborers of any ethnic group in America.

But Italians also yearned for the security of their own businesses, and as soon as they were able, they bought pushcarts or opened small stores. In New York City they dominated the fruit business in all its phases, from produce market to retail outlet. They opened shoe-repair shops, restaurants, groceries, and bakeries. Some made spaghetti, others made candy. Many cut hair, and by 1910 more than half the barbers in New York City were Italian. Italians are also responsible for much of the opera that exists in the United States.

Unlike the Italians, who left Europe for the most part illiterate and unskilled, 67 percent of the Jewish males who arrived in the early part of the twentieth century were classified as skilled workers. This figure compared with an average of 20 percent for all other male immigrants. Most of the Jews utilized their craftsmanship in New York's garment trades, which employed half the city's Jewish workers. On the eve of World War I, in fact, 70 percent of all workers in New York's clothing industry were Jews. Other Jewish workers found jobs in cigar factories and distilleries, as printers and bookbinders, and as skilled carpenters. For the unskilled, a peddler's pushcart often opened the path to settled retail trade throughout the country, while the enormous numbers of Jews, with their special dietary needs, gave rise to the establishment of kosher butchers, grocers, and neighborhood candy stores, which also sold soda water, newspapers, stationery, tobacco, and sundries. Jews also found opportunities in music and the theater, and in the early decades of the twentieth century they made up half the actors, popular songwriters, and song publishers in New York City.

Outside the big cities, in the Rocky Mountain area for example, Basques have been associated with sheep raising in the West's Great Basin. They have been herders, foremen, buyers, transporters, and ranch owners. When they arrived in the 1870s and 1880s, they were valued for their shepherding skills but despised as a minority. Some people referred to them derogatively as "Bascos," likened them to "Chinamen," and described them as filthy, treacherous, and meddlesome. Nevertheless, they maintained their calm and went about their work. Shepherding is a lonely, monotonous task, but the Basques excelled at it. Their culture values people who succeed in physically arduous tasks that also require grit and determination. One analyst opined that the Basque "sees physical labor and adverse working conditions as a personal challenge which affords an opportunity to merit the approbation of his peers." Basques dominated the western sheep industry from the end of the nineteenth century, but they also entered a wide variety of industrial and professional activities.

Many Japanese immigrants on the West Coast became truck farmers. Beginning as farm laborers, they managed to acquire their own places, raising food for local markets. In the Hood River Valley of Oregon they won a reputation for their apple orchards. In cities such as Los Angeles and Seattle they operated small businesses. They ran hotels, fruit and vegetable stands, barber shops, restaurants, and laundries. Whether farms or businesses, these were family enterprises. Japanese men, who began the immigration stream, sent for their wives and children back home. If they were single, they married young Japanese women by proxy. These "picture brides," as they were called, arrived in America without having seen their new husbands. Many were shocked to find men older than they appeared in their pictures. One remarked, "When I first saw my fiancé, I could not believe my eyes. His hair was grey and I could not see any resemblance to the picture I had. He was forty-six years old." But once here, brides worked beside their husbands when the children were in school.

Like most of the immigrant men who preceded them, the latest newcomers expected their wives to stay at home to raise children and run the family. Girls were socialized to become wives and mothers. But immigrant families were so poor that they needed the wages of daughters, who often went to work at an early age. Those few women who came on their own to the New World were expected to live with relatives and contribute to the family coffers until they had families of their own. Work was rigidly segregated by gender, and women usually took low-paying jobs in the garment shops of Chicago and New York or in the mill towns of New England.

Of course, married women could stay at home and earn money just like women of yore. In Johnstown, Pennsylvania, women had few opportunities outside of the home, but with many single men coming to work in the mills, they could take in boarders. The 1900 census found more than half of all east central European households with lodgers. This meant "more overcrowding, less privacy, more drinking and fighting, and an exhausting seventeen hours a day of work for the wife who had to cook, clean, scrub, wash, iron, carry water and do the shopping." Obviously caring for boarders was undesirable and women tried to avoid it. Thomas Bell's novel of Slovak life, *Out of This Furnace*, noted how when times were good in Pittsburgh's mills, families tried to avoid having lodgers, but all too often, as the statistics make clear, it became an economic necessity.

Women found other ways to earn money while remaining at home. Mothers and daughters did needlework or made artificial flowers to be sold on the streets. One girl told a New York State investigating committee, "When I go home from school, I help my mother to work. I help her earn the money. I do not play at all. I get up at 6 o'clock and I go to bed at 10 o'clock." Reformers at the turn of the century considered home work involving children or in unhealthy occupations such as rolling cigars to be especially harmful to their health, and they gradually convinced legislative bodies to outlaw it. With inspectors in short supply, the laws were not always enforced.

Wherever the newcomers labored, employers sapped them of their energies before replacing them with fresh recruits. Industrial accidents proliferated. The infamous Triangle Shirtwaist Factory fire in New York City in 1911 took 146 lives, mainly young women. One fireman who watched the women leap to their deaths told of the horror. "They hit the pavement just like hail. We could hear the thuds faster than we could see the bodies fall." Construction and railroad workers also frequently met with fatal injuries, as did newcomers in the Pittsburgh steel mills. Even where the workers were fortunate to escape alive, working conditions often ensured irreparable damage to health. In Riverside, California, Armenian cement makers inhaled dust and poisonous gases emitted in the large, overheated grinding rooms. In

Chicago, Greek teenagers slaved in shoeshine parlors from 6 A.M. to 8 P.M. Afterward, the boys cleaned the stores before being allowed to return to barrackslike dwellings for a supper of stale bread and watery soup. The yearly earnings of a shoeshine boy were $160 to $180. A Hungarian immigrant complained about his experiences in a Pittsburgh steel mill: "Wherever the heat is most insupportable, the flames most scorching, the smoke and soot most choking, there we are certain to find compatriots bent and wasted with toil." In New York home sweatshops, whole families bent over coats and suits with their sewing needles.

In labor camps, where many immigrant men worked, conditions were as bad as in the cities, if not worse. Armed guards patrolled isolated labor camps in Georgia and West Virginia, and beatings with iron bars and gun butts kept the men at their jobs. When a Hungarian immigrant tried to escape from a Georgia lumber camp, his bosses went after him with trained dogs. When they caught him, he was horsewhipped and then tied to the buggy for the return trip. Peonage, though illegal, was widely practiced. Eventually, charges were brought against this particular lumber camp and the owners had to stand trial. As the Hungarian peon recalled, a peculiar kind of justice was enacted. "Of all things that mixed my thinking in America," he later wrote, "nothing was so strange as to find that the bosses who were indicted for holding us in peonage could go out free on bail, while we, the laborers, who had been flogged and beaten and robbed, should be kept in jail because we had neither money nor friends." In a West Virginia labor camp Italian workers slept in wooden boxcars where "the dirt of two years covered the mattresses. Roaches and bedbugs livened the walls and held undisputed sway of the beds and their immediate surroundings. . . . All doors were closed at night. No windows, no air. Nothing seemed to have been left undone to reduce human beings to animals." The workday for these men lasted from 5 A.M. to 4 P.M. with an hour off for lunch. They were never given morning breaks because the *padrone* who controlled them resisted: "The beasts must not be given a rest. Otherwise they will step over me."

Greek and Italian *padrones*, or labor agents, exercised great control over the immigrants. The *padrones*, who had come to the United States earlier, spoke English and arranged jobs and found living accommodations for their later-arriving compatriots. Men and boys were sent to railroad and construction gangs, lumber camps, and factories. A *padrone* collected the salaries of everyone under him, or else a prior fee for placement, and kept a portion for himself as his commission. He also performed sundry tasks like writing letters and sending money back home for those unable to do so themselves. Often, and accurately, accused of taking advantage of those who placed their trust in him—the record of abuses committed by the *padrones* is replete with reports of decrepit rooming houses and vanishing payrolls—the *padrone* nonetheless performed the valuable services of easing the adjustment to the New World and of obtaining a man's initial position for him. In 1897 two thirds of the Italian workers in New York were controlled by *padrones*, but as the immigrant numbers increased and the states began to regulate labor agents, the need for these intermediaries lessened. By the beginning of the twentieth century in Chicago and on the eve of World War I in New York, the number of *padrones* had declined considerably.

Although new immigrants had little trouble finding jobs—either with or without the assistance of the *padrones*—the wages paid rarely provided for a family's subsistence. One scholar discovered that in a Pittsburgh steel district where a family needed $15 a week to survive, two thirds of the recent immigrants earned $12.50 a week, while the other third took home less than $10. Tales abound of garment workers earning 8 cents an hour; others made $1.25 for a full week's work. Prior to World War I, residents of New York City required a yearly wage of $876 to maintain a minimum standard of living, yet most families earned less. Among all immigrants, Armenians, Jews, and Greeks generally fared better than Poles, Slovaks, southern Italians, and Serbs.

Wages were especially low for immigrant women who found jobs in the garment industries, in laundries, or as domestics. Yet these jobs were more desirable than others. Less fortunate women who arrived alone and without money ended up as prostitutes in the nation's red-light districts. Indignant and moralistic reformers sometimes exaggerated the extent of the "white slave" traffic, but prostitution certainly existed. One muckraking journalist described the plight of some of these women in New York City.

> Just north of Houston Street are the long streets of signs where the Polish and Slovak servant-girls sit in stiff rows in the dingy employment agencies, waiting to be picked up as domestic servants. The odds against these unfortunate, bland-faced farm girls are greater than those against the Galician Jews. They arrive here more like tagged baggage than human beings, are crowded in barracks of boarding-houses, eight and ten in a room at night, and in the morning the runner for the employment agency takes them with all their belongings in a cheap valise, to sit and wait again for mistresses. . . . Just below this section of Poles and Slavs lies the great body of the Jews. . . . These girls are easily secured. . . . In many cases the men who obtain control of them do not even speak their language.

With working-class life so desolate, union organization made firm headway. Garment workers in New York and Chicago went out on strike in 1910 and after long struggles finally won the right to collective bargaining. In an industry run by tyrannical foremen and profit-hungry owners, unions like the Amalgamated Clothing Workers and the International Ladies' Garment Workers' Union (ILGWU) pioneered efforts to establish safety and sanitary codes and to obtain shorter hours and higher wages. The people in the garment trades—owners, workers, and union organizers—were predominantly Jewish (and secondarily Italian), and this was the case well into the twentieth century. In 1924 Jews constituted 64 percent of the ILGWU members, and as late as the 1940s they made up 75 percent of the members of Dressmakers Local 22 in New York City. As the decades passed, however, Jews concentrated in the upper echelons of management in both factories and unions and were replaced in the rank and file by blacks, Latin Americans, and Asians.

Although trade union leaders were usually men, there were exceptions. One of the most notable examples of women leading strikes occurred in the "Great Uprising" of 1909 in the shirtwaist factories of New York City, when 20,000 workers walked out and began the process of organizing the industry. Jewish women became leaders in the strike and in unionization. Some historians have suggested that it was not the poor working conditions of the shops alone that triggered female activism, but also the radical culture of their European background. Others think that Jewish families gave their young women more freedom than did Italian families, and this may account for the greater Jewish participation. Whatever the exact cause, young Jewish women took the lead, answered the call, and played a major role in organizing garment workers. Many of these women, such as Rose Schneiderman and Clara Lemlich, remained active in union and radical politics for years.

Garment workers who struck in 1909 had the support of middle-class reformers, and two years later their cause was greatly strengthened by the Triangle Fire. While the strikes of New York's women garment workers became famous, historians have noted that Polish women struck Detroit's cigar makers in 1916 and Italian, Polish, Lithuanian, Greek, Syrian, Armenian, and Portuguese daughters and wives participated in the Lawrence, Massachusetts, textile strike of 1912.

The beginnings of union organization and the continuous replenishment of workers at the lowest job levels by newer immigrants provided minorities with opportunities to upgrade their positions and move away from the slums. It is remarkable, in retrospect, how people survived and continued to work and hope for better lives when they were mired in such depressed conditions. Whole neighborhoods were filthy, foul smelling, and overcrowded. In cities like Boston, New York, and Chicago houses adjoined stables, and offal, debris, and horse manure littered the streets. Piles of garbage in front of buildings or in narrow passageways between houses gave rise to stomach-turning odors and a large rat population. Population density was astronomical, some sections of Chicago, for example, having three times as many inhabitants as the most crowded portions of Tokyo and Calcutta. In 1901 a Polish neighborhood in the Windy City averaged 340 people per acre, and a three-block area housed 7,306 children. In the late nineteenth and early twentieth centuries Italian sections of New York, Philadelphia, and Chicago seemed little better. One survey taker found that 1,231 Italians were living in 120 rooms in New York; another reporter could not find a single bathtub in a three-block area of tenements. In Chicago a two- or three-room apartment might house an Italian family of parents, grandparents, several children, boarders, and cousins. A 1910 survey revealed that many of Philadelphia's Italian families had to cook, eat, and sleep in the same room, while most shared outhouses and a water hydrant—the only plumbing facility available—with four or five other families. In addition, many Italians kept chickens in their bedrooms and goats in their cellars. In 1901 New York passed a tenement-house law requiring that all new buildings have windows 12 feet away from the opposite building, toilets and running water in each apartment, and solid staircases within each structure. But it was many years before a majority of the newcomers occupied such houses.

Although members of various groups shared similar working and housing conditions, it would be a mistake to suggest that they also had common aspirations. All, of course, desired decent homes, well-paying jobs, and the opportunity to maintain their own lifestyles free of strife. But ethnic groups differed in cultural ethos and the ways in which they chose to attain their goals. Their attitudes toward family, education, religion, success, philanthropy, and community affairs differed considerably. Moreover, values of the various groups frequently collided with the dominant strain in this country, a factor that sometimes created new problems.

The non-British minority groups spoke a foreign language when they arrived in America, and this placed an immediate stigma upon them. For their own emotional security they chose to live in neighborhoods inhabited by people like themselves; as a result they had even less reason to learn English quickly. Immigrant women felt particularly isolated because they rarely left the insulated community. Many of the men were also cut off from interaction with other groups, especially when they worked with their compatriots in similar occupations, a situation that further retarded the assimilation process. As one Italian put it, "When I arrived in New York I went to live with my *paesani* [countrymen]. I did not see any reason for learning English. I did not need it for everywhere I lived, or worked or fooled around, there were only Italians." Habits of dress, food preparation, and religious practices were also retained by the immigrants. But children, educated in the United States, could not accept or feel completely at home with all of their parents' ways. Although they did not sever cultural ties, immigrant children tried to harmonize as much of their parents' values as they could with the demands of American society. Inevitably, such efforts created intergenerational strains.

Italians, for example, placed little importance on *individual* success or accomplishment. A person was supposed to enhance the family's fortune or honor, not his or her own. Only members of the family and their close blood relations were considered important and trustworthy. All outsiders were strangers to whom one had no responsibilities. Family honor had to be defended to the death, if necessary, but society's laws were of little moment. "Individual initiative was virtually unknown," one scholar tells us, and "all actions had to receive the sanctions of tradition and custom." Most of the Italian immigrants seemed to follow the advice contained in a southern Italian proverb: "Do not make your child better than you are."

The Italian *contadini* (peasants), who had a history of oppression, linked education with class, status, and nobility. It was regarded as something that peasants—and women—could not aspire to. Education might be financed with surplus wealth, but most immigrant families could barely sustain themselves on what they earned. The *contadini* also had other reasons for being wary of the schoolhouse. In Italy, historian Rudolph Vecoli tells us, "educated persons were regarded with mistrust; in the old country, the priest and professor had been among the exploiters. Immigrant parents prized education solely for its utilitarian value; reading in itself was thought to be an idle, and perhaps injurious, pastime." Southern Italian immigrants therefore did not encourage their children to excel in reading. As soon as the law allowed, they pulled their offspring out of school and sent them to work. Material advancement was what counted.

Some Italians, of course, did not subscribe to these views. The first American of Italian descent to become a governor and a United States senator, Rhode Island's John O. Pastore, had a mother who was impassioned with achieving American middle-class respectability. She made her sons wear fresh shirts every day and admonished them, "Make yourself liked; make people respect you." New York City's first Italian American school principal recalled his father's urging, "Go to school. Even if it kills you." But these were the exceptions. Before World War II, few immigrant Italians graduated from high school or attended college. One survey of Italian children in St. Louis found that a majority went beyond the sixth grade for the first time in the 1930s. In 1940 only 1 percent of residents on the "Hill"—the Italian area in St. Louis—had graduated from high school, and only 13 percent had done so in 1970.

Southern Italian attitudes toward religion and the Church also differed considerably from those of most Americans and other immigrants. Nominally Roman Catholic, Italians as a whole did not share the Irish dedication to the faith. Unlike American Protestants, who are not always dutiful in their attendance at church services but who tend to maintain a respect for the institution and its members, most Italians regarded the church as "a cold and almost puritanical organization." Moreover, they looked upon the priests as they had in Italy, "as lazy, ignorant hangers-on who merely earned their living off the community." It was not that Italians lacked religious beliefs, but rather that their customs differed from those of the dominant Irish Catholics. They were flexible about doctrine, ignorant of many traditional aspects of Roman Catholicism, and devoted to their festivals and *festas*. The southern Italian immigrant feared "the evil eye" and its effects, and, as one historian tells us, "through the use of rituals, symbols, and charms, they sought to ward off evil spirits and to gain the favor of powerful deities."

Irish domination of the American Catholic Church caused further problems. The Irish hierarchy looked down upon the Italians. One said, "When they are told that they are about the worst Catholics that ever came to this country, they don't resist, or deny. If they were a little more sensitive to such remarks they would improve faster. The Italians are callous as regards religion." An 1884 census of 50,000 Italians in New York City showed that 48,000 of them "neglected church services." Italian men left it to the women to attend mass and to keep the faith. One scholar remarked of his father, "Typical of males of contadino origins, my father had been an infrequent churchgoer, attending Mass only on major holidays like Christmas and on those traditional occasions when family loyalty made presence compulsory—weddings and funerals."

Eventually the Church appointed Italian-speaking priests to serve in predominately Italian parishes. Father Antonio Demo, who headed a parish from 1898 to the Great Depression, helped his New York flock find jobs and deal with authorities; he even worked with Protestant groups on mutual concerns. Italian women were also recruited by Church officials to train as nurses and teachers. As successive generations of Italians Americanized, they adhered more closely to the dominant standards of the Roman Catholic Church in the United States.

Immigrant Italians rarely united for community programs. Southern Italians were devoted to their families and had some loyalty to members of their villages or communities in Italy, but they lacked an overall ethnic commitment. Italian mutual-benefit societies existed in the United States, but for the most part they helped comparatively small numbers. Regional dialects and lack of widespread written communication, as well as a diversity of thought, actions, and lifestyles, divided Italians of different provinces and regions and made any kind of group organization almost impossible in the United States. Not until 1967, in fact, did the Italian-American Civil Rights League band together to protect and defend those of Italian descent from abusive treatment by other Americans.

On the other hand, Jewish success in this area won the admiration of numerous groups. In 1908, when the New York City police commissioner asserted that many criminals were Jewish, Jews protested vigorously. A New York Italian newspaper remarked approvingly: "The Jews are all connected to each other, and, when they believe a patent offense has occurred to their colony, they act as one man."

Pogroms in Russia from 1903 to 1906 provided a focus for organized Jewish efforts to help their brethren in distress, and led to the formation of the American Jewish Committee, an organization composed of and representing the Americanized German Jewish community. The Committee pledged itself to protect the civil rights of all Jews throughout the world. In 1913 midwestern Jews organized another defense organization, B'nai B'rith's Anti-Defamation League (ADL), four weeks after an Atlanta jury convicted a Jew, Leo Frank, of murder primarily, as B'nai B'rith and other Jews saw it, because he was a Jew. The ADL, dedicated to combating prejudice in the United States wherever it existed, was the first such general defense organization founded in this country, and over the years has been quite successful in curbing the effects of prejudicial behavior.

Jews differed from Italians in a number of other ways. The east Europeans were more religiously observant; unlike for the Italians, becoming more American for Jews meant a weakening of religious ties. Moreover, the Jewish faith embodies ethical prescriptions that make charity a social obligation, and most Jews still accept that view. For those who seek honor and prestige within the Jewish community, philanthropy is a necessity. Respect and appreciation go to those involved in humanitarian endeavors.

This sense of *noblesse oblige*, combined with fears that east European Jews would exacerbate anti-Semitism among non-Jews, motivated German and Americanized Jews to help the newcomers adjust to life in America. To acculturate their European cousins, German Jewish individuals and agencies supported educational institutions that trained foreigners to speak English, started a Yiddish-language newspaper for Lower East Side ghetto dwellers, and funded the Jewish Theological Seminary to train Americanized Conservative, rather than Orthodox, rabbis. No efforts were spared to bring Jews into the mainstream of American life. And to prevent them from becoming a burden on society, wealthier and more established Jews in the United States financed homes for orphans, delinquents, and unwed mothers as well as new Jewish hospitals.

East European Jews accepted whatever assistance they got; they also endeavored to provide their own facilities. They too established charitable organizations to help the needy, and devoted themselves to the quest for culture. Between 1885 and 1915 they started over 150 Yiddish-language newspapers, journals, and yearbooks. The best known of those was Abraham Cahan's *Forward*. At its height before World War I, it was the ghetto's leading daily and over the years the most widely read Yiddish newspaper in this country. In addition, Jews established successful theater groups, and participants like Paul Muni, Jacob Adler, and Molly Picon went on to Broadway and Hollywood. East European Jews attended concerts and lectures and afterward moved on to the most popular cultural institution on the Lower East Side, the café or coffeehouse, where they would debate endlessly about plays, poets, pianists, politics, and the direction society was taking.

More than anything else, however, the Jews sought knowledge. New York City's Educational Alliance had a regular daily attendance of 500 and a waiting list of 1,000 for English classes, which were given at all hours of the day and 6 evenings a week. The poorest Jewish families saw to it that their children attended public school, and teachers generally praised the youngsters for their industry and deportment. By 1915 Jews made up 85 percent of the student body at New York's free but renowned City College, one fifth of those attending New York University, and one sixth of the students at Columbia.

Like all other immigrant groups, Jews were more enthusiastic about educating boys than about teaching girls. But Jewish women had a tradition of literacy in the Old World. Whereas Italian and other immigrant families took their girls out of school as soon as possible, Jewish parents were much more supportive of female education. It no doubt helped that Jews were better off than many other immigrants and did not always have to send young women to work. There were also practical reasons for educating girls: well-trained women could help their husbands and fathers in the many small family businesses. And as the white-collar economy began to expand after 1910 it offered a wider variety of opportunities. Teaching was another profession open to women. During the Great Depression of the 1930s, over half the women college students in New York City were Jewish. They later provided the greatest number of new public school teachers.

Jews who lived outside New York City did not have a million-plus coreligionists to support a full and rounded community life. Accordingly, most relinquished Old World customs at a faster pace. It is for this reason, in fact, that first- and second-generation New York City Jews remained where they landed. Rural areas, small towns, and even some of the bigger cities simply could not provide the cultural and educational opportunities as well as the Jewish sense of community so essential to these east European newcomers.

Other immigrants also sought to maintain their own cultures in the United States. For the Magyars in America, both social and religious life revolved around the Church. The Poles were also devoted to the Roman Catholic Church and supported the institution generously. On the other hand, they thought less highly of education or advancing their children's positions in society. For most of the east central European Catholic peasants, home ownership was clearly the primary goal. Children may have been expected to learn to read and write, tutored in the group's rich history and traditions, and inculcated in the precepts of their faith, but as one Polish-American second-generation male complained, "Immigrant parents often thoughtlessly sacrificed their children's future to the exigencies of their own survival, sending them off to jobs when they should still have been in school or college."

Some parents, however, made decisions about education deliberately and without qualms, and in this regard their views were reinforced by the local priest, who "urged 'hard-working creatures of God' to exercise humility and patience suitable for their condition planned by 'Almighty Providence.'" Many ethnics agreed with such pronouncements. Too much education, they believed, was inappropriate for their youth.

Two scholars, Ewa Morawska and Helene Lopata, have written extensively on this phenomenon. Morawska explains that among east central European Slavs:

> Popular consensus in the village still considered education acquired by formal schooling to be a pursuit for the nobility, a fancy of the higher orders; "It is all right for the rich man, but not for a poor, stupid peasant." In the virtually unanimous testimony of eyewitnesses—peasant-born memoirists, writers, publicists, and politicians—prolonged schooling and too-visible concern with formal education alienated those peasants who possessed it from the rest of the village. For most, the only accepted and comprehensible purpose of schooling for a peasant son at the turn of the century was still the priesthood.

Helene Lopata, writing about the Poles, describes the almost identical thought patterns:

> The traditional peasant attitudes toward formal education were very negative, intellectual matters being defined as the province of the nobility and the intelligentsia; schooling was seen as an economic waste and a source of intergenerational problems. . . . The only school system the immigrants trusted to rear their children was the parochial school, which was expected to teach them Polish Catholicism and moral values.

Among most of the Slavs and southern Italians, education past the age of fourteen was deemed wasteful due to the family's loss of their children's income. Morawska found in her research, in fact, that many priests in Johnstown, Pennsylvania, as a matter of course signed papers indicating that underage children were in fact a year or two older so they could obtain work legally. Other religious Catholics, like Mexicans and French Canadians, shared these beliefs. One scholar has written, in fact, that among French Canadians "formal schooling was devalued. Education beyond a basic level—reading, writing, and simple arithmetic—was required only for children who would join a religious order." It would take several generations before these views began to change; not until after World War II, and especially since the 1960s, do we find significant reevaluations of such thoughts among the descendants of the Slavs, Italians, and French Canadians. (The Mexicans will be discussed in a subsequent chapter.)

On the other hand, in those groups that recognized the importance of education both in itself and as a tool for socioeconomic advancement, children and grandchildren of immigrants moved into the middle and upper classes much more quickly than did individuals whose parents frowned on too much learning. Among those who prized education were the Czechs, Japanese, Armenians, and Greeks. Japanese immigrants, who by law could never become citizens themselves, often made incredible sacrifices so that their children might go to high school and college. Armenians surpassed all other incoming groups between 1899 and 1910 with a literacy rate of 76 percent. Once in this country they, along with the Japanese and Greeks, "devoured" education. A common admonition of the Armenian parent to his child went, "My son, don't be ignorant like me—get an education and be a man." "The Czechs," on the other hand, "came from a country where universal compulsory education was strictly enforced. A sense of literacy was thus ingrained in the Czech immigrant, and it was not unusual for parents to aspire toward a college education for their children in the United States." Greek children, no matter how poor their parents or how lowly their status, were "socialized to postpone immediate gratifications for a future goal. For a majority of Greek parents, that goal was to see their children . . . move up the social scale through the avenue of education, business, and commerce outside the Greek ethnic community."

The Greeks also tried to instill in their children the language and heritage of the old country while making sure they became accomplished in the United States. They encouraged their offspring to prepare for the professions, especially law and medicine, because in Greece these were considered the most prestigious fields. One scholar tells us that among Greek Americans "education of the young became a byword in community after community," while a Chicago schoolteacher claimed, "I think I have found the Greeks the brightest and quickest to learn." Greek American children performed their required chores, but when someone asked one man why his fourteen-year-old son was not out working, the father responded, "My boy will stay in school. He must study at home after school. He must be a good student; he must become a good man."

In the Greek American community the *kinotitos*, or community council, was the governing body of the people. It provided for the establishment of churches and schools, hired and fired priests and teachers, and exerted a continuing influence on Greek affairs. The feelings of the group were almost always reflected in the actions and statements of the *kinotitos*. For recreation the Greeks flocked to their *kuffenein*, or coffeehouses. These served as community social centers where men smoked, drank, conversed, and played games in what became literally places of refuge after a hard day of work or escapes from dank and dreary living quarters. No Greek American community was without its *kuffenein*, and one chronicler reported that in Chicago before World War I "every other door on Bolivar Street was a Greek coffee house."

Many of the ethnic groups that came to the United States felt an attachment or loyalty to their native countries, but none surpassed the Greeks in their devotion to, or involvement with, the homeland. In the United States, Greek Americans divided into factions and argued vigorously the ramifications of politics in Greece. Many Greeks were fervently attached to their mother country and hoped to return. Although large numbers remained in the United States, they were slow to take out American citizenship, which to many meant a renunciation of their heritage.

Like the Greeks, the east central European Slavs remained attached to their compatriots and were reluctant to become American citizens. The ocean crossing did not lead to changed values or outlooks, and unlike the fiercely independent Greeks, the Slavs in general did not perceive the United States to be a place where additional effort would increase their opportunities to move up the socioeconomic ladder. Nor did they seem to consider social mobility a realistic possibility for their children. They accepted the so-called natural superiority of the upper classes as part of God's order on earth and these views, which were sanctioned by both religion and custom, were deeply ingrained in them. They resisted pressures to Americanize and lived the life encapsulated by an old Galician village proverb: "There is not equality among angels in heaven; there will never be any on earth. A peasant is always a peasant, a gentleman a gentleman: Amen."

The numerous fraternal and social organizations immigrants established further attested not only to their reluctance to relinquish their heritage and beliefs but also to their desire to enrich their lives in America among compatriots who shared their values. Among the groups actively promoting the maintenance of traditional cultures were the South Slav Socialistic Federation, which played a key role in aiding Yugoslav workers in the United States; the Ukrainian Women's Alliance (which became the Ukrainian Woman's League of America in 1925), which taught illiterates how to read while promoting the goal of a national Ukrainian state in Europe; and the Croatian Catholic Society, formed in Gary, Indiana, in 1922. The Greeks had two major ethnic associations: GAPA (Greek American Progressive Association) and AHEPA (American Hellenic Educational Progressive Association), organized in Atlanta in 1922. The former strove to perpetuate the Greek culture; the latter wanted to help smooth the path to acculturation. The variety of ethnic associations across the country also included the Garibaldina Society—Italian, formed in Los Angeles in 1885; the Young Men's Serbian Society of Tonopah, Nevada; and the Hungarian Verhovay.

Along with the ethnic societies were numerous newspapers that recorded the groups' events. In the larger cities, like Chicago and New York, the different immigrants often had a choice of several daily and weekly newspapers in their own languages. In some of the smaller communities, however, choices of foreign-language newspapers were understandably smaller or nonexistent. Among some of the numerous periodicals that recounted events in the old country and offered suggestions for coping with life in America were the *Ukrainian Chronicle*, the *Slovenian Proletarac*, and the *Bolletino del Nevada*. In the 1920s, among the foreign-language press in Utah, an observer listed *Beobachter* (German), *Bikaben* (Danish), *Utah Nippo* (Japanese), and *To Fos* (Greek).

In another area of the West, the Basques also took pride in and strove to maintain their culture. Their language is Europe's oldest, although the Spanish takeover of Basque lands in 1839 caused it to become diluted with Spanish words; it is so complex that in this country most of the children have not learned it and speak only English. Although the Basques married one another during the first generation, the passage of time and their involvement with other people made this difficult to continue. Nonetheless, the Basques do gather periodically. Since 1928 they have held an annual Sheepherder Ball in Boise, and there is also a midsummer St. Ignatius Day picnic to honor their patron saint. Many western universities have made an effort to preserve Basque culture. The University of Oregon has a collection of Basque songs and stories; the University of Nevada offers a course in the Basque language; and the University of Idaho collects Basque historical items.

Ethnic organizations were often segregated by gender. Just as men ran political groups and worked outside the home, they dominated the formal ethnic groups. Yet women had their own organizations in churches and participated in social and union activities. Jewish women attended the educational programs offered to their communities and Italian women participated in the street religious festas. In the informal world of immigrant life, men and women frequently went separate ways. The saloon or bar culture was basically for men. Describing Polish workers, one historian noted, "Men had their own world—the corner saloon, where immigrant males could meet their friends and drink away the tiredness of the day." Sporting clubs were also for men. Italian men, for example, went to neighborhood saloons to play cards or to the local parks to play bocce. Urban immigrant boys played stickball in the streets, or if they were lucky, attended the numerous clubs to play basketball.

Women's economic role in the home was also a social role, for the home was "woman's place." They spent their free time meeting with friends and relatives or participating in church activities. They often frowned on the male saloon culture. Stories abound in immigrant communities of men drinking up their earnings or deserting their wives. Immigrant organizations aided those in distress, but not always successfully; and as noted, the plight of women heading households with many small children was precarious at best. For young single women the world of "cheap amusements" proved attractive. They went to amusement parks, attended dances, and patronized nickelodeons, so common in immigrant neighborhoods. These women were being introduced to the emerging world of consumerism, which in the long run would take them away from their ethnic communities. During the twentieth century, movie houses, department stores, mass advertising, radio, and the other forms of an emerging mass culture would have a profound influence on the lives of immigrants and their children.

Growing consumerism and greater distance from Old World culture was part of the ongoing process of Americanization. Once begun, assimilation could not be stopped. For most groups each succeeding generation had fewer ties to the old country and was more directly involved with American society. Children and grandchildren forgot the language of previous generations, joined trade unions that cut across ethnic lines, and moved away from urban ghettos. In this fashion they gained a strong foothold in the mainstream of American life.

Chapter 4

Ethnic Conflict and Immigration Restriction

ALTHOUGH IMMIGRANTS CONTRIBUTED to the accelerated pace of American growth and development, native-born Americans rarely considered their presence an unalloyed blessing. Periodically, different groups of Americans wanted to curtail the immigrant traffic, but the overriding national need for more people and the commitment to the idea of America as a haven for the distressed prevented serious legislative curbs. During the colonial period, the Scots-Irish and the Germans were subject to hostile barbs from earlier arrivals and selective taxation by colonial governments. While John Adams was president, in 1798, the period required for foreigners to be in the United States before applying for citizenship was temporarily increased from five to fourteen years. In the middle of the nineteenth century the Know-Nothing Party again raised the issue of too many foreigners, but it evaporated before it could mount a lengthy campaign.

Between 1875 and 1924, however, pressure groups succeeded in getting Congress to reduce the number of immigrants allowed to enter the United States. Congress enacted its first restrictive law in 1875 when it banned prostitutes and alien convicts from American shores. Seven years later a more comprehensive law excluded lunatics, idiots, and people likely to become public charges. In 1884 further legislation eliminated contract laborers. These measures reflected a growing fear of certain types of people, but kept out relatively few of those who sought entry into the United States.

More important, the Chinese Exclusion Act of 1882 was the first proscription of an ethnic group. The enactment of this law was the culmination of a vigorous West Coast campaign against the Chinese, and it reversed the welcome they had received after the gold rush in the early 1850s. In 1852, for example, the governor of California, seeking new sources of labor for the state, characterized the Chinese as among "the most worthy of our newly adopted citizens."

The negative picture of the Chinese originated before they came to America, with American missionaries, merchants, and diplomats who had sent back derogatory pictures of China and the Chinese. At first, these images were not widely known. Nevertheless, they did prepare public opinion for the growing hostility toward Asians, especially as immigrants from Asia increased from approximately 40,000 in 1860 to over 100,000 in 1880. Although a few opponents of the Asians insisted that Chinese laborers were virtual slaves in this country, most West Coast workers, whether native or foreign-born, claimed that these people depressed wages and consequently provoked unfair competition. In the 1860s, when the race to complete the transcontinental railroad was in full swing and jobs were abundant, this charge mattered little. When the railroad was finished, and especially during the depression of the 1870s, anti-Chinese feelings became virulent in California. One legislative committee in the state, appointed in 1876 to investigate the Chinese in their midst, concluded that "the Chinese are inferior to any race God ever made. . . . [They] have no souls to save, and if they have, they are not worth saving."

Behind much of the anti-Chinese sentiment was racism, the belief that there were vast cultural and racial differences between whites and Asians. The Chinese were accused of having low morals, specifically of practicing prostitution and smoking opium; of low health standards; and of corrupt influences and practices. One advocate of restriction told a congressional committee in 1877:

> The burden of our accusation against them is that they come in conflict
> with our labor interests; they can never assimilate with us; that they
> are a perpetual, unchanging, and unchangeable alien element that can
> never become homogeneous; that their civilization is demoralizing and
> degrading to our people; that they degrade and dishonor labor; that they
> can never become citizens.

The movement to ban the Chinese from America centered in California. Mobs assaulted them, legislatures burdened them with special head taxes, and city ordinances harassed their hotels and laundries. The most vigorous opposition came from Dennis Kearney and the Workingmen's Party in the 1870s. One manifesto of this group declared, "The Chinaman must leave our shores. We declare that white men and women, and boys, and girls, cannot live as the people of the great republic should and compete with the single Chinese coolie in the labor market. . . . To an American, death is preferable to life on a par with the Chinaman."

The 1875 law banning prostitutes was in part aimed at Chinese women, and the Chinese Exclusion Act of 1882 was a response to intense pressure from the West Coast. Loopholes in the law allowed for some immigration, however, and this sparked further agitation and violence in the West. In 1885 a Tacoma, Washington mob drove out Chinese residents and burned their homes, and incidents of violence occurred elsewhere. More Chinese were harassed in Arizona in 1886 than in any other year. While awaiting further congressional action California passed its most far-reaching anti-Chinese law. This measure barred all Chinese except governmental officials from entering the state and required those already there to register with state officials. In 1892 additional congressional legislation virtually ended Chinese immigration and restricted the civil rights of those still in this country.

Following these restrictions, overt violence against the Chinese ceased, and agitation for tighter laws and controls gradually subsided. Yet the prejudice against the Chinese remained. Discrimination in jobs and housing was common after 1890, and derogatory images of Chinese Americans appeared in the media. Newspapers played up stories of prostitution, gambling, and opium dens in Chinatowns. "Chinks" and "John Chinaman" were sobriquets frequently used to describe Chinese Americans. The prejudices and discrimination lasted well into the twentieth century. State laws against interracial marriages, for example, were part of the legacy of racial prejudice, and Chinese aliens were not eligible for citizenship until after 1943.

In part, Americans transferred their prejudice after the Japanese began arriving in California and Hawaii in the 1890s. Again the focus of hostility and agitation was California, where most of the Japanese lived. Arguments similar to those used against the Chinese were employed to assail Japanese immigrants. "The Japs must go," shouted one demagogue; and the United States Industrial Commission reported in 1901 that the Japanese were "far less desirable" than the Chinese. "They have most of the vices of the Chinese, with none of the virtues. They underbid the Chinese in everything, and are as a class tricky, unreliable and dishonest."

And yet the racism directed against the Japanese was not the same as the anti-Chinese feeling. Whereas the Chinese were considered coolies who depressed American wages, at times the Japanese were considered too successful, especially in California agriculture, in which they became efficient workers and growers. Unlike China, Japan was becoming a world power at the beginning of the twentieth century. Instead of showing contempt for Japan, many racists became alarmed by her growing power. The fear was expressed in the "yellow peril" scare just after 1900, an imagined invasion of the United States by hordes of Asians. Congressman Richmond Pearson Hobson of Alabama insisted that the "yellow peril" was already here, and he further warned: "the Japanese are the most secretive people in the world," and were "rushing forward with feverish haste stupendous preparations for war. . . . The war is to be with America." The Hearst press in California insisted that "every one of these immigrants . . . is a Japanese spy."

Growing fear of and antagonism toward Japanese immigrants reached a crisis after the turn of the century. Led by labor groups, delegates gathered in San Francisco in 1905 to organize the Asiatic Exclusion League. A year later, the San Francisco Board of Education ordered the segregation of all Asian pupils. Of the city's 25,000 schoolchildren only 93 were Japanese, but the public was outraged at reports that older Japanese boys were sitting next to little white girls in classes. The Japanese government protested the order, and Theodore Roosevelt's administration found itself faced with a full-fledged diplomatic crisis. Federal pressure on the San Francisco school board led to the rescinding of the new policy. In return the Japanese, in the Gentlemen's Agreement of 1907, promised to restrict exit visas for laborers who wanted to go to the United States. The agreement short-circuited a confrontation but did not prevent those Japanese already here from pursuing the American dream. Reputedly hard workers and shrewd businessmen, they amassed a great deal of property before the California legislature, in 1913, prohibited aliens ineligible for citizenship from acquiring land. The act, based on a provision of the naturalization laws limiting citizenship to incoming whites and descendants of Africans, failed because the Japanese continued acquiring property in the names of their American-born children or under legal corporate guises.

Californians may have been especially concerned with Asian minorities, but the most widespread American hostility was directed at Roman Catholics. The growing Catholic immigrant population after 1880 once more stirred up Protestant bigotry. Even more than before the Civil War, the Roman Catholic Church appeared aggressive and powerful as Irish Catholics succeeded in politics and Catholic leaders spoke without restraint in public.

School issues in particular kindled ethnic tensions. Catholics found the Protestant orientation of American public schools offensive and developed their own parochial schools. Although the Church encouraged all parishioners to send their children to these schools, only a minority—mostly of Irish background—chose, or could afford, to do so. This led in turn to Catholic demands for state aid for parochial schools, a proposal that further enraged Protestants. Local elections often centered on the school issue, as did the 1880 election in New York City, for example. The Democrats had nominated William R. Grace, a Roman Catholic, for mayor, and this incensed a number of the city's Protestants. *The New York Times* stated the prevalent anxieties clearly:

> If the Irish Catholics should happen, for instance, to control the Mayoralty, the Controllership, and the Board of Aldermen, they would very soon be able to reconstitute the Board of Education, to place Catholic Trustees over certain schools, to put in Catholic teachers, to introduce

Catholic textbooks, to convey public funds to Church schools under some guise which would elude the law, and, in fact, to Romanize our whole system of public education.

In the end Grace won the election, and the fears expressed by *The New York Times* proved groundless. But the anxieties remained.

Boston, with its large Irish population, was also a hotbed of dispute. In 1889 a teacher in a public high school defined indulgences in a manner that was considered offensive by a Catholic pupil. The Church protested and the Boston School Committee reprimanded the teacher, transferred him from history to English (a "safer" subject), and dropped a disputed text. Aroused Protestants organized and in the next election won control of the school committee.

At the national level the issue of religion and the schools intruded and divided political parties. In 1875 James G. Blaine, the House Republican leader, proposed a constitutional amendment to ban governmental property and financial aid for the use of any school or other institution under the control of any religious sect. Although the amendment never passed, the issue prompted considerable debate.

At bottom much of the conflict centered on the belief held by many Protestants that Catholicism was a menace to American values and institutions. This view was not as strong as it had been before the Civil War. Nevertheless, many Protestants believed that a large proportion of American Catholics were under the thumb of Rome and were unwilling to accept American values. Some militant Protestants insisted that Catholics had divided loyalties and should be denied the ballot until they took an oath of allegiance renouncing the supremacy of the pope. A prominent Protestant clergyman, Josiah Strong, expressed much of this anxiety in his popular *Our Country: Its Possible Future and Its Present Crisis* (1885), in which he argued that Catholics gave their foremost allegiance to the Church, not to the United States of America. Protestants like Strong were also agitated because of the Roman Catholic Church's opposition or indifference to the temperance crusade.

The largest anti-Catholic organization to appear in the late nineteenth century was the American Protective Association (APA). Founded in 1887 in Clinton, Iowa by Henry Bowers, the APA had a large following until the mid-1890s; at its peak it claimed 2.5 million members. Appealing mainly to working-class Protestants in the Rocky Mountain states and the far West, the APA pledged its members' support of public schools, immigration restriction, and tougher naturalization laws. To fight the so-called Roman menace, APA members organized boycotts of Catholic merchants, refused to go on strike with Catholic trade unionists, and vowed never to vote for a Roman Catholic for public office. The growing political power of Catholics was especially alarming to the organization, which claimed that "although only one-eighth of the population of the United States was Catholic . . . one-half of all the public officeholders were Catholics . . . Catholics were favored in the Civil Service examinations, and . . . all civil servants were forced to contribute to Catholic charities."

Hysteria peaked in 1893 when many believed a rumor that the pope had written a letter ordering Catholics to exterminate all heretics in the United States. Some Protestants armed themselves, and the mayor of Toledo called out the National Guard to halt the coming slaughter. The rumor soon proved groundless and fraudulent, of course, but members of the APA quickly found other aspects of Catholicism to fight.

The association never formed a political party, but it did enter politics. It supported candidates, usually Republicans, who were against the Catholic Church and lobbied for particular pieces of legislation. The association backed state compulsory school-attendance laws and, at the national level, became embroiled in a dispute over Indian schools. Under federal policy established during the Grant administration, contracts were granted to church groups to operate Indian schools. Thus federal funds were going to parochial schools, which horrified the APA. The association threw its support behind efforts to eliminate the contract system and substitute public schools for the church-supported ones.

In spite of the widespread hostility to Catholicism among non-Catholics, the appeal of the association was limited. The movement crested in the 1890s and then fell apart. Other issues were more important to American voters in the 1890s, and the APA found itself plagued by internal disputes. Republicans used the APA, but they discovered that it was not important politically. Anti-Catholicism took other forms after 1895.

In addition to the religious prejudice directed at Catholics, hostility toward Jews grew in the late nineteenth century. Anti-Semitism was aggravated by the economic depressions that plagued Americans, on and off, from 1873 through 1896. The German Jews, who arrived in the United States in the middle of the nineteenth century, prospered despite the existing prejudices because there were few, if any, economic barriers to those who were enterprising. Their prosperity in the face of widespread unemployment and despair reinforced the old Shylock image of a cunning and avaricious Jew demanding his pound of flesh. One southern patrician noted, for example, "it is quite the fashion to caricature the Jew as exacting his interest down to the last drachma." He then pointed out, perhaps half in envy and half in respect, that in the hardest of times the Jew "has money to lend if not to burn and before he is ready to execute his will he owns the grocery store, the meat-market, the grog-shop, the planing-mill, the newspaper, the hotel and the bank." The extremist fringe in the free-silver movement saw the Jew as the archenemy foisting an international gold standard on beleaguered American farmers who were fighting for silver, "the people's money."

The presence of east European Jews, who started coming to the United States in the 1870s, aggravated existing anti-Semitic feelings; and as already noted, all Jews faced growing social and economic discrimination. As Jewish immigration from eastern Europe increased, anti-Semitism helped to kindle the movement for immigration restriction. In 1906 a member of President Theodore Roosevelt's immigration commission told an investigator that the "movement toward restriction in all of its phases is directed against Jewish immigration."

Alongside religious antagonisms, immigrants also confronted economic conflicts. Many workers opposed immigrants on the grounds that they depressed wages and were potential strikebreakers. The Knights of Labor called for a ban on contract labor, as did a number of labor leaders. Organized labor, with a high proportion of foreign-born workers, was reluctant to support general immigration restriction, but labor leaders were becoming more critical of immigration in the 1880s and in the economically depressed 1890s. In 1897 the American Federation of Labor (AFL), America's largest labor union, finally supported a literacy test as a means of limiting immigration.

Although employers needed workers for the nation's growing industries, at times they were uneasy about immigration. Labor disturbances, fairly common in the late nineteenth century, were frequently blamed on foreign agitators. In 1886 policemen broke up a peaceful protest meeting in Chicago. Before the crowd could be dispersed, however, a bomb exploded, killing seven policemen. Although no one knew who threw the explosive, the press blamed foreigners. One newspaper declared, "The enemy forces are not American [but] rag-tag and bob-tail cutthroats of Beelzebub from the Rhine, the Danube, the Vistula, and the Elbe." Another said the German anarchists accused of the crime were "long-haired, wild-eyed, bad-smelling, atheistic, reckless foreign wretches, who never did an honest hour's work in their lives."

Especially important in the growth of nativism was Americans' awareness of the increased immigration from southern and eastern Europe. These new immigrants were considered undesirable, unassimilable, and hostile or indifferent to American values. Stereotyped images of Slavs, Italians, and Jews predominated. A retired superintendent who had worked in the Pennsylvania steel mills from the 1880s through the 1930s recalled, "Racism was very distinct then. . . . We all called them Huns, Dagos and Polacks." To the nativist, Italians suggested an image of crime and violence. As a Baltimore newspaper put it, "The disposition to assassinate in revenge for a fancied wrong is a marked trait in the character of this impulsive and inexorable race." Such hostile sentiments led to the lynching of eleven Italians in New Orleans in 1891. After the murder of a police superintendent, suspicion focused on the local Sicilian community and several Italians were indicted. City officials called for stern action but the jury refused to convict. An angry mob then took matters into its own hands and lynched the accused men.

Late nineteenth-century Americans were increasingly receptive to pseudo-racial thinking that classified European nationalities or ethnic groups, such as Slavs, Jews, and Italians, as races. Such thinking emphasized differences and deemed one "race" to be superior to another. This point of view found increasing support in the early twentieth century. Not surprisingly, racists regarded earlier immigrant groups as more desirable. One alarmed nativist said, "it is only in recent years that new, more ignorant and therefore more dangerous elements have entered into the problem of immigration. . . . The Irish and German tides were ebbing, while those of Southern and Eastern Europe were both increasing and threatening. None but an optimist . . . can view it without concern."

Just as religious prejudice, economic rivalry, and intellectual racism generated opposition to immigration, so did politics. Urban reformers noted with apprehension the rise of the Irish in urban politics. Reformers, usually old-stock Americans, believed that political machines built on immigrant votes were corrupt and inefficient, the protectors of prostitution, graft, and saloons. Prostitution was considered a virtual immigrant monopoly. A reform group in the 1890s declared, "Unless we make energetic and successful war upon the red light districts . . . we shall have Oriental brothel slavery thrust upon us. . . . Jew traders, too, will people our 'levees' with Polish Jewesses and any others who will make money for them. Shall we defend our American civilization, or lower our flag to the most despicable foreigners—French, Irish, Italians, Jews, and Mongolians?" When the power of the immigrant-supported machine was broken, they argued, American cities would be reformed.

Many reformers, however, attributed political corruption to business influence. They noted that immigrants supported machines because the machines helped them. Clean up the immigrants' environment, and the machine would lose its following. Yet graft and the social ills of American cities, combined with the concentration of immigrants in the urban ghettos, too often led native-born Americans to blame political chicanery on immigrants.

Conflicts also arose among the immigrants themselves. Many of the newcomers distrusted and disliked one another. Irishman Dennis Kearney, leader of the California Workingmen's Party, led the assault on the Chinese, and English-born Samuel Gompers of the AFL favored immigration restriction. Within the ranks of labor some foreign-born unionists did not want members of ethnic groups other than their own in their unions. Foreign-born Protestants within the APA did not trust Catholics. Within the Catholic Church, Germans, French Canadians, Italians, and Poles resented Irish domination. As one Polish journal remarked in 1900, "is it that the Irish want to dominate the Catholic world? Can't Polish Catholics have as much freedom as the other nationalities? Isn't the United States a land of Freedom? It is, but that is no reason that the Irish should have more preference than any other nationality."

Europeans arrived in America with fears and prejudices that did not disappear. When German votes killed a proposal to teach Bohemian in a Chicago school, Bohemians retorted, "Finally, since impudence, selfishness, obstinacy and insolence is excessively rooted in the minds of all Germans, almost without exception, how then could we expect, even in this land of freedom to receive any support from them?" An American writer of Norwegian ancestry recalls his grandmother admonishing members of the family never to trust a Swede. "The essence of her counsel," the grandson wrote, "was that Swedes were a strange, cold, selfish, sneaky lot and that any contact with them could only have unhappy consequences."

The intense xenophobia in the United States, among both older Americans and more recent arrivals, pointed inevitably in one direction: immigration restriction. Although the Chinese were banned in 1882 and the first restrictive federal immigration law excluded certain classes of immigrants, the legislation did not greatly affect the flow of newcomers. Bigots called for drastic limitations. The time had come, they insisted, to decide whether the nation was "to be peopled by British, German and Scandinavian stock, historically free, energetic, progressive, or by Slav, Latin and Asiatic races, historically downtrodden, atavistic, and stagnant." The most popular scheme for stemming the tide was the literacy test. Led by the Immigration Restriction League, founded in Boston in 1894 by Boston blue bloods, agitation for federal action grew. The literacy test, which required immigrants over sixteen to be literate in some language, made no distinctions among nationalities or races, but the intent of the proposal was clear. Since proportionately more northern and western Europeans than southern and eastern Europeans were literate, the requirement would have barred the latter groups of immigrants from the United States.

The literacy test, supported by the Republican Party, finally passed in 1896, only to be vetoed by President Grover Cleveland, who insisted that

America should remain an asylum for the oppressed of Europe. The president also rejected the inference that the new immigrants were less desirable than the old: "It is said," he declared, "that the quality of recent immigration is undesirable. The time is quite within recent memory when the same thing was said of immigrants who, with their descendants, are now numbered among our best citizens." The literacy test's proponents attempted to muster votes to override the veto, but they failed. And then, after 1896, prosperity returned and the tide of nativism ebbed.

But it resurged quickly. By 1901 President Theodore Roosevelt spoke in a different vein than Cleveland had a few years earlier. Stirred by the recent assassination of President William McKinley by an anarchist, Roosevelt called for a comprehensive immigration act to keep out "not only all persons who are known to be believers in anarchistic principles or members of anarchistic societies, but also all persons who are of a low moral tendency or of unsavory reputation . . . who are below a certain standard of economic fitness to enter our industrial field as competitors with American labor." He also called for an educational test to ascertain the capacity of immigrants to "appreciate American institutions and act sanely as American citizens." Roosevelt insisted that his proposals would decrease the "sum of ignorance" in America and "stop the influx of cheap labor, and the resulting competition which gives rise to so much of the bitterness in American industrial life, and it would dry up the springs of the pestilential social conditions in our great cities, where anarchist organizations have their greatest possibility of growth." Congress responded in part to the president's request by excluding anarchists in 1903 and four years later "imbeciles, feeble-minded [persons] and persons with physical or mental defects which might affect their ability to earn a living."

In 1907 Congress also appointed a joint Senate-House commission to investigate the "immigration problem." The new commission, known by the name of its chairman, Senator William Paul Dillingham of Vermont, issued a 42-volume report in 1911. Its main assumption was that the newer immigrants from southern and eastern Europe were more ignorant, more unskilled, more prone to crime, and more willing to accept a lower standard of living than previous immigrants from northern and western Europe. Although the Dillingham Commission preferred a literacy test rather than a ban, it also suggested that restrictive legislation could be based on a percentage of each nationality group already in the United States. This alternative was ignored at the time but would be revived in the 1920s.

Congress responded to the Dillingham report with passage of another literacy bill in 1913, but once again a president would not sanction it. William Howard Taft, heeding protests from friends favoring liberal immigration policies, acknowledged an "abiding faith" in American institutions to exert a positive influence upon newcomers "no matter how lacking in education they may be. . . . The second generation of a sturdy but uneducated peasantry," he continued, "brought to this country and raised in an atmosphere of thrift and hard work, and forced by their parents into school and to obtain an instrument for self-elevation, has always contributed to the strength of our people, and will continue to do so."

The outbreak of World War I and American entry into the war in 1917 broke the dam holding back the tide of nativism. On the eve of America's declaration of war Congress again passed a literacy bill, and when President Woodrow Wilson for a second time refused to approve it, Congress overrode his veto. The act also created an Asian "barred zone," which excluded most Asians and added to the list of banned immigrants.

In the heated atmosphere of wartime, patriots insisted upon 100 percent Americanism. Radical opponents of the war and German Americans who were suspected of having pro-German sentiments or of being secret agents of the Kaiser became targets of unrestrained hysteria. Theodore Roosevelt led the attack and insisted that "the men of German blood who have tried to be both German and American are not Americans at all, but traitors to America and tools and servants of Germany against America." Superpatriots attacked German Americans, their organizations, and their press. Libraries removed German books from their shelves, and several states, among them Delaware, Iowa, and Montana, prohibited public schools from teaching German. Sauerkraut was renamed "liberty cabbage," orchestras refused to perform German music, and towns, business firms, and people hastily anglicized their German-sounding names. The governor of Iowa issued a proclamation urging citizens not to use foreign languages in public, and the governing body of Nye County, Nevada, passed a resolution to the effect that use of another language in a publicly designated area would be deemed evidence of disloyalty. Angry mobs sometimes smashed German stores or burned German books. That most German Americans were loyal to the nation and supported the war effort did not seem to matter.

Although they were not as suspect as German Americans, some Irish Americans also came under attack. Many people of Irish ancestry were unenthusiastic about fighting a war in alliance with Great Britain, regarded as the enemy and oppressor of Ireland. A few who were critical of the Wilson administration found themselves in difficulty with the law.

The xenophobia unleashed by the war reached new heights in the 1920s. Although German and Irish Americans now found more acceptance, immigrants and their children were generally suspect. The nation assumed an isolationist mood; old-stock Americans rejected Europe and her peoples and insisted on conformity and loyalty to the United States. Terms like "wop" appeared regularly in newspapers like the *Pocatello* [Idaho] *Tribune,* and about the only time minorities found stories about themselves in the daily newspapers was when they were involved in crimes, industrial accidents, or sports events. Ewa Morawska observes, "The same young men from Slavic and Magyar homes who, as American soldiers fighting in Europe during World War I, had been praised by the *Johnstown* [Pennsylvania] *Tribune* as 'our Johnstown boys' and lauded for heroism in the struggle 'in defense of their country' (the United States) were again labeled 'foreigners' after they returned to the city" at the end of the war. The Russian Revolution, a byproduct of the war, added to the fears of things foreign. Americans believed that radical ideology, which was considered a foreign import, had to be stamped out or suppressed. Radical groups were hounded and members physically assaulted, and Attorney General A. Mitchell Palmer's Justice Department rounded up aliens in spectacular raids and deported them during the Red Scare of 1919. Patriotic groups bombarded Congress with petitions proclaiming that the time had arrived "when Americans should assert themselves and drive from these shores all disloyal aliens."

While conservative and patriotic groups feared radical agitators flooding America with their Bolshevik ideas, union leaders feared cheap labor. The 1920s were lean years for organized labor, as the unions lost more than a million members. In 1918 the AFL, anxious about the problems of industrial reconversion after the war, called for a two-year halt in immigration. Some labor union leaders not only used the old cheap-foreign-labor argument but also warned about the social dangers of immigration. The English-born Gompers, president of the AFL, defended restriction: "America has not yet become a nation." He noted that it was "honeycombed with 'foreign groups' living a foreign life," and this would continue if the nation's door remained open to all comers.

The 1920s have been described as a tribal era during which ethnocentrism and xenophobia ran wild. No development better illustrates this situation than the activities of the Ku Klux Klan, the largest nativist organization of the 1920s, which claimed over 4 million members at its height. Founded in Georgia in 1915, the Klan had a spectacular growth rate in the early 1920s and for a brief period exerted considerable political clout in several states, including Indiana, Alabama, Texas, and Florida. Klansmen thundered at liberal Protestantism and modern ideas and demanded Prohibition enforcement and compulsory Bible reading in the public schools. But the focus of their credo was anti-Catholic and anti-immigrant, and they wanted to keep African Americans "in their place." Hiram W. Evans, the Klan's imperial wizard, believed that the "old-stock Americans," the "Nordic race," had "given the world almost the whole of modern civilization." And he insisted that aliens from eastern and southern Europe should be kept out of the United States.

The Klan's response to immigration and minorities was merely an extreme version of what many old-stock white Protestants believed. Prohibitionists, for example, insisted there was a sinister connection among liquor, cities, and immigrants. One liberal clergyman proclaimed, "national Prohibition is the highest mark of distinctively American morality and citizenship" and warned, "there is already too much congestion of immigrants in the great cities. . . . If we are to have an American civilization we must assimilate the stream of newcomers. If we do not assimilate them they will adulterate us with an admixture of old-world morals. A straw in the wind is afforded by the recent referendum in Massachusetts on the liquor issue. The entire state went overwhelmingly dry except the large immigrant filled cities, and they went so overwhelmingly wet as to give the state as a whole a wet majority."

From Michigan, Henry Ford's *Dearborn Independent* published anti-Semitic diatribes. Included in the newspaper's vitriolic writings was the *Protocols of the Elders of Zion*. This fake document, concocted by the Russian secret police at the turn of the century, charged there was a Jewish plot to establish a world dictatorship. During the decade, anti-Semitism even reached the hallowed gates of Harvard University when the institution's administration established a Jewish quota, thereby prompting one Jew to dub the school an "intellectual Ku Klux Klan."

Discriminatory practices and thoughtlessness characterized Americans throughout the country in the 1920s and 1930s, and people of a variety of foreign ancestries suffered through many humiliating experiences. A number of individuals changed their foreign-sounding names to anglicized versions, either for better economic opportunities or merely to avoid unnecessary comments from others. Sam Divanovich of Tonopah, Nevada, for example, became Sam Devine because he thought it would "sound better and not cause as much comment." In Morrelville, Pennsylvania, in the 1930s, teachers often incorrectly characterized students of east central European descent as "Slavish." "At school I went as Thomas," one man later recalled, "because my teacher would not pronounce or spell my own [name]." His wife had a similar experience. Her surname was "Tomasovich, but the teacher spelled it Tumoski; she did not bother to get it right." A child of Polish American parents remembered that she never raised her hand in elementary school to speak. "I was afraid I'd make a mistake. . . . American children called us 'Hunky.' . . . We felt inferior." One man voluntarily misidentified himself and explained why: "I usually say I'm Russian. If you say you're Ukrainian, the guy tells you, 'Jesus Christ, what's that?' and you have to go into the whole history of Ukraine and explain to the guy what you mean. It is easier to just say that you are Russian."

Ideological racism, another facet of American nativism, peaked in the early 1920s. The eugenics movement in America after 1900 had warned of the dangerous effects of bad heredity. Eugenicists argued that poor hereditary, rather than environmental, factors produced unalterable human inequalities. Many Americans supported racist thinking. Popular writers such as Madison Grant and Lothrop Stoddard enjoyed a vogue in the 1920s. Grant's *The Passing of the Great Race* and Stoddard's *The Rising Tide of Color* preached a racism that could easily be applied to immigration restriction. Grant declared

> these new immigrants were no longer exclusively members of the Nordic race as were the earlier ones who came of their own impulse to improve their social conditions. The transportation lines advertised America as a land flowing with milk and honey, and the European governments took the opportunity to unload upon careless, wealthy, and hospitable America the sweepings of their jails and asylums. The result was that the new immigration . . . contained a large and increasing number of the weak, the broken, and the mentally crippled of all races drawn from the lowest stratum of the Mediterranean basin and the Balkans, together with hordes of the wretched, submerged populations of the Polish Ghettos.

A follower of Grant argued that continued immigration would inevitably produce "a hybrid race of people as worthless and futile as the good-for-nothing mongrels of Central America and Southeastern Europe," while a psychologist, flushed with uncritical use of intelligence test results, proclaimed that the "intellectual superiority of our Nordic group over the Alpine, Mediterranean and Negro groups has been demonstrated."

Given the intense nativism of the 1920s, the issue was not *whether* there would be immigration restriction but *what form* it would take. Aside from the recent immigrants, few Americans, regardless of background, resisted restriction. Congressmen representing urban areas with heavy concentrations of the foreign-born attacked the proposed laws and their racist assumptions, but they lacked the votes to sustain their views. Over 800,000 newcomers arrived in 1921, and foes of immigration had visions of another immigrant invasion after the wartime lull. Stories circulated of between 5 and 20 million Europeans ready to descend upon the United States.

In 1921 Congress finally established the principle of restriction based on nationality and placed a ceiling on immigration from Europe. The 1921 law limited, for a one-year period, the number of entrants of each nationality to

3 percent of the foreign-born of that group in America based on the 1910 census. Under this stopgap measure approximately 358,000 were eligible to come from Europe. Congress extended the law twice before passing the Johnson-Reed Immigration Act of 1924.

The Johnson-Reed law continued the qualifications enacted in the past, such as the exclusion of anarchists, prostitutes, illiterates, and those likely to become public charges, and tightened the quotas established three years earlier. It cut the number of immigrants to 2 percent of the foreign-born of each group based on the 1890 census, further discriminating against southern and eastern nations, which was exactly what Congress wanted to do.

The case of the Greeks shows how moving the base year back from 1910 to 1890 and lowering the percentage helped Congress accomplish its purpose. In 1910 there were 101,282 Greeks in the United States. Under the 1921 act, they were therefore entitled to a yearly quota of 3,038 people (3 percent of 101,282). But the 1924 act, by lowering the percentage and setting the base year back to 1890, when census takers counted only 1,887 Greeks in this country, cut the quota to 38 (2 percent of 1,887), or about one percent of what the 1921 law had allowed. Similar cuts affected Italians, east European Jews, and Slavs. Thus an ostensibly objective change of base years and a one-point decrease in the percentage drastically curtailed immigration opportunities for those that Congress desired to exclude. The quota based on the 1890 census was meant to be temporary. The Johnson-Reed Act established National Origins Quotas, based on the white population according to the 1920 census, that went into effect in 1929. While basing quotas on the entire white population and not simply the foreign-born increased the numbers from southern and eastern Europe, it still drastically reduced their totals from the annual figures before World War I. The new system provided for 153,714 immigrants from Europe (Asians were already barred in 1924, Western Hemisphere natives were not restricted, and African and other colonies came under the quotas for the European nations that controlled them). Each European nation received a number based on its share of the American white population in 1920. English, Germans, and Irish received the bulk of the allotments.

Passage of the Johnson-Reed Act marked the end of an era in American history. Asians had already been excluded, for the most part, but for Europeans the nation had had an open door. The act ended this virtually free immigration policy. Although the United States modified its restrictions after World War II, it never again opened its gates to unlimited numbers.

Immigration restrictions of the 1920s, combined with the severe depression of the 1930s, achieved the effect that restrictionists desired. But the laws did not curtail ethnic conflicts, and the nation continued to experience tensions over immigration and intergroup relations throughout the twentieth century.

Shortly after the final quota system went into effect in 1929, President Herbert Hoover requested that the State Department use its administrative powers for a tight enforcement of the laws. In particular, the "likely to become a public charge" provision of the immigration codes was invoked, for America experienced a deep economic depression during the 1930s and did not want foreign laborers to compete with the growing numbers of unemployed native-born workers seeking jobs. Actually, few from any land tried to emigrate to America during the early years of the depression. Only 23,068 came in 1933; 28,470 in 1934; and 34,956 in 1935. In several years more people left than arrived; there were simply not enough jobs to go around, and relief benefits were few and inadequate.

Before the immigration acts and the depression combined to curb the numbers of newcomers, Filipinos moved into Hawaii and California to fill the labor gap created by the restriction on other Asians. Because the Philippines was then a commonwealth of the United States, there were no legal barriers to population movement; the enormous needs of the sugar planters in Hawaii and the farmers in California provided the spur.

Filipinos had been emigrating to Hawaii to work for the sugar and pineapple planters since the Gentlemen's Agreement of 1907 with Japan had reduced Japanese emigration. During the next quarter century the Hawaiian Islands welcomed 125,000 Filipinos. In the 1920s, however, when California growers feared that Congress might impose quotas on Mexicans, they turned to the Filipinos for labor. Filipinos came to the mainland from Hawaii and directly from the Philippine Islands. According to 1920 census figures, there were only 5,603 Filipinos on the mainland, but 10 years later they numbered 45,208. Other sources estimate that there may have been more than twice that number. Some 90 percent of the Filipinos were single, male, and under 30 years of age. They worked in northern and central California farms and vineyards. Stockton, California, with a concentration of perhaps 4,000 to 8,000 Filipinos, became known at the end of the 1920s as the Manila of California. Other sizable settlements formed in San Francisco, Seattle, and Portland.

The commonwealth status of the Philippines also permitted substantial numbers of Filipinos to be recruited for the United States armed forces, especially the navy. This accounted for the presence of Filipino communities in the San Diego and Los Angeles areas. A majority of these recruits made the military their career and left the service only upon retirement. The armed forces provided them with security and, more important, with the chance to bring their families to the United States. In the navy the Filipinos were usually assigned to mess halls and as personal attendants to high-ranking military personnel.

The depression and American prejudices caused many Filipinos to lose their jobs during the 1930s. A congressional act of 1934, which promised the Philippine Islands their independence in 1946, also established an annual Filipino quota of 50 immigrants. The quota, plus the fact that many Filipinos returned home, cut their numbers in West Coast agriculture; by 1940, 90 percent of those who remained in California were working in such personal domestic service jobs as bellboys, houseboys, cooks, kitchen helpers, and waiters.

As economic conditions improved in the late 1930s, the numbers of European immigrants rose again. More important motivating factors than economics, however, were the triumph of fascism in Germany in 1933 and the coming of war in Europe six years later. As the Germans annexed Austria (1938) and Czechoslovakia (1939) and then crushed Poland (1939) and conquered Norway, Denmark, the Netherlands, Belgium, and France in the spring of 1940, hundreds of thousands fled in terror, and more would have left had they been able to do so.

Though millions of political and religious dissenters were persecuted by Hitler's regime, Jews stood out as the major victims. Plagued by legal and other harassments, they sought asylum in other countries. After accepting as many as they thought they could absorb, the nations of the world refused further modification in their immigration policies. Until 1939 Hitler permitted almost all Jews to leave if they chose to do so; unfortunately, most could not find any nation that would accept them. The horrors perpetrated by the Nazis were legion, but before the mass exterminations in the concentration camps, perhaps the worst single episode occurred on the night of November 9–10, 1938. The government sanctioned a savage assault on German Jews, and throughout the night people were beaten, stores were looted, and homes, hospitals, and old-age institutions were burned; at least 20,000 people were rounded up for deportation to concentration camps. The barbarity of these actions evoked worldwide denunciation. President Franklin D. Roosevelt declared, "I myself could scarcely believe that such things could occur in a twentieth-century civilization."

Nevertheless, U.S. immigration laws remained intact, and the American government made few allowances for the victims of Hitler's terroristic policies. Americans certainly feared economic competition from immigrant workers, for with almost 10 million unemployed in the United States, job prospects for newcomers were dim. The likelihood that additional new people in the country would become public charges and swell overburdened relief rolls was not discounted either. A few Americans also believed that spies and fifth-column agents would enter as refugees if quotas were eased. But especially important in the opposition to relaxing existing quotas was anti-Semitism in the United States. Both Protestant and secular newspapers wrote about it, but the Catholic Church, and Catholics in general, found Jewish support for the Republican cause in Spain particularly galling. Moreover, for many Americans of all stripes the word "Jew" was often used synonymously with the word "communist," and most people were simply against having any more of them in their midst.

President Roosevelt was aware of American hostility toward Jews, yet he also sympathized with the refugees' plight, as did a number of Americans who urged the government to assist them. Roosevelt instructed members of the consular service to grant refugees "the most humane and favorable treatment under the law," which enabled some to come to America; generally the president was willing to let the State Department handle the situation. Unfortunately, anti-Semitism existed in the State Department too, and its influence resulted in a rigid application of the visa policy against Jewish applicants. Typical of this attitude was that of the Assistant Secretary of State, Breckenridge Long, who had charge of refugee affairs after 1939. In a 1941 diary entry he indicated approval of another man's opposition to further immigration. "He said," Long wrote, that "the general type of intending immigrant was just the same as the criminal Jews who crowd our police court dockets in New York. . . . I think he is right."

The State Department position probably reflected the majority viewpoint in the United States. When, in 1939, Senator Robert F. Wagner of New York and Congresswoman Edith Rogers of Massachusetts proposed a measure to allow 20,000 German refugee children between the ages of 6 and 14 years into the United States above the quota limit, patriotic societies like the American Legion and the Daughters of the American Revolution denounced it. In speaking against the legislation a spokeswoman for the Ladies of the Grand Army of the Republic warned that Congress might "decide to admit 20,000 German-Jewish children!" A year later, however, when mercy ships started bringing children from Great Britain to the United States, patriotic organizations voiced no opposition, and congressional mail ran heavily in approval. Over 15,000 American families volunteered to take one of the British children, with "a blond English girl, 6 years old" the most popular choice.

Anti-Semitism reached new heights in the United States in the late 1930s. Groups like the Silver Shirts and the German-American Bund thundered against the Jews. Bigots saw the "hidden hand of international Jewry" around every corner, and patriots organized "Buy Christian" campaigns. The most influential and well-known anti-Semite was the radio priest Father Charles E. Coughlin. Originally a supporter of the New Deal, Coughlin turned against Roosevelt and increasingly used anti-Jewish and anticommunist arguments in his broadcasts and journal, *Social Justice*. This journal reprinted excerpts from the discredited *Protocols of the Elders of Zion* and carried a speech by the German Propaganda Minister Joseph Goebbels. *Social Justice* had an estimated circulation of over 300,000, and millions heard Coughlin's radio voice. In 1940 and 1941 public opinion polls revealed that 17 to 20 percent of the nation considered Jews "a menace to America." Another 12 to 15 percent admitted that they would support an anti-Semitic campaign, and still others indicated that they would be sympathetic to such a campaign.

Despite the bigotry, though, Jews as well as others who came to America under the quota system received hospitable treatment. A host of organizations like the National Refugee Service, the Hebrew Immigrant Aid Society, and various ad hoc groups stood ready to assist the newcomers in finding jobs, housing, and friends.

There were few such welcomes for Mexican immigrants and their children during the Great Depression. The government was reluctant to grant visas to those south of the border. Moreover, as the unemployment lines grew, local, state, and federal officials began to deport Mexican immigrants rather than give them aid. They were sent on buses or trains back to Mexico. Facing the inevitable, the Mexican government cooperated in these efforts, and many Mexican families returned voluntarily. Exact figures are not available, but the number deported ran somewhere over 300,000. The deportees included the American-born (and hence U.S. citizen) children. No other ethnic group was subject to such mass deportations.

European arrivals in the 1930s included a number of eminent intellectuals and scientists. Albert Einstein was perhaps the best known of the illustrious immigrants, as they have been called, but other Nobel Prize winners also came during the decade. Among the most noted were Thomas Mann, the writer; Bruno Walter and Arturo Toscanini, the conductors; Paul Tillich, the theologian; Bela Bartok, the composer; and Enrico Fermi, the physicist. Several of the scientists who came played key roles in the development of the atomic bomb.

Those who arrived in the 1930s usually adjusted to America more readily than most of the millions who had come before them. For the most part the professionals and refugees were well educated, knew some English, and had contacts and skills that they could utilize in the United States. Fleeing in terror from Europe, they were eager to become American citizens and to participate in American society. One such refugee was Henry Kissinger, who would later serve as President Richard Nixon's chief foreign policy adviser and in 1973 would become America's first foreign-born secretary of state.

Not all could adapt as well. Bela Bartok, the composer, never felt at home in America and died in relative obscurity and poverty in New York City in 1945. Some, like Thomas Mann, returned to Europe after the war. Others who lacked the contacts of an Einstein or a Toscanini had to take jobs where they could find them, often beneath their educational levels and skills. The fact that some of them left families and friends behind to an unknown fate added to their anxieties.

Concern that fifth-column agents would enter America if quotas were relaxed may have been one factor blocking a change in immigration laws, but fear of sabotage by enemy aliens already here was even greater during World War II. Consequently, the federal government interned a few Germans and Italians and carefully watched others during the war. Japanese aliens and American citizens of Japanese ancestry, however, fared quite differently. Most of them on the West Coast were incarcerated in relocation centers that some critics likened to concentration camps.

Certainly the fear of espionage, heightened by the surprise attack on Pearl Harbor and rumors of attacks to come on the mainland, was a real factor in prompting the federal government to intern Japanese Americans. In spite of the fact that no acts of espionage or sabotage by Japanese Americans were uncovered in either Hawaii or California, the boards of supervisors of eleven California counties solemnly declared that "during the attack on Pearl Harbor . . . the Japanese were aided and abetted by fifth columnists of the Japanese." One United States senator insisted

A Jap born on our soil is a subject of Japan under Japanese law; therefore he owes allegiance to Japan. . . . The Japanese are among our worst enemies. They are cowardly and immoral. They are different from Americans in every conceivable way, and no Japanese . . . should have a right to claim American citizenship. A Jap is a Jap anywhere you find him, and his taking the oath of allegiance to this country would not help, even if he should be permitted to do so. They do not believe in God and have no respect for an oath. They have been plotting for years against the Americans and their democracies.

Even when others pointed out that no espionage had been reported, proponents of internment argued that that merely proved the danger was greater, for the Japanese were tricky, sneaky, and underhanded, plotting for the right moment to subvert America. Ironically, the absence of overt sabotage was held against them. It was, said General John DeWitt, "a disturbing and confirming indication that such action would be taken!"

Behind the discussions of potential disloyalty lay years of racial antagonism toward the Japanese in America. The Oriental Exclusion Act of 1924 slammed the door against Japanese and other Asian immigrants, but it did not end racism. Various California patriotic and nativist groups hated or mistrusted Japanese in their midst and considered them unassimilable and treacherous. Economic conflicts also influenced attitudes; some small businessmen and farmers envied their economic success. The war clouds gathering in the Far East during the 1930s also added to the fears of Japan and the Japanese.

The attack on Pearl Harbor rekindled old fears and prejudices and prompted new outbreaks of anti-Japanese hysteria. Responding to demands to remove Japanese Americans from the Pacific Coast, in February 1942 President Roosevelt issued Executive Order 9066, one of the most infamous presidential actions in American history. Under this decree, which was later backed by a congressional law, the army rounded up approximately 110,000 West Coast Japanese, most of whom were native-born American citizens, and scattered them throughout the western states in camps called relocation centers. In Hawaii, where martial law existed, prejudice was less intense and the Japanese played a more important role in the economy.

Hasty removal meant hardship and suffering. Given only five days' notice, those interned could take only what they could carry; the government sequestered all other belongings. Not only were the financial losses great, but conditions in the relocation centers were miserable. At first the Japanese were placed in temporary quarters, including a hastily converted racetrack that lacked basic amenities. Eventually the government built ten camps, most of them in barren desert country, hot in the summer and cold in the winter. The surroundings were drab and unattractive, complete with barbed wire, military police, and, in some instances, machine guns. One Japanese American woman wrote of her experience at Camp Minidoka, north of Twin Falls, Idaho.

> When we first arrived here we almost cried and thought that this was a
> land that God had forgotten. The vast expanse of sagebrush and dust, a
> landscape so alien to our eyes, and a desolate, woe-begone feeling of
> being so far removed from home and fireside bogged us down mentally,
> as well as physically.

Gradually conditions improved, except for internees at the Tule Lake, California camp, who were considered especially disloyal.

One of the sorriest episodes of the Japanese American internment was the reaction of the United States Supreme Court. Several Japanese Americans challenged the government's policy and took their cases all the way to the highest court. In 1943 in *Hirabayashi v. U.S.*, and in 1944 in *Korematsu v. U.S.*, the justices upheld military curfews as well as the evacuation. Three dissenting justices—Owen Roberts, Frank Murphy, and Robert Jackson—scorned the government's policy and attacked the racial prejudice that supported it. But the majority accepted the argument that internment of these immigrants and their American-born children served the national interest in wartime.

When the government closed the camps in 1945, Japanese Americans were fearful about how they would fare in the United States. Some of the most bitter renounced their American citizenships and returned to Japan. The vast majority, though, elected to return to California despite federal efforts to relocate them elsewhere. Anti-Japanese groups opposed their return. Bumper stickers appeared declaring NO JAPS WANTED IN CALIFORNIA, and a few incidents occurred, especially in the Central Valley of the Golden State. Veterans' groups urged boycotts of reopened businesses, and a few rocks were thrown and shots fired into homes. In Oregon an American Legion post removed the names of local Japanese American servicemen from the public honor roll, and other American Legion posts on the West Coast banned Japanese American servicemen from membership.

Yet the opposition gradually subsided, and, aided by church and liberal civic groups, Japanese Americans were able to find homes, jobs, and increasing acceptance. However, they reclaimed only about a tenth of their $400 million in forfeited holdings. In 1948 an anti-Japanese proposition on the California ballot to make the alien laws harsher was defeated by 59 percent of the voters. Although over 40 percent still favored restrictions against the Japanese, this was the first time in California history that an anti-Japanese referendum had been defeated. In 1952 the California Supreme Court declared the 1913 Alien Land Act unconstitutional. Also in 1952, in the McCarran-Walter Immigration Act, Congress lifted the ban on Asian immigration and the exclusion of Asians from citizenship. Japanese Americans still faced discrimination in the 1950s and 1960s, especially in housing and jobs, but the situation had changed drastically from pre-World War II attitudes and practices. By the 1960s public opinion polls revealed that most Americans considered Japanese Americans desirable citizens, trustworthy people, and loyal to the United States. Nevertheless, the trauma for those interned has not been completely overcome. A generation after the camps closed, one Japanese American admitted, "My father still trembles when he talks about this experience." On Memorial Day 1974, some Japanese Americans whose children had difficulty believing the stories of their parents' hardships made a pilgrimage to the Tule Lake camp. In Klamath Falls, Oregon, where a few had stopped to pay respects to those who died at Tule Lake, a woman passing by rolled down her car window and shouted, "You're on the wrong side of the ocean."

Today most Japanese Americans find the same opportunities available to them as do other Americans. The well educated are quickly employed, the affluent can live where they will, and those who choose to marry people of a different heritage are not blocked by miscegenation laws. In other words, Japanese Americans are no longer ethnics who are feared; now they are Americans who are respected.

The internment of the Japanese during World War II coincided with the peak of American xenophobia. Measured by public opinion polls, hostility toward American minorities probably reached its greatest intensity during the early 1940s. When the war ended in 1945 the European and Asian worlds had been torn asunder, but few Americans wanted to help any of the survivors begin life anew in the United States. The story of how our immigration policies changed after 1945 is related in the next chapter.

Chapter 5

Immigration After World War II, 1945–1998

WHEN WORLD WAR II ENDED in 1945, the Daughters of the American Revolution, the American Legion, the Veterans of Foreign Wars, and several other patriotic groups called for a ban on immigration for five to ten years. However, Congress passed legislation to bring 205,000 displaced Europeans to our shores within three years; added to that figure in 1950; and continued to increase the numbers of immigration permits, rather than restrict them, during the next four decades. Despite the narrow McCarran-Walter Immigration Act, which essentially reiterated American beliefs in the 1924 policies established by the Johnson-Reed Act, special legislation to aid individual groups in dire circumstances characterizes the Congresses of the past five decades. The new policies reflected a more liberal and generous spirit in American society, but they also represented a response to communist expansion and the sense of Christian obligation that many Americans felt required us to provide a refuge for those escaping from tyranny. Not to be overlooked as an element in this change is the strength of ethnic lobbying organizations. Before World War II these groups shied away from opposing the views of patriotic organizations, but in 1946 they recognized that favorable legislation would come about only through petitioning and influencing Congress. Then special-interest legislation, and a completely revised immigration bill in 1965, worked their way into the statute books.

But before legislation could be passed the temper of the country had to change. Anti-Semitism peaked in 1945–1946, then began to subside. The changed perception of minorities was aided by a popular Hollywood film, *The House I Live In,* in which Frank Sinatra made a plea for tolerance in 1945; the publication of books like Laura Z. Hobson's *Gentleman's Agreement* and Carey McWilliams's *A Mask for Privilege,* which exposed the depth of anti-Semitic feelings in this country; the Supreme Court's decision to outlaw restrictive covenants in housing; President Harry S. Truman's 1948 proposal for a civil rights program; and increased American prosperity.

Postwar public opinion polls, for example, indicated that fewer Christians believed Jews to be greedy, dishonest, or unscrupulous; and overt anti-Semitism, so common in the 1930s, became less frequent and less respectable. Accompanying the drop in prejudicial attitudes toward Jews was the decline of social and economic discrimination. Universities and professional schools eliminated Jewish quotas, and business firms that had been averse to hiring Jews modified their policies. Changes in major corporations and law firms came slowly. A symbolic landmark was established in December 1973, when E.I. du Pont, the world's largest chemical company, chose Irving S. Shapiro, the son of east European Jewish immigrants, as its president and chief executive officer.

Another persistent theme in American history, anti-Catholicism, also subsided after World War II. Conflict between Protestants and Catholics continued over aid to parochial schools, a proposed American ambassador to the Vatican, the relations of church and state, publicly sponsored birth control clinics, and abortion. But the deep emotional strife of the past eased greatly. The ecumenical movement of postwar society brought Protestants, Catholics, and Jews together in new areas of cooperation. In this same spirit Pope Paul VI visited the United States in 1965, conducted a prayer service before 70,000 people in New York's Yankee Stadium, and received a warm welcome. In 1979 and 1987 the charismatic Pope John Paul II made similar tours and met with even more enthusiastic receptions.

While decreasing anti-Semitism and anti-Catholicism were essential for the enactment of new immigration legislation, the laws, which made possible the admission of many Asians and blacks from the Caribbean, would not have been possible without a decline in racial prejudice. While Chinese and Japanese immigrants had been scorned and were the first ethnic groups to be banned, they found growing acceptance in post-World War II America. Educational and employment opportunities began to open up for their children, and by the middle of the 1960s many state legislatures had outlawed racial discrimination. The most far-reaching of these measures came at the height of the civil rights movement. In 1964 Congress banned discrimination in public accommodations, education, and employment; it then passed the Voting Rights Act of 1965, permitting all adult Americans to register to vote.

The decline of prejudice can be explained by several factors. The fear of divided loyalties that was so potent in World War I and, to a lesser extent, in World War II did not materialize during the Cold War. Prejudice is also strongly correlated with levels of income, religious intensity, and education. As incomes and education increased and as religion became less of a commitment and more of a social identification, tolerance grew. Education did not guarantee the end of prejudice, but there is no doubt that rising levels served to dampen the fires of bigotry. A highly educated public seemed more willing to accept ethnic differences. At the same time, minority members of European and Asian groups absorbed the dominant values of society as they went though the public schools, state colleges, and universities. Finally, as a result of the immigration laws of the 1920s, the nation had achieved a general balance of ethnic groups. The fears of old-stock Americans that hordes of aliens might undermine American traditions and destroy existing institutions declined. The foreign-born percentage of the population steadily decreased from about one seventh in the 1920s to less than one twentieth by the 1970s. America was becoming a more homogenized nation as the grandchildren of Asian and European immigrants came to be indistinguishable from one another or, indeed, from those whose ancestors came here before the American Revolution.

The abatement of ethnic conflict and the general prosperity of post-World War II America created a climate suitable for the modification of the severe immigration acts. First Congress opened the doors to the families of GIs by passing the War Brides Act of 1945, which enabled 120,000 wives, husbands, and children of members of the armed forces to immigrate to the United States. Then it turned its attention to refugees. World War II caused enormous damage to homes and factories in cities and towns throughout Europe, and reshuffling of national boundaries left many people unable or unwilling to return to their native lands. Some had collaborated with the Nazis during World War II and feared retribution; others scorned the communists; still others could not endure going back and rebuilding their lives amid the ruins. As a first step in alleviating the problem President Truman issued a directive on December 22, 1945, requiring that, within existing laws, American consulates give preference to displaced persons in Europe. About 40,000 people benefited from this order before Congress abrogated it with the passage of the Displaced Persons (DP) Act of 1948. The legislation resulted from intensive lobbying on the part of a newly formed Citizens Committee on Displaced Persons, which emphasized that 80 percent of the displaced persons were Christian. The DP Act won approval only after it had been mutilated by opponents of a liberal immigration policy. It was worded to favor agriculturists, exiles from the Baltic states, and those of Germanic origin. President Truman signed the bill reluctantly, denouncing the provisions that, as he put it, discriminated "in callous fashion against displaced persons of the Jewish faith." In 1950, after most of the Jewish refugees had gone to Israel, Congress amended the 1948 act and eliminated the offensive stipulations. Ultimately about 400,000 people arrived in the United States as a result of the two DP laws.

These acts only scratched the surface of the immigration problem. Postwar dislocations and the onset of the Cold War exacerbated the difficulties of readjustment, and millions more still sought entry into the United States. To cope with the needs of these people, as well as to contain the voices of their friends and relatives in the United States who wanted immigration policies liberalized, in 1947 both houses of Congress established a committee to look into the question. Subcommittees carefully studied the old laws and the mass of rules, regulations, and proclamations governing immigration. Senators and representatives gathered data, heard testimony from 400 people and organizations, and then recommended that the basic national origins system remain intact. While rejecting theories of Nordic supremacy, the committee held, nonetheless, "that the peoples who made the greatest contribution to the development of this country were fully justified in determining that the country was no longer a field for further colonization and, henceforth, further immigration would not only be restricted but directed to admit immigrants considered to be more readily assimilable because of the similarity of their background to those of the principal components of our population." McCarran warned, "We have in the United States today hardcored, indigestible blocs which have not become integrated into the American way of life but which, on the contrary, are our deadly enemies." The proposed legislation became the McCarran-Walter Immigration Act of 1952. It maintained the national origins system and strengthened security procedures.

The McCarran-Walter Act liberalized immigration in one area: it repealed the ban on Asian citizenship and granted nations in the Far East minimum annual quotas of 100 each. This was not a controversial change in 1952. During World War II, mainly because of foreign policy considerations, Congress repealed the Chinese Exclusion Acts, gave China a token annual allotment of 105 persons, and made Chinese immigrants eligible for citizenship. After the war Congress passed similar bills for natives of the Philippines and of India.

The removal of some restrictions against Asians did not mean the end of racism in immigration policy, for the 1952 act contained other discriminatory provisions. Those of European background born in the Western Hemisphere were eligible to come from their nations of birth, but Asians in similar circumstances were not. People with one Asian parent were charged to that parent's home country. Thus a person of Italian and English descent who was born in Mexico, which was a nonquota nation, could enter the United States easily, whereas a person of French and Japanese descent who was born in Mexico would be charged to the Japanese quota. The intent of Congress was clear: to admit few people of Asian heritage. The McCarran-Walter Act also set a quota of 100 for several of the West Indian nations. President Truman, who favored broadening immigration laws and eliminating these provisions and the offensive national origins quotas, vetoed the bill, but Congress overrode his veto.

Within a year after the McCarran-Walter Act had become law, efforts were made to modify it. President Eisenhower wanted to admit more refugees, and in 1953 when the Displaced Persons Act expired Congress enacted the Refugee Relief Act, which admitted another 200,000 Europeans and a few hundred Asians. Passed at the height of the Cold War, the measure was meant to aid refugees as well as escapees from communist-dominated areas.

Liberals who wanted broad alterations in the law were disappointed, but Congress made a number of other changes during the 1950s and early 1960s along the lines of the Refugee Relief Act. After the abortive Hungarian Revolution of 1956, Congress passed a law that admitted another 29,000 refugees, chiefly Hungarians, but including Yugoslavians and Chinese. Some 31,000 Dutch Indonesians, another uprooted group, came in under a law passed the next year. The United Nations declared 1960 World Refugee Year and Congress responded with the Fair Share Law, which opened the doors of this country for more immigrants.

In addition to congressional actions, Presidents Dwight D. Eisenhower, John F. Kennedy, and Lyndon B. Johnson used the executive powers they possessed under the existing immigration laws to relax restrictions. Thus 30,000 refugees entered after the 1956 Hungarian Revolution as parolees without visas, ineligible for permanent alien registration until Congress made them eligible. President Kennedy ordered the admission of thousands more, especially the Hong Kong Chinese and Cubans who sought refuge after Fidel Castro's seizure of power in 1959.

Additions to the basic immigration law made it possible for many to come who did not qualify under the quota system. In the early 1960s most immigrants were of this sort. By then the political climate was more conducive to immigration reform and not piecemeal action. In 1963 President Kennedy urged Congress to eliminate ethnic discrimination and the national origins system, which he insisted lacked "basis in either logic or reason. It neither satisfies a national need nor accomplishes an international purpose. In an age of interdependence among nations, such a system discriminates among applicants for admission into the United States on the basis of the accident of birth." After President Kennedy's death, President Johnson called on Congress to enact the Kennedy proposal. Following extensive hearings, a new immigration bill passed overwhelmingly in 1965. Designed to be fully effective in 1968, the act abolished the national origins quota system and made other modifications in immigration policy.

Although the national origins proviso disappeared, an overall limitation remained. Only 170,000 people, excluding parents, spouses, and minor children of American citizens, were allowed to enter the United States from outside the Western Hemisphere. No nation in the Eastern Hemisphere was permitted to have more than 20,000 of this total, although immediate relatives were not counted. The United States still had a selective policy for immigrants, but now Congress put in place a preference system that favored family unification, occupational skills, and refugee status. Seventy-four percent of the slots were reserved for family members. Occupational visas accounted for 20 percent of the 1965 law's categories, and refugees received the smallest allotment.

Liberalization of the law for Asians and Europeans accompanied a shift in policy toward Canadians and Latin Americans. In the 1965 law Congress placed a limit—120,000—on immigration from the Western Hemisphere (immediate family members of U.S. citizens were exempt from the limit). The Johnson administration had not pressed for this restriction, but a majority in Congress feared the possibility of a massive increase in Latinos, especially Mexicans. The limitations were modified to admit Cuban refugees. Western Hemispheric immigration increased after 1965 and the Latino presence in the United States became more pronounced.

In the 1970s Congress added to the reforms begun in 1965 and shaped a worldwide uniform immigration policy. In 1976 Congress created a preference system for the Western Hemisphere and placed a 20,000 limit on all its nations, excluding immediate relatives of American citizens. This provision affected Mexico, which sent several times that number to the American Southwest annually in the early 1970s. Friends of Mexico said that the United States had a special relationship with its neighbor to the south and should make allowances, but Congress thought otherwise. The limit on Mexico helped other Latin American nations, however. Whereas Mexico had previously taken up about a third of the Western Hemisphere's overall quota, now other nations could increase their share. In 1978 Congress completed the reforms begun in 1965 when it created a worldwide ceiling of 290,000 quota places annually (not counting immediate family members of U.S. citizens) by combining the Western and Eastern Hemisphere totals; it also established a uniform preference system for all nations. This system reiterated clauses from the 1965 act that emphasized family unification, occupation, and refugees.

Congress also passed several other immigration acts after 1978. The Refugee Act of 1980 provided a regular system for refugee admissions and stipulated that the "normal flow" of refugees should be 50,000 annually. But like other limits on immigration, that number could be, and usually was, exceeded. In 1986 legislators gave amnesty to nearly 3 million illegal aliens, and finally in 1990 passed a law that increased immigration another 35 percent.

The changing policies of postwar America led to an increase in immigration compared with the rate during the lean depression years. Whereas only 528,000 people arrived in the 1930s and 120,000 during World War II, the numbers grew substantially after 1945. In 1978 they passed 600,000; they were averaging 600,000 annually in the 1980s. During the 1990s immigration reached an all-time high for a decade, with over 10 million people arriving from foreign lands. These figures do not include an estimated 275,000 undocumented immigrants arriving annually. The large increases in immigration meant that the proportion of the United States population that was foreign born also increased. Only 4.8 percent of Americans had been born abroad in 1970, but that figure increased to 9.3 percent in 1996. This was the highest percentage of immigrants in our population since 1930.

After World War II, Europeans at first dominated immigration flows. Many had experienced the horror of war, and they faced language barriers, shortages of funds and skills, and the culture shock of a new environment. Often they were discouraged about the chances of finding good jobs. "I knew I would have to start at the bottom of the employment ladder, but I had no idea that the bottom rung was so far underground," lamented one newcomer. Moreover, many DPs had been through the hardships of concentration-camp life, including malnutrition and physical torture, which made adjustment still more difficult. Those fleeing communism often escaped with only the clothes on their backs.

Yet these people had some advantages. Whether they were fleeing from communism or released from DP camps, the general climate was probably more friendly to immigrants than it had been at any other time in modern American history. A host of private organizations and governmental agencies stood ready to assist them. Jewish groups that had actively assisted refugees in the 1930s continued their efforts. The United Service for New Americans, formed in 1946, was especially helpful to Jewish DPs. Various other European ethnic and religious groups, as well as federal, state, and local governments, assisted still more. In 1957 Hungarians fleeing after the Russian army had crushed the Hungarian Revolution were flown in and quartered temporarily at Camp Kilmer in New Jersey. A federal program begun in 1960 and implemented by the Department of Health, Education, and Welfare aided Cuban refugees; by 1980 over $1 billion had been spent on them. Later the Department helped the Chinese and the Vietnamese, among others. Often public and private agencies worked closely together to ease immigrant adjustment. Moreover, many refugees from communism found Americans sympathetic to their anticommunist views. By comparison, then, most newcomers probably experienced fewer problems than had nineteenth- and early twentieth-century immigrants. Prior to the 1970s they were fortunate too in coming during a period of relative prosperity after World War II, when jobs were available.

Although the enactment of special legislation enabled many southern and eastern Europeans to emigrate as refugees, expellees, or displaced persons, many came under the regular immigration laws, especially the 1965 act. American communities of Italians, Portuguese, and Greeks, among others, used the law to bring in their relatives.

Between 1960 and 1975 over 20,000 Italians arrived annually and settled in places where other Italians had gone, such as New York and New Jersey. They found not only friends and relatives who helped them secure jobs and housing but also churches, stores, and community organizations with familiar names. On the streets they heard their native tongue. After economic conditions improved in Italy in the 1970s fewer sought work in northern Europe or the United States. As a result, immigration from Italy fell off drastically after 1975; only 1,284 Italians arrived in 1995.

Portuguese too were aided by passage of the 1965 immigration act, though they were not as numerous as Italians. The act made their migration possible, and a military coup in 1974 provided a motive for many urban professionals, tradesmen, and entrepreneurs to leave, though a majority were not of the elite. Most émigrés left from Portugal, but a few came from the former Portuguese colonies of Angola and Mozambique in Africa. A few others were from the Cape Verde Islands, but Cape Verdians received their own quota upon the Islands' independence in the 1970s; about 1,000 of these Portuguese speakers settled in the United States in 1995. Portuguese immigration averaged about 10,000 annually in the 1970s, but was only 2,611 in 1995. Newark, New Jersey was the largest center of new Portuguese immigrants. The "Ironbound" district, as it was called, consisted of run-down shops and factories when the Portuguese began to arrive in the 1960s. Because of its size, many documented and undocumented Portuguese settled there. As one alien put it, "We are totally invisible. No one knows about us. Being illegal is just a label that doesn't mean anything." The Ironbound's thriving community consisted of restaurants, shops, and homes for newcomers. "I thought I was still in Portugal," remarked one. Brazilians, who spoke Portuguese, began to settle there in the 1990s.

Greeks were a third European group to benefit from the 1965 law. Between 1960 and 1980, 170,000 Greek immigrants arrived, generally settling among compatriots in Chicago and New York City. In New York they headed for the Astoria section of the borough of Queens, and another 20,000 or so located in Chicago. A Hellenic American Neighborhood Action Committee began in New York in 1972 to help immigrants adjust in their new circumstances. Despite good educations many Greeks accepted menial jobs in restaurants, coffee shops, construction, and factories. But enterprising families refused to stay at the bottom and soon purchased businesses of their own. In 1980 *Newsweek* asserted that the Greeks had all but "taken over [New York City] coffee shops."

The most dramatic impact of the 1965 Immigration Act was on Asia. In many of the years after 1965 Asians accounted for over 40 percent of the newcomers; about 6 million arrived between 1970 and 1995. Not even counting refugees, nations such as the Philippines, Korea, China, and India were among the top sending groups. While Korean immigration dropped somewhat in the 1990s, migration from the Philippines, India, Vietnam, and China remained strong. Table 5.1 gives the ten leading sources of immigration to the United States in 1995 and 1996.

The more than 16 million immigrants who arrived after 1970 settled in all parts of the United States, but about three quarters concentrated in the nation's four largest states: California, Texas, New York, and Florida; and two others, Illinois and New Jersey. Ellis Island is now a tourist attraction; today, most new arrivals come through airports. Los Angeles is the leading center for immigration, and New York is second. Mexicans and Central Americans simply come across the southwestern border. New York attracts many immigrants from the Caribbean, Europe, and Asia, while Los Angeles and California receive Latinos and Asians. Los Angeles was 72 percent Anglo in 1960, but by 1980 people of European ancestry comprised only 40 percent of the city's population. Indeed, as the twentieth century came to an end, the

Table 5.1   America's Recent Immigrants

Immigrants Admitted from the Top 10 Countries of Birth

Country of Admission	1996	1995
1. Mexico	163,572	89,932
2. Philippines	55,876	50,984
3. India	44,859	34,748
4. Vietnam	42,067	41,752
5. China, People's Republic	41,723	35,463
6. Dominican Republic	39,604	38,512
7. Cuba	26,466	17,937
8. Ukraine	21,079	17,432
9. Russia	19,668	14,560
10. Jamaica	19,089	16,398

SOURCE: Immigration and Naturalization Service, *Statistical Yearbook*

state of California was on the verge of seeing its European-origin population become a minority. By the late 1990s one third of New York City's population was foreign born, a figure similar to the high-water mark of the first decades of the twentieth century. New York City was truly a world city demographically. Table 5.2 shows the 30 most popular metropolitan areas for immigrant settlement.

The amazing diversity and demographic change were not limited to New York and Los Angeles. Miami housed many Cubans after 1960 and other Latinos after 1980. Arabs prayed five times a day in Dearborn, Michigan, and transformed many streets in that community into a Middle Eastern phantasmagoria. In New Jersey were many Indians, and along the Texas-Mexico border, Mexicans. Like ethnic groups before them, Muslims established summer camps for their children. One such camp in Pennsylvania made no bones about its intention to "relax the body" and "strengthen the belief." To counter views of other Americans about Islam and terrorism, banners in the dining room stated, "No to terrorism, yes to moderation." While California was known for its Asian and Latino population, in the San Diego area a small community of refugees from Somali appeared after 1991. Its section was called "little Mogadishu," after the capital of Somali.

If diversity has been part of the new immigration, another change in recent years is that so many of the new wave of immigrants are now living in the suburbs. In 1986 the Census Bureau reported that about half of the 4.7 million immigrants arriving between 1975 and 1985 had settled in suburban areas rather than in central cities. And they often lived among other Americans, not in ghettoes of their own ethnic groups. While the Asian population of New York City doubled in the 1970s, it tripled in the city's suburbs. In nearby Bergen County, New Jersey, an official suggested that the Asian population was growing even faster after 1980. A Japanese journalist who lived in prosperous Scarsdale, New York, remarked that the late-night commuter train from New York City was dubbed "the Orient Express," because so many Asian fathers were on it. Outside Los Angeles, Monterey Park became the nation's first Asian-American city or suburb. Sometimes called "Mandarin Park" by those who disliked the changing demography, it was over half Asian (mostly Chinese) in 1994 but had been 85 percent white in 1960.

Immigration will continue to be dominated by developing nations, at least in the near future. Knowledge about the United States is plentiful around the globe and so is the desire to emigrate. Commenting on the situation in Israel, one scholar noted, "Communications are dominated by the 'big eye' of television where the American influence is large, indeed almost inescapable." He noted that in nations throughout the world, "Millions share sleepless nights pondering the machinations and incredible complexities of the Ewings of

Table 5.2   Immigrants Admitted, by Top 30 Metropolitan Areas of
Intended Residence, Fiscal Year 1996

Metropolitan Statistical Area	Number	Percentage
New York, N.Y.	133,168	14.5
Los Angeles-Long Beach, Calif.	64,285	7.0
Miami, Fla.	41,527	4.5
Chicago, Ill.	39,989	4.4
Washington, D.C.-Md.-Va.	34,327	3.7
Houston, Tex.	21,387	2.3
Boston-Lawrence-Lowell-Brockton, Mass.	18,726	2.0
San Diego, Calif.	18,226	2.0
San Francisco, Calif.	18,171	2.0
Newark, N.J.	17,939	2.0
Orange County, Calif.	17,580	1.9
Dallas, Tex.	15,915	1.7
Oakland, Calif.	15,759	1.7
Bergen-Passaic, N.J.	15,682	1.7
San Jose, Calif.	13,854	1.5
Philadelphia, Pa.-N.J.	13,034	1.4
Detroit, Mich.	11,929	1.3
Jersey City, N.J.	11,399	1.2
Nassau-Suffolk, N.Y.	10,594	1.2
Seattle-Bellevue-Everett, Wa.	10,429	1.1
Riverside-San Bernardino, Calif.	10,314	1.1
Fort Lauderdale, Fla.	10,290	1.1
Atlanta, Ga.	9,870	1.1
Middlesex-Somerset-Hunterdon, N.J.	9,286	1.0
El Paso, Tex.	8,701	0.9
Minneapolis-St. Paul, Minn.-Wis.	7,615	0.8
Sacramento, Calif.	6,953	0.8
West Palm Beach-Boca Raton, Fla.	6,553	0.7
Honolulu, Hi.	6,553	0.7
Fort Worth-Arlington, Tex.	6,274	0.7
Total Immigrants Admitted to U.S.	915,900	100.0

SOURCE: Immigration and Naturalization Service, U.S. Department of Justice

'Dallas'—in about as many tongues and accents as one could care to conjure. Blue jeans are the great leveler of the twentieth century, popular as much in Leningrad as in Louisville. Every man's dreams and expectations tend somehow to be spun out in Hollywood and on Madison Avenue rather than in centers closer to home." American movies were no less popular than TV, and in the 1990s French officials, among others, complained about what they believed to be the negative influence of Hollywood productions. Travelers from the United States were almost sure to find McDonald's fast-food restaurants in the major cities of the world. In 1997 the State Department announced that the backlog of people awaiting immigrant visas to the United States was nearly four million, with countries such as India, the Philippines, and Mexico topping the list.

Newcomers from Asia were radically changing the nation's Asian communities and having an impact on American demography. Except for the Japanese, immigrants accounted for the majority of the population of Asian-American communities in the United States. Whereas from 1951 to 1960 only 25,201 people entered the United States from mainland China, Taiwan, and Hong Kong, during the next 35 years, over a million arrived. The impact of such immigration was potentially staggering when one realizes that fewer than 250,000 people of Chinese ancestry lived in the United States in 1960. While immigration from Taiwan fell after the mid-1980s, it rose from the People's Republic of China, and it is not known how many Chinese entered illegally. Smuggling rings that appeared in the 1980s brought in illegal workers from China for a hefty price. Once here they found themselves virtual indentured servants, forced to work 60 or more hours a week at low wages to pay off those who had smuggled them in. Moreover, the newcomers settled in a few American cities, such as San Francisco, New York, and Honolulu, substantially swelling the numbers already there. San Francisco's Chinatown more than doubled its population from 1952 to 1972, and New York City's Chinese population grew from 33,000 in 1960 to 300,000 in 1990. By 1980 New York's Chinese population was the nation's largest, living in the old Manhattan Chinatown and new settlements in the boroughs of Queens and Brooklyn. From 1990 to 1994 another 60,000 Chinese could be found in the city. The rapid influx strained housing. In the mid-1980s some experts estimated that nearly 2,000 new immigrants were searching monthly for apartments in New York City's Chinatown. In addition, restaurants and garment shops also sought Chinatown locations. The old Chinatown spread north into Little Italy and east into the famed Lower East Side, the home of tens of thousands of Europeans decades before. Capital to purchase housing for people and businesses came from Hong Kong, where uneasy investors feared the transfer of that colony's control from Great Britain to China, which took place in 1997. As a result, commercial rents were higher in Chinatown than in most areas of the city.

The new Chinese immigrants had to face not only high-priced and crowded housing but also strained community facilities. In the 1970s and 1980s newspapers carried stories of conflicts between the old and the new Chinese, including violent gang and street fights. The nation's Chinatowns, which had won a reputation for their low crime rates, were now threatened by new violence.

Like earlier immigrants without language and labor skills, Chinese immigrants could be exploited. Even when they had mastered English, they had trouble finding work. One Chinese man described his parents' situation in a garment factory: "There [are] no vacations, no pensions; they just work and work all their lives. We're willing to work, but can't find [good] jobs." In 1972 an estimated 7,500 Chinese, most of them immigrants and many of them women, worked in 250 garment factories—virtual sweatshops in New York City's Chinatown—for wages as low as 65 and 75 cents an hour. A Labor Department administrator said these "employees" in Chinatown were one of the most exploited groups in the metropolitan area. While many of the new Chinese immigrants struggled to make ends meet in overcrowded urban neighborhoods, others located in suburbs or found housing in less congested areas. These were mostly well-educated professionals, part of the brain drain to the United States after World War II.

The scientific community of America was disproportionately foreign-born. From the end of World War II until the 1960s, scientists and engineers came to the United States, from Great Britain and Canada especially, and Germany was not far behind. Most of these immigrants found jobs in private industry, but a considerable number taught and did research in American universities. Many had originally come with a temporary visa or as students but elected to remain in this country.

In 1961 the foreign-born made up about 5 percent of the American population but 24 percent of the members of the National Academy of Sciences. The national Register of Scientific and Technical Personnel estimated in 1970 that 8 percent of the nation's professional scientists were born and had received their secondary educations abroad. Of the 43 American holders of Nobel Prizes in physics and chemistry up to 1964, 16 were of foreign origin. Of the 28 Americans receiving Nobel Prizes in medicine and physiology, 8 were foreign born.

The situation in medicine was similar as American hospitals increasingly became dependent upon immigrant physicians for their staffs. In 1950 only 5 percent of new medical licenses were granted to foreign graduates, but by 1961 this figure reached 18 percent. Ten years later, more immigrant doctors came to America than were graduated that year by half of the nation's 120 medical schools. In New York City, where nearly 30 percent of foreign-born doctors settled, 70 to 80 percent of the residents and interns of some hospitals were immigrants. After changes in the law in 1976 the proportions began to decline. Even so, by the mid-1990s there were 28,000 Indian physicians practicing in the United States, and they comprised 10 percent of the nation's anesthesiologists.

While immigration laws and procedures favored the admission of scientists, engineers, and doctors from abroad, attractive conditions in America were also essential to lure them. A study done by the National Science Foundation in mid-1970 revealed several reasons for immigration. Many, such as the Cubans, disliked their political situations at home, and others were curious about life in America. Insufficient opportunities for research also drove some out. But above all, existing opportunities made the United States seem like the land of golden opportunity. Most of the newcomers cited a higher standard of living, lower taxes, and higher salaries as major factors inducing emigration. About half said that their salaries in America were at least twice what they would have been in their homeland.

Regardless of the educational and income levels of the new Chinese immigrants, there was one major difference between them and the Chinese who came before World War II: they lived in family-based societies rather than the old bachelor ones. The new Chinese immigrants arrived as families, and their new communities were family oriented. Women raised the children and labored outside of the home as well. Some were professionals while others worked alongside their husbands in the many restaurants and small shops. Thus Chinese immigration and settlement patterns began to resemble those of so many European immigrants.

The Philippines sent even more immigrants to America than did Hong Kong, Taiwan, and the People's Republic of China, and ranked second only to Mexico in immigration to the United States after 1960. Between 1960 and 1995, 1.3 million Filipinos arrived. Filipino women married to American servicemen, stationed in the Philippines until the bases closed in 1992, accounted for some of this migration. But the Philippines as a former American colony was highly Americanized. English was spoken by educated Filipinos, and many of the nurses and doctors had received training in universities that used American technology. Mostly an urban middle class, many medical professionals headed for the United States to utilize their training. In the late 1970s it was estimated that more than 9,000 Filipino physicians lived in America, compared to about 13,000 in the Philippines. Filipino nurses were crucial for the operation of many American urban hospitals.

These men and women came in family groups, unlike the migration before 1940, and settled mostly on the West Coast. A high proportion of the women went to work for pay, and as result Filipino-American family incomes were higher than the American average. Like so many other immigrants, they read ethnic newspapers catering to them and worried about the struggle for democracy and economic development in their homeland. They also joined ethnic organizations; but Filipinos, because of their fluent English and high levels of education, did not form ethnic ghettoes. Unlike most other Asian groups, they were apt to intermarry during their first decades in the United States.

More noticeable than Filipinos but fewer in numbers were Koreans. They received attention because of conflicts with African Americans and because they were at the center of the Los Angeles riots of 1992, which destroyed many of their businesses. Few Koreans lived in the United States before 1950. Then came a few students, a few businessmen, and—after the Korean War ended in 1953—wives of American servicemen. The Korean War had an impact on Korean society, for the penetration of American culture triggered immigration, especially after 1950. Koreans learned of our country from the wives of American servicemen and from students, many of whom remained in America after completing their educations. Korean newspapers also told of life here; in 1976 one series of articles was published as a book, *Day and Night of Komericans*, which became a best-seller. However, knowledge was one thing, the law was another; not until the 1965 immigration reform act was it possible for many Koreans to emigrate. First came doctors and nurses, and once they were settled they sent for their relatives.

The 1990 census counted just under 800,000 Koreans, most of whom had arrived since 1960. The largest community was in Los Angeles, but there were also important Korean populations in New York City and Chicago. Many economically successful Koreans, such as medical professionals, lived in the suburbs. Koreans in Los Angeles mixed with other groups, including Mexicans, Samoans, and Chinese, but the city had a Koreatown and the Koreans themselves had a rich community life. For Koreans an important institution was the church. Because so many were Protestants, they affiliated with Presbyterian and Methodist congregations, but they also began to hold separate services. In 1985, the First United Methodist Church of Flushing, in Queens, New York City, had only 30 members in its English-speaking congregation but 450 in its Korean congregation. In many suburbs, where the more prosperous Koreans lived, Koreans held services in their language, even though many of them spoke English well.

Koreans also formed business associations to assist their many economic enterprises. No other immigrant group so easily found a niche in small business. In the 1970s they were successful in running small grocery and vegetable stores in predominately black neighborhoods, replacing Jewish and

Italian merchants. In the 1980s and 1990s they branched out and opened nail salons, dry cleaners, and liquor stores. The immigrants running these shops were often college-educated men and women who worked long hours while keeping their stores open late at night. Korean businesses were especially noticeable in New York City and Los Angeles, but they also moved into declining neighborhoods in cities like Newark, New Jersey. El Paso, Texas had only one Korean store in 1982; three years later thirty more were reported. In that Texas city, as elsewhere, Koreans quickly earned a reputation for successful merchandising. As one El Paso merchant put it, "They're moving in like crazy—it seems every space that's available, they take it. They're very hard-working and industrious."

Urban Korean merchants in predominately black areas found themselves in the midst of growing conflicts. Some black residents claimed that the Koreans insulted them, would not hire them, and did little to help the local community. Black groups organized boycotts of Korean stores, forcing several to close and leading to violence in a few cases. But no one predicted the upheaval that occurred in Los Angeles in 1992. When a white jury refused to convict white police officers of beating a black man—an event broadcast on television—blacks and Latinos in the city erupted. Korean stores in the ghettoes were attacked and more than 2,300 were destroyed, resulting in $350 million worth of damage. Although community leaders tried to patch up the differences and bring groups together, many Korean merchants refused to reopen their stores; they blamed the police for inadequate protection.

Korean immigration to the United States had been declining before 1992, and it continued to fall. However, the Korean economic crisis of 1997 prompted a renewed interest in emigration. Some Korean Americans expressed shame and shock. One remarked, "We thought we were doing so well. Now all of sudden for nothing, there is no money in the bank. . . . I feel so, so, embarrassed, and so annoyed—very mixed." Answering the Korean Association of New York's appeal to send money home, men and women lined up in Korean-owned banks to transfer money to relatives in Korea.

Like the Koreans, few Indians from Asia lived in the United States before 1950, but after that date their numbers grew rapidly, with over 800,000 Indians reported in the 1990 census. Although they settled in most regions of the country, the largest contingent could be found in the New York City area, especially across the Hudson River in New Jersey, and in California. A majority of the first Indians were men who soon afterward began to send for their wives and families. Of the nation's newcomers, these Indians had the highest incomes, much higher than the general national average. The educated elite did well economically in professional positions, as did others who went into business. One of the most successful was the newsstand concession run by Indians for New York City's Transit Authority. Others purchased service stations, but the most notable businesses were motels, many run by Indians with the surname Patel. By 1985 an estimated 80 percent of California's independent motels were operated by Indians. They then branched out and won the concessions for over a quarter of the Days Inn chain motels. One wag labeled these "Potels."

Indians spoke English and were generally not ghettoized. They often lived near their places of work: universities, hospitals, and corporations. Because they were so highly educated and taught in colleges and universities, there were often a few Indian families in places such as Middlebury and Burlington, Vermont, where IBM located a major establishment. Another IBM facility in Boulder, Colorado, employed Indians, as did high-tech industries on the West Coast. Indians formed their own organizations, and were bound together as Sikhs and Hindus. Among some groups, ethnic identity was maintained within the larger Indian community. Bengalis began to hold their own cultural events and publish a magazine. One leader remarked of the annual conference, "The struggle now is to make sure that this second generation, which was raised in America and sees itself as very American, rightly so, does not lose touch with its language and its music."

If Indians represent the elite of the new immigrants, Vietnamese refugees are at the other end of the spectrum. Many, after enduring horrendous hardships, arrived in the United States with few skills, no English, and little knowledge of American culture. They came in several waves, the first being those who were airlifted from Saigon after it fell to the communists in the spring of 1975. Others crossed into Thailand or fled by ship; they were known as "boat people." About 170,000 eventually ended up in the United States. In 1978 a new crisis developed as communists tightened their control over members of the business class, many of whom were ethnic Chinese. As the crisis spread to Laos and Cambodia, endangered Hmong hill tribesmen who had fought against the communists with the backing of the CIA sought refuge in Thai camps. The bloodbath of Pol Pot's Cambodian Khmer Rouge government sent shock waves through the world. Over a million were killed, and thousands of Cambodians fled across the border. In the 1980s the United States and Vietnam agreed upon an "Orderly Departure Program" to process directly relatives of those who had already settled in the United States. In addition, a law passed by Congress created a program for the children fathered by American servicemen and Vietnamese mothers to come to the United States. Many had no knowledge of their fathers and some were abandoned by their mothers. The refugee flow began to slow in the mid-1990s after the United States had received over one million people from the former Indochina.

The federal government processed the first wave through camps set up in army bases. There officials and voluntary workers attempted to help refugees adjust to their new lives. The government also attempted to scatter the newcomers, but the effort was only partly successful. Many Vietnamese favored southern California and moved there as soon as they could. Yet a substantial number ended up in Texas, Massachusetts, Minnesota, and other states as well.

Who were these Asian refugees to America, and how did they fare in their new land? In the first wave, arriving in 1975, many were urban, well educated, knew English, and had formed close ties to the United States' efforts in South Vietnam by working with American armed forces or for American corporations. Some had been officials or military officers in the South Vietnamese government. Among the second wave, coming as part of the large exodus from Indochina in 1978 through the early 1980s, were ethnic Chinese who frequently owned small businesses in the cities. These middle-class people often settled in America's Chinatowns rather than near other East Asians. Included too in this influx were Vietnamese businesspeople and those who had worked for the United States and the government of South Vietnam before 1975. Although a predicted bloodbath did not take place when the communists took over, these people were harassed by the new regime and their old ways of livelihood destroyed. Others in this wave were a large number of desperate people from Laos and Cambodia, many peasants uprooted by the constant fighting. Hmong tribesmen frequently were illiterate farmers who lacked urban skills and experience.

Regardless of their backgrounds, all Vietnamese refugees faced problems in their new land, including racism that erupted into public hostility and even violence. In Philadelphia, Denver, New Orleans, New York, and Seadrift, Texas, refugees encountered chilly receptions. The most newsworthy violent episode pitted Vietnamese fishermen against white Texans. Some refugees who entered in 1975 settled along the Texas Gulf Coast to engage in shellfishing. Unfamiliar with American regulations and customs about fishing for shrimp and crabs, immigrants used smaller boats than did Americans and did not always follow established rules and procedures. Tempers flared as prices for shrimp and crabs remained low and fuel prices were high in 1978 and 1979. One American complained, "There's too many gooks and too few blue crabs. The government gives them loans and houses but doesn't care about us. Who's gonna protect our rights? The Vietnamese are gonna take over, it just isn't right." In the summer of 1979, an American trapper was killed during a fight between native whites and refugees. Although the Vietnamese were arrested and indicted, tensions remained high when they were acquitted of murder charges.

Ugly episodes of racism and violence during the 1980s victimized other groups too. In Washington, D.C. arsonists fire-bombed 11 Korean stores in a two-year period; in one incident a Korean woman was killed. In Philadelphia, Koreans reported a rise in thefts committed openly. In a Detroit bar, unemployed and angry automobile workers beat Vincent Chin, a Chinese American, to death. Asian Americans were incensed when the defendants were sentenced to only three years' probation and a $3,780 fine. These occurrences were by no means isolated. The U.S. Commission on Civil Rights reported in 1986 that there was a 62 percent increase in anti-Asian incidents from 1984 to 1985. In Los Angeles County in 1986 violence against Asians accounted for half of the racial incidents, compared to only 15 percent the year before.

While the rapid growth of racial violence was troubling, most refugees did not experience it. Their most acute problems included lack of English, lack of familiarity with American ways, and little or no capital. Federal government programs, along with aid from church and community groups, helped many of the newcomers become self-sufficient, and by the 1990s some of the first wave of refugees was on the way to becoming successful in the new land. In Chicago, Vietnamese immigrants revived the once economically depressed Argyle Street. Within ten years of their arrival they operated fifty shops in this "Little Saigon." A city alderman remarked of their success, "The change has been astronomical. No one used to dare go there after 5 P.M. and now there is a real night life."

Ten years after appearing on the scene, these refugees also began to make their mark academically. The media publicized stories of Vietnamese arriving penniless with no knowledge of English and winning academic awards a short time later. In 1984 one such refugee, Chi Luu, became the valedictorian of his graduating class at The City College of the City University of New York. Two years after that, Hoang Nhu Tran became the second Vietnamese immigrant to graduate from the Air Force Academy and the first to be named a Rhodes Scholar for two years' study at Oxford University, England. The son of a high-ranking Vietnamese air force officer, he had fled in 1975 to the United States.

For the boat people and others who arrived in the 1980s the picture was not as bright. Many had survived horrendous conditions at sea and malnutrition in refugee camps. Moreover, many were poorly educated; some of the Laotians were not even literate in their own language. Uprooted by constant fighting and emotionally drained by refugee camp living, they lacked the knowledge and means to adapt readily to American ways. The cultural gap was deep. An official working with the Hmong people relocated in Montana observed that they had never encountered freeways, food stamps, checkbooks, or birth control pills. He explained, "This is like Disneyland to them. It's like us going to Mars and starting over again."

Although most refugees came as families or were able to reunite with their loved ones within a few years, it was not always possible to do so. One quarter of Cambodian families were headed by women. Their husbands had been killed or had been lost trying to escape to Thailand. For these women, with little education and only an elementary knowledge of English, life was hard. Social workers reported that they had an especially difficult time adjusting to the United States. They knew little English, and they were reluctant to go out. "When I go out," explained one, "some people ask me lots of questions and I can't answer enough." Some had been raped during their escapes, which added to their fears of leaving their apartments. Thus, in addition to the problems they faced economically, many experienced mental health difficulties. Low-paying jobs often lacked health insurance; this made welfare a necessity to keep Medicaid benefits. Because their children were learning English in the schools, women had to rely upon them to interpret and explain American ways. For some, such reliance was a loss in status and proved embarrassing as well when questions were asked about birth control. The jobs they found were low-paying and in the service sector. Cambodians, for example, found a niche in California's Dunkin' Donuts shops, even though few if any had ever heard of donuts in Asia. Government officials worried that Cambodians, Hmong, and even some Vietnamese would become a permanent dependent class. Surveys after 1980 reported high rates of welfare, although they also revealed that the longer the refugees remained here the more likely they were to learn English, find jobs, and become self-sufficient. No doubt the first wave, with their higher status, would help the newest Asian immigrants adjust, but only time would tell the final stories of the refugees.

In the 1980s and 1990s the numbers of several new groups of Asians coming to the United States increased. Among them were Thais, Pakistanis, and Bangladeshis. Some of the first Thais were women married to American servicemen who were stationed in Thailand during the Vietnam War. Then came some medical professionals. Bangladeshis benefited from a lottery provision of the immigration laws, begun as a temporary measure in 1986 and made part of the 1990 immigration act. This provision reserved several thousand visas for people who came from nations that had sent few immigrants to the United States after passage of the 1965 immigration act. Those receiving visas were determined by a lottery in which names were selected at random. The largest Bangladeshi community was reported to be in New York City, with smaller settlements in New Jersey, Boston, Chicago, Los Angeles, and Philadelphia. From 1985 to 1995 annual immigration from that county increased from 1,146 to over 6,000. While some of the Bangladeshis and Pakistanis were professionals, others had to begin at whatever jobs they could. Members of both groups drove taxis, opened restaurants, and ran small newspaper shops. The number of Asian restaurants in American cities increased geometrically, and diners were no longer limited to Chinese and Japanese establishments. Although Pakistanis formed their own organizations, they also affiliated with America's growing Muslim population. Some experts think that Muslims may one day overtake Jews behind Protestants and Catholics among America's religious groups. Like Indians, Pakistanis became shopkeepers. In New York City Pakistan Day festivals were held; Pakistan had moved up to eighteenth on the list of countries sending immigrants to America. Their communities were relatively small but growing, and given the family unification system provided for in immigration laws, they had the potential for future expansion.

While the number of East Asians grew substantially after 1965, increases were also recorded from the Middle East. Following the Islamic revolution in Iran in 1979, many fled to the United States, some entering as refugees and others as regular immigrants. A good number of these people were professionals and entrepreneurs who found that their livelihoods were threatened in Iran. Some were Jews who feared persecution. In California and elsewhere Iranians utilized their skills, became self-employed, or worked as professionals. Many were fortunate to know English and were relatively successful. The Iranians of Los Angeles located in Beverly Hills and Brentwood, two of the city's most affluent neighborhoods. This group was active in construction and some, like the Ersa Grae firm, built shopping centers and subdivisions in several states.

The Soviet invasion of Afghanistan in 1980 triggered another wave of refugees. As the war dragged on thousands of Afghanis fled to neighboring Pakistan; authorities estimated their number to be 3 million. The United States supported those fighting the Soviets and at the same time recognized that assistance would have to be granted to the unfortunate refugees. Those who entered without proper papers had a difficult time convincing the government they were entitled to asylum, but eventually several thousand were admitted annually as refugees in the 1980s. Their numbers began to decline when the Soviets ended the war, and only 616 refugees were accepted in 1995. Afghanis came to a nation that had few of their compatriots, and most who came before 1979 were highly educated. The newest refugees had diverse backgrounds. A few opened restaurants, but they became better known for operating fried chicken stands. "It's like Koreans with markets," remarked one. "When one starts, he gives jobs to friends and they get started in the same business."

Another Middle Eastern migration consisted of Armenians, who also headed for Los Angeles. When they began to arrive, the city scrambled for residents who spoke Armenian to teach in the public schools. A survey of Armenians in Los Angeles discovered that over 90 percent spoke Armenian

at home, a higher figure for language maintenance than other Middle Easterners. But like generations of other immigrants before them, the children
were learning English and no longer speaking their parents' language at
home.

Turks were another group whose migration grew after 1965, although they
averaged only 3,500 in the 1990s. One center of settlement was New York
City, in the Sunnyside section of the borough of Queens. Most Turks were
secular Muslims, but some followed conservative teachings. In the United
States they found themselves living among some of Turkey's traditional enemies, Armenians and Greeks, some even working at Greek-owned gas stations. In one New York school, a Turkish-speaking counselor was brought in
for parent-teacher conferences and to assist in expanding the curriculum to
include Turkish folk tales, music, and dance.

Israel, traditionally a country receiving immigrants, continued to do so
after the fall of European communism at the end of the 1980s. Many Russian
Jews then went to Israel. At the same time, Israelis emigrated, both legally
and illegally, to the United States. American culture thoroughly penetrated
Israel. Israelis saw American television and movies, and many had friends or
relatives already in the United States before they emigrated. The immigrants
usually spoke English and were often well educated; of all the Middle Easterners Israelis were most apt to know English. That and the fact that many
were highly educated gave them an advantage in the United States. Whether
living in New York City, Los Angeles, or Chicago, Israelis did well. In Los
Angeles, for example, of all the Middle Easterners, Israelis had the highest
earnings.

Israelis, Turks, Armenians, and Iranians speak different languages and
come from diverse cultures, but even many of the Arabic-speaking immigrants had little in common. The wars in the Middle East between Israel and
her neighbors served as a catalyst for migration, as did the bitter civil war in
Lebanon. Thus Palestinians, Lebanese, Jordanians, and Syrians left. Chal-
deans, a Christian group from Iraq, settled in Detroit where they were small
shopkeepers. Many Palestinians purchased small stores in California. A
Palestinian estimated in the mid-1980s that his ethnic group ran about half
of San Francisco's groceries. Like so many other "mom and pop" immigrant
shops, these were businesses where the whole family worked. In Los Angeles, the men ran laundries and the women hair salons. As refugees, Palestinians also included many professionals little concerned with the turmoil
in the Middle East. They shared one trait in common with other Arabs and
Middle Easterners: the desire to maintain their culture.

Black immigrants found that particular parts of the new immigration policy allowed them to enter the United States in growing numbers. African immigration grew slowly after World War II, but civil strife made it possible for some to come as refugees. Some were Asians who found the new regimes threatening. Such was the case for Indians living in Uganda in the 1970s. About 70,000 fled or were compelled to leave; most went to England or Canada, but several thousand others settled in the United States, where they became part of the Indian migration. Some whites left Africa as well, but most African immigrants were black. Ethiopians left after a Marxist revolution there in 1974. Ethiopians also had reasons other than politics to concern them. A dreadful famine prominently displayed on television in the mid-1980s made many grieve for their countrymen. "It's in the back of our minds all the time," said Bishop Paulos Yohannes of the Ethiopian Orthodox Church of the Savior. "Every time you eat, you see them." Another group of refugees were Somalians arriving in the 1990s. An estimated 20,000 came after 1991, with 12,000 settling in the cold climate of Minneapolis. Many worked in the food processing jobs that were available. Mostly Muslim, they organized their own mosques, wore traditional clothing, and tried to maintain their culture. They frowned on women working outside the home. If working in the cold climate of Minnesota seemed unusual, so did the fact that other Africans found employment on the ski slopes of Colorado.

Unlike most other new immigrants, African men outnumbered women. Often African migrants were well-educated professionals who found jobs in American hospitals and in universities, teaching such subjects as economics. One journalist found fifty-five Nigerians employed in a single New York City hospital. Elite Nigerians formed their own professional groups, yet not all new immigrants were professionals, nor did professionals find life easy at first. They were willing to take low-paying jobs to get started, and they saved their money to bring their families to the United States. Others had menial positions because they lacked immigration papers. When hearing of another who was slain, one Senegalese livery cab driver observed, "I am scared but I can't do anything else. I have no choice. I have no green card. That's why I drive a cab." Some became entrepreneurs selling goods on American streets; on rainy days they appeared from almost nowhere to sell umbrellas. Like Jewish peddlers of old, they fanned out across the United States to sell their wares in St. Louis, Detroit, Atlanta, and Chicago. One individual noted, "The average African who leaves his mom and dad and leaves his continent—that is a risk-taker. They are Christopher Columbuses. They come here with a suitcase, and they end up with a home. They make life from nothing."

Their numbers are certain to grow, at least in the near future. The 1990 provision for "diversity visas" gave Africa a sizable share of that category. In addition, in 1998 President Bill Clinton increased the refugee allotment from Africa to 12,000. Along with refugees and family members exempt from the quotas, Africans were averaging well over 20,000 annually in the 1990s. This new immigration was diversifying black America. The newcomers spoke different languages, were mostly Muslim, had their own cultural institutions, and distanced themselves from native-born African Americans.

English-speaking West Indians also added a new dimension to black America. As before World War II, immigrants from the Bahamas went to Florida, and Jamaicans and Guyanese settled in New York City. Other cities that received these immigrants were Philadelphia, Hartford, and Washington, D.C. The Hartford community was originally formed by farm workers who picked apples and tobacco in the Connecticut River Valley. Immigration laws made it possible for West Indian women to take the lead in moving to the United States. Using the occupational preferences, they came as nurses and as child care workers. Some were single but others, once established, petitioned to have their families join them. West Indian women had one of the highest labor force participation rates of all the ethnic groups. Their fluency in English also made it possible for many to find white-collar clerical work in American cities. The men had a reputation for running their own small-scale businesses, such as shops catering to the immigrants or livery services, which in New York City took subway tokens as payment. Most of the men and women were not independent entrepreneurs, however. Because of the existence of so many two-wage earning families, they had incomes above those of native-born black Americans. Yet they still encountered the same racism. Many people believe that white Americans favor West Indians because of their reputation as hard workers. As a result some West Indians did not wish to be identified with African Americans, or as one said, "Since I have been here, I have always recognized that this is a racist country and I have made every effort not to lose my accent."

These new immigrants often returned home periodically or permanently. But as so many settled in the United States they formed organizations built around their economic needs and culture. Cricket was played in places were West Indians congregated, and shops sold food such as curried goat. Each island differed, and West Indians did not necessarily believe that they were part of a larger West Indian culture. Although these immigrants spoke English, newspapers such as the *New York Carib News*, dedicated to their particular needs, began publication. In Brooklyn in the late 1940s West Indians began holding a parade that celebrated their traditions. Repeated every Labor Day, by the 1990s it had become the largest ethnic parade in the nation, drawing over one million people to see the pageantry, hear West Indian music, and eat ethnic food. Like an earlier generation of West Indians, the latest newcomers began to naturalize and move into politics. By the 1980s they were beginning to elect their fellow countrymen to political office in New York City. The prospects for influence in New York were relatively good, for foreign-born blacks made up over one quarter of the city's black population of two million.

French and Creole speakers from Martinique, Guadeloupe, and Haiti joined the Caribbean flow. The largest group by far was from Haiti but their reception in the United States was considerably different from that of Jamaicans, Guyanese, or Barbadians. These mostly Creole-speaking migrants fled the dictatorial regime of the Duvalier family and a wretched economy, which made Haiti the poorest country in the Caribbean. The elite left first, but by the 1970s desperate Haitians unable to obtain immigrant visas were boarding rickety boats and heading for Florida. Once in the United States they took any jobs they could find. In Miami, where many of them settled, they were often scorned as another poor immigrant group. If caught they could be deported as illegal aliens. Haitians and their supporters among civil rights and religious groups insisted that they were refugees and entitled to asylum, much like Cubans. The Immigration Reform and Control Act of 1986 granted asylum to those who arrived before 1982, but before that act passed the United States government rejected their contention that they were refugees and, beginning during the Reagan administration, intercepted Haitian boats at sea and returned them to Haiti. In 1992 presidential candidate Bill Clinton criticized Republicans for this policy, but he continued it after he was elected. Then the government sent some Haitians to the American Guantanamo Naval Base in Cuba to await a resolution of their situation. Quarrels over their HIV status complicated the issue, but some Haitians were admitted. In 1994 President Clinton ordered an invasion of Haiti, both to restore democracy and to stem the Haitian exodus. The president warned that unless democracy was restored tens of thousands of Haitians would head toward the United States. These actions drastically slowed the exodus. In late 1998 President Bill Clinton and Congress agreed to allow thousands of Haitians illegally in the United States to adjust their status to legal immigrants.

While Asians, Middle Easterners, Caribs, and Latinos were the major beneficiaries of changing immigration policy after 1960, some Europeans also benefited. During the Cold War the United States granted refugee status to Poles and Soviets who managed to leave. They lost this opportunity when the Cold War ended, but Poles were able to gain admission by using the lottery. The Soviet Union permitted many Jews to leave in the late 1970s, but when Congress passed a law tying increased trade to Russia with a relaxation of that country's emigration policies, the Soviets responded by tightening restrictions. Of those who managed to get out during the 1970s many were well-trained professionals. They settled in Los Angeles, Philadelphia, Baltimore, Chicago, and New York. So noticeable was their presence in the Brighton Beach section of Brooklyn that the area earned the nickname "Little Odessa."

After communism collapsed in the Soviet Union, its people were once again permitted to leave. The U.S. Congress passed the Lautenberg amendment in 1989 declaring that all Jews, along with some Armenians and Pentecostal Christians, should be considered refugees. As a result, in the next 6 years about 300,000 people came to America from Russia and the Ukraine. Police complained that the new immigrants were used to corruption and tyranny, being from a place "where to cheat the state, to evade the law, is a heroic deed." While some newcomers got into trouble with the law, others struggled to learn English and begin life anew.

When economic conditions improved in Ireland during the late 1960s and 1970s, few wanted to leave. After the economy turned down, however, the Irish discovered that the 1965 immigration law curtailed the number of visas available to them. Thus many of them entered the United States illegally, settling in Boston, New York, and Chicago, where men worked in construction and women as child care helpers. *The Irish Voice*, a newspaper devoted to the concerns of these "New Irish," carried numerous want ads for child care. Congress responded to the pressure of Irish groups and provided a lottery in 1986. Applications poured in from Ireland, and Irish immigrants won 40 percent of the slots. The lottery was made permanent in 1990, with 40 percent of visas reserved for Ireland for a 3-year period. As a result many of the "New Irish" legalized their status. From 1992 to 1996, 95 percent of Irish immigrants to New York entered on visas won in the lottery. In the bars of their communities the Irish brogue and familiar Old World music could be heard. In these new neighborhoods one could purchase "Irish chocolates, Irish sausages, Irish brown bread and Irish Beer."

The latest European immigrants came at a time when people of European ancestry were mixing in ways not dreamed of by their grandparents. While not as impressive in numbers as immigrants from Asia, the Middle East, Africa, the Caribbean, and Latin America, they added to America's ethnic diversity. Black America was being changed by the new immigration. In 1940 less than 1 percent of American blacks were foreign born, but the figure was approaching 10 percent at the century's end, and black immigrants came from a great variety of cultures. Asians comprised less than 1 percent of the nation's population in 1945 but over 3 percent in 1995, and the number is growing rapidly. Whole new Asian communities, such as the Vietnamese, appeared after 1970. Middle Easterners too were changing. Formerly most

Arabs had been Christians, but now Muslims were the dominant group. But Middle Easterners were also marked by great diversity of language, religion, and culture.

Demographic changes were pronounced in six states, but they could be seen in many communities. Even white churches in the South could not escape the new immigration. Outside the Shallowford Presbyterian Church in DeKalb County, Georgia, a banner proclaimed ONE IN CHRIST in four languages—English, Korean, Spanish, and Asian Indian—noting four separate services. When services overlapped, parking became a problem and so did cultural conflict. One woman who had been attending church there for forty-one years remarked, "I don't like all this jumping around. I like formality." Others complained that worship did not begin or end on time. The Mexican-born assistant pastor noted, "Punctuality is not a virtue for Hispanics. Time is to benefit the celebration of life, not for life to serve time."

No change was so noticeable as that taking place among America's Latinos, who made up more than 10 percent of the population in 1998 and were on the way to overtaking African Americans as the nation's largest minority group. Their story is the subject of the next chapter.

Chapter 6

Newcomers from South of the Border

SINCE WORLD WAR II there has been a continuous increase in the Latino presence in this country. With the *bracero* movement during the war, Puerto Rican migrations to New York City and other East Coast locales after the war, and the migration north from Mexico in the late 1940s and 1950s, Hispanics have carved a niche for themselves that rivals that of the Germans in the nineteenth century. Moreover, since 1968 a plurality of all immigrants to the United States has come from Mexico. By the end of the twentieth century, in fact, Mexico had already passed Great Britain, Italy, Ireland, and even Germany as a source for immigrants. In 1998 25.7 million people born abroad lived in the United States—nearly 10 percent of the American population, the highest percentage since prior to World War I. Of that number, seven million, more than one quarter of the total, were from Mexico.

Newcomers and their children from Mexico and other nations in Latin America made up a growing proportion of the American population. Census records of 1980 revealed that there were more than 14 million people of Mexican, Puerto Rican, Cuban, and other Latino origins in the United States, a substantial increase over the figures for 1970. In 1980 Latinos constituted 6.4 percent of the nation's people; but in 1997, swelled by immigration, high birth rates, and the 1986 amnesty granted by the Immigration Reform and Control Act, they were 29 million, over 10 percent of the population. Sometime in the first decade of the twenty-first century, Latinos will replace African Americans as the nation's largest minority group. This growth, along with that of Asians, is indicative of major demographic shifts in the United States since the end of World War II.

The signs of Latino vitality are evident almost everywhere in America. More than a hundred television and radio stations broadcast in Spanish. In February 1998, for example, the top-rated television station in Miami, Florida, WLTV, broadcast exclusively in that language. Other major Spanish-speaking television stations thrive in cities like New York, Los Angeles, and Albuquerque, New Mexico. Pacific Telephone puts out a Spanish-language supplement in California; Chicago bus notices and Philadelphia civil service examinations appear in both languages; and shops from California to New York display *Aqui se habla español* placards in their windows. In Miami, shops display Cuban flags and CUBA LIBRE signs. One can walk for blocks in that city hearing only Spanish and stop at cafés that serve rich, dark Cuban coffee. In 1997 a slick magazine catering to upwardly mobile Latinos, called *Hispanic*, celebrated its first decade.

By 1970 Spanish had replaced Italian as the nation's most frequently spoken foreign language. The changes were reflected in the nation's schools. Beginning with the arrival of Cubans in the 1960s, Miami's schools developed bilingual programs. In 1967 the federal government passed a bilingual education act that provided support for such schools; buttressed by a Supreme Court decision in 1974 that said that children must be taught in a language they can understand, bilingual programs expanded. The vast bulk of the classes were held for Spanish-speaking children. The *Mariachi Hunachi* (Spanish spelling for "Wentachee") band was reportedly the most popular school marching band in the central part of Washington State in the late 1990s, and rapid growth of the Latino population in that community, which accounted for about one quarter of the city's students, forced the Wentachee board of education to scramble for Spanish-speaking teachers. The state bilingual education director reported, "It's taking school districts by surprise. It's a situation we're not ready for." The 1990 census revealed that 32 million Americans spoke a language other than English at home, and in most cases that language was Spanish. Given the high rate of Latino immigration in the 1990s, the figures will be even greater in the census of 2000.

Although large Latino communities exist in practically every major city in the country, different groups predominate in different areas. The Puerto Ricans (born citizens of the United States) are most significant in New York City where in recent years they have been challenged by Dominicans as the leading Latino group. Puerto Ricans also have substantial populations in Philadelphia and Cleveland. The Cubans dominate in East New York, New Jersey, and Miami. But Cubans have been augmented by other Latinos in the 1980s and 1990s in Miami; now many Nicaraguans and other Central Americans are there. Mexicans are the main minority in Los Angeles, San Antonio, San Francisco, Seattle, Detroit, Denver, and throughout smaller southwestern communities. Along the border separating the United States and Mexico are major Mexican communities that have grown significantly since 1980. Mexicans make up about 20 percent of the city of Los Angeles's population and 40 percent of that county's people. Chicago too has a large Mexican population.

It is important to keep in mind that Latinos represent many different countries and cultures. Most Latinos speak Spanish, but Brazilians speak Portuguese. In the 1990s Mexicans of Indian heritage, mostly Mextecs, moved across the border to work in California's agricultural fields. Although these "Latinos" were from a Latino or Hispanic nation, many did not speak Spanish; they only spoke their Indian dialects. A 1993 survey of California's Mexican farm workers in labor camps in north San Diego found that 40 percent spoke indigenous Indian languages rather than Spanish. Twelve languages turned up, including Cakchiquel, Chatmo, Kanjobal, Nahuatl, Otomi, Tlapaneco, Trique, Zapoteco, and Mexteco. The new wave of Latinos has included economically successful immigrants and those who are very poor. Cubans and many Central Americans are refugees who have foreign policy issues on their minds, but most Latinos pay little attention to Fidel Castro and are simply fleeing poverty or seeking their fortunes in the United States.

Mexican Americans, over 60 percent of the nation's 29 million Latinos, are the most prominent. Most of them live in the Southwest, the majority in urban areas. In 1997 they constituted approximately 31 percent of the population in California, 20 percent in Arizona, 28 percent in Texas, 14 percent in Colorado, and nearly 40 percent in New Mexico. Since World War II, however, Mexican immigrants have been spreading throughout the United States; although the vast majority of them live in the five states mentioned above, there are communities in most states, including Minnesota, Illinois, and New York.

As discussed in earlier chapters, some Mexican Americans, especially those in New Mexico and southern Colorado, can trace their ancestry back many centuries. Santa Fe, New Mexico was founded in 1609, twenty years before the Puritans set foot in New England. After the United States annexed the Southwest, Mexican immigrants crossed the border in search of work. Ever since, the history of the Mexicans in the United States has been tied to the history of the Southwest. The modern migration began with the completion of the southwestern railroads, the expansion of cotton planting in Texas, Arizona, and California, and the agricultural revolution in the Imperial and San Joaquin valleys in California. These industries needed cheap labor, and the Mexican workers provided it. Mexicans made up more than 60 percent of the common laborers on the railroad track gangs, in the mines of Arizona and New Mexico, in agricultural fields in Texas and California, and in the numerous packing plants on the West Coast. They also dominated the labor supply in the sugar beet states as far north as Montana and as far east as Ohio.

The coming of Mexican laborers coincided not only with the rapid growth and development of the Southwest but also with the curbing of immigration from China and Japan and later from Europe, and with the revolutionary upheavals in Mexico beginning in 1910. Mexican workers, cowboys, shepherds, and ranch hands had crossed the Mexico–U.S. border frequently and easily between 1850 and 1910, just as others had moved north and south or east and west within the United States. There was no border patrol before

1924, and American immigration officials were more concerned with keeping out Asians than with tracking down Mexicans. But as southwestern agriculture developed it demanded hundreds of thousands of cheap, mobile laborers who could pick the crops quickly, then move on to other areas and harvest whatever else was ripe. In Texas the migratory farm workers usually started in the southern part of the state in June, then moved eastward and eventually westward for the later harvest in the central part of the state. In California, on the other hand, more than 200 crops are cultivated and the growing season ranges from 240 to 365 days, keeping workers busy all year.

Before 1910 most of the Mexican migrants were temporary laborers, but after the upheaval caused by the Mexican Revolution many permanent settlers arrived. Although the overwhelming majority were lower-class agrarian workers, the migration also included artisans, professionals, and businessmen whose property had been destroyed by the violence accompanying the revolutionary chaos.

The Mexican Revolution spurred movement, but so too did a number of other factors. From 1877 to 1910 Mexico's population increased from 9.4 million to 15 million without a commensurate increase in the means of subsistence. A small percentage of *haciendados* (feudal barons) controlled most of the country's land, which was tilled by the agricultural proletariat. There existed between hacienda owners and their laborers a patron-peon relationship, and each role was well defined. As the economy boomed, though, prices rose while daily wages remained constant or even declined to an amount well below that needed to care for a family. At the beginning of the twentieth century the construction of the Mexican Central and Mexican National railroads, as well as the opening of mines in northern Mexico, encouraged movement.

Once the exodus from central and eastern Mexico began, many workers saw no need to stop at the border. Wages in the United States were at least five times higher than in Mexico and American businessmen avidly sought foreign peons. As two scholars who have studied Mexican migration pointed out, their inability "to speak English, their ignorance of personal rights under American law, and their recent experience as virtual serfs under the exploitative dictatorship of Porfirio Díaz made them ideal workers from the growers' viewpoint." The northward migration brought about 10 percent of Mexico's population to the southwestern borderlands.

The first Mexican migrants in the twentieth century were overwhelmingly males, mostly transient, who found work on the railroad track gangs. They lived in boxcars and moved from place to place with the Southern Pacific or the Santa Fe or the Chicago, Rock Island, and Pacific. By 1910 they could be found from Chicago to California and as far north as Wyoming. They were cheap laborers who worked for $1 to $1.25 a day, less than their predecessors—the Greeks, the Italians, and the Japanese. Employers found Mexicans desirable because of their tractability and their willingness to work at more arduous jobs for longer hours, at lower wages, and in worse living conditions than the Europeans or Asians. Many of today's Mexican American *colonias* (settlements) originated as railroad labor camps. Women accompanied some of the men heading north and they too found employment in the low-wage sectors of the economy. In El Paso and other Texas cities with Mexican populations, women worked largely as domestics in the homes of European Americans or as service workers in the growing tourist industries. Some women also joined their husbands in the fields during harvest time. As the canneries of California expanded, they began to employ women. One historian noted, "the canning labor force included young daughters, newly married women, middle-aged wives and widows. Occasionally three generations worked at a particular cannery—daughter, mother, and grandmother."

With the influx of Mexicans, El Paso, Texas became a major placement center and assembly point for workers in an arc of twenty-two states reaching from Louisiana to the state of Washington. Three major railroads passed through this border city, where railroad, mine, and seasonal agricultural employers recruited. Representatives from labor-contracting companies also took thousands of immigrants to distributing centers in Kansas City, Missouri; Los Angeles; and San Antonio.

After 1910 more Mexican newcomers found work in agriculture rather than on the railroads. Nonetheless, the major southwestern railroad employed more than 50,000 Mexicans. During World War I, European immigration fell drastically, American residents went off to war, and the expanding southwestern agricultural acres needed hands. As a result the laws governing contract labor were temporarily suspended in 1917, and those Mexicans who were otherwise ineligible for immigration visas, were brought in to cultivate the crops and work the harvest. The depression of 1921–1922 left many of them unemployed, but then the return of prosperity and the immigration restriction acts of 1921 and 1924 curbed European immigration, thereby stimulating a further demand for Mexican labor. Large southwestern agricultural growers put great pressure on Congress to exempt Mexicans from the quota for their area, and their intensive efforts succeeded. To be legally admitted to the United States, Mexicans still had to pay fees for visas and medical examinations, show that they were literate and not likely to become public charges, and prove that they had not violated the contract labor laws. These restrictions, plus an inadequately patrolled border (not until 1924, in fact, was money appropriated for a border patrol), made it easier for Mexican agricultural workers to enter illegally than to go through the rigmarole of formal application. Scholars estimate that in the 1920s there were at least 450,000 documented immigrants, and about the same number without appropriate immigrant papers. The 1920s immigrants worked primarily in the agricultural areas of five southwestern states—California, Texas, Arizona, New Mexico, and Colorado—as well as in the Michigan sugar beet fields and in the industrial areas in and around Chicago, Detroit, Milwaukee, and western Pennsylvania. Chicago's Mexican population, in fact, shot up from 3,854 in 1920 to 19,362 ten years later, and the city claimed the largest Mexican population east of Denver.

The depression of the 1930s curtailed immigration, and many Mexicans and their American-born children were encouraged—even forced—by local government officials to return to Mexico. More than one third of the Mexican American population was removed between 1929 and 1940. About half the Mexicans who remained in the United States experienced severe deprivations. In Gary, Indiana, social workers found them living without furniture and with only boxes for tables and the floor for beds. Moreover, they fell victim to tuberculosis and rickets, and malnutrition was common among their children. One report, noting the poor housing, the large numbers of unemployed, and the deteriorating health, observed, "The agony and suffering that all of these people endure is beyond comprehension of any who have not experienced it." Southwestern agricultural wages fell from 35 cents to 15 cents an hour. In Texas, Mexican cotton pickers, working from sunrise to sunset, were lucky to earn 80 cents a day; other Mexican farm workers had to be content with 60 cents a day. In California by the late 1930s migratory Mexican families averaged $254 a year, and even there American whites were given preferential treatment. By 1939, in fact, more than 90 percent of the Golden State's field workers were dust-bowl refugees who had replaced the minority group members. In 1940 one investigator found that most of the Mexican agricultural workers in Hidalgo County, Texas, earned less than $400 a year. That same year a quarter of the Mexican children between 6 and 9 years of age worked in the fields with their parents; 80 percent of those in the 10–14-year age group did so as well.

The coming of World War II opened up new opportunities for Mexican laborers in the Southwest. Many of those in California and Texas moved out of rural areas to urban centers, where they found jobs in airplane factories, shipyards, and other war-related industries. In the Midwest, steel mills, foundries, and automobile factories (which were now manufacturing for military needs) could not fill their job vacancies fast enough as those eligible for military service went off to war. The southwestern agricultural fields were also starved for workers.

At this juncture the governments of Mexico and the United States inaugurated an entirely new program: the importation of contract laborers, known as *braceros*, to work in the fields and on the railroads. According to the bracero agreement, Mexicans came into the United States for temporary seasonal jobs, then returned home when their tasks were completed. Begun in 1942, the initial program ended in 1947; while it lasted, the United States received about 220,000 braceros. The U.S. Department of Agriculture administered the program and the agreement stipulated that there would be a guaranteed minimum number of working days, adequate wages, and suitable living accommodations. Braceros worked in 21 states, with more than half of them going to California. The Mexican government would not allow any of its nationals to work in Texas because of intense discrimination in the Lone Star State.

From the braceros' point of view the program was a good one. Most of the workers were men who could not provide adequately for their families at home, and the jobs in the United States offered what they considered good wages. Although they earned only 30 cents an hour and less than $500 a year, this rate still provided them with enough to send money back to their families.

Although protective provisions had been written into the law, many observers were later appalled to find braceros living in converted chicken coops, abandoned railroad cars, and rickety wooden structures that were on the verge of collapse. The braceros themselves, however, were attracted by the wages and kept returning whenever they could. In *The Bracero Program*, published in 1971, Richard B. Craig explained why these people accepted conditions that others would find deplorable and degrading. The Mexican laborer, Craig noted, is "accustomed to living, and indeed thriving, in a virtual state of physical and mental peonage. The Mexican . . . bracero or wetback* probably found little except language (and not always that) to distinguish between the *patron* and the strawboss. It would appear, in sum, that the sociopsychological milieu in which the average Mexican peasant was reared prepared him ideally for his role as the servile, hard-working, seldom complaining, perpetually polite bracero."

Although the original bracero program ended in 1947, there were temporary extensions until 1951 when the clamorings from southwestern growers and the impact of the Korean War combined to induce Congress to reestablish it. The new law lasted until 1964. Table 6.1 shows the numbers of braceros entering the United States during the 22-year program. The appar-

---

*The term "wetback" (*mojado*), which designates an illegal immigrant, originated because many Mexicans swam across the Rio Grande River, which separates Mexico from Texas, and waded across during relatively dry periods when the water was shallow.

Table 6.1   *Braceros* Entering the United States Under
Contract, 1942–1964

1942	4,203	1950	67,500	1958	432,857
1943	52,098	1951	192,000	1959	437,643
1944	62,170	1952	197,100	1960	315,846
1945	49,454	1953	201,388	1961	291,420
1946	32,043	1954	309,033	1962	194,978
1947	19,632	1955	398,650	1963	186,865
1948	35,345	1956	445,197	1964	177,736
1949	107,000	1957	436,049		

SOURCE: U.S. Congress, Senate Committee on the Judiciary, *Temporary Worker Programs: Background and Issues*, 96th Congress, 1st Session (1980).

ently bottomless reservoir of cheap labor from south of the border helped build up the multibillion-dollar agricultural concerns from California through Texas, which, unlike during the war years, were now included in the revised program. One appreciative and callous grower acknowledged: "We used to own slaves but now we rent them from the government."

In the 1950s braceros earned 50 cents an hour (30 cents for cotton chopping in Arkansas) and upset American laborers. The Mexican Americans in the Southwest were particularly resentful. They did the same work as the braceros, often side by side, but for lower wages, worse housing and facilities, and no transportation. The humiliation and bitterness that these citizens felt when they compared their situation to that of the imported foreign laborers eventually reached the ears of liberal politicians in Congress and prominent labor officials. Both groups protested the continuation of the bracero program, but they lacked the numbers or the influence to prevail in the 1950s. In the 1960s the Democratic administrations proved more sympathetic and helped bring the program to a close.

Other factors also militated against continuing the bracero program. The southwestern growers had already begun to increase mechanization and thereby decreased their need for more hands; in 1962 Secretary of Labor Arthur Goldberg imposed a $1-an-hour minimum wage for these people; and at about the same time, labor shortages below the Rio Grande made the Mexican government eager to end the agreements. During the 22 years of the program's existence, from 1942 to 1964, almost 5 million braceros came into the country, and they were viewed as indispensable to the southwestern economy. Moreover, their earnings contributed to the Mexican economy as well, because they sent more than $200 million to their relatives at home.

Besides braceros, whose wages and living conditions were stipulated by agreement, the southwestern farmers also employed an untold number of illegal immigrants. For the most part, they were not selected by the Mexican government for the bracero program but had backgrounds and needs similar to those who were admitted. The conditions these aliens were willing to accept in the United States—wages of 20 to 30 cents an hour, housing without plumbing or electricity, washing in irrigation ditches—hint at what life must have been like in Mexico. Certainly, the inhumanity and cruelty that they experienced here must have been an improvement over what they left behind; otherwise they would not have struggled to enter the United States. A more plausible explanation, however, might be that with wages double or triple those in Mexico, workers might be willing to endure great hardships in exchange for economic gain. The growers, of course, found them ideal laborers. Fearing disclosure of their illegal status, the Mexicans performed their tasks well; they neither argued nor complained, and they cost practically nothing. In fact, some unscrupulous southwestern agricultural entrepreneurs turned these undocumented aliens in to immigration officials before payday, thereby saving themselves the cost of the workers' meager wages. Between 1947 and 1954, when the Immigration and Naturalization Service (INS) inaugurated a major campaign to round up and deport illegal aliens, more than 4 million of them were apprehended in the United States, but an unknown number escaped detection. From 1946 to 1954, however, undocumented Mexican entrants were the most important source of southwestern farm labor.

Although a great many illegal migrants were deported to Mexico, the number of legal Mexican immigrants began to rise in the 1950s. Since then, except for refugees, Mexico annually has sent the largest number of people to this country. From 1960 to 1995 Mexican immigration amounted to over four and a half million. In 1991, when the numbers were swelled by amnestied aliens, nearly one million entered. And the list of those awaiting visas in Mexico was long. Beginning in 1957 the American government stopped counting those who left the United States; some experts believed, however, that Mexicans returned home at a fairly high rate. Latinos from the Caribbean also returned frequently in a circulatory migration pattern.

Mexicans looked north because their nation's economy did not develop fast enough to absorb its rapidly growing population. The devaluation of the peso in 1976, and again in the early 1980s following the collapse of the oil market, only served to worsen the economic situation and stimulate further movement. Valued at 24 to the dollar in 1982, the peso exchange rate fell to 750 to the dollar in 1986, and to 948 in January 1987. Then the government was unable to meet its debt obligations in the 1990s. Only a bailout by the United States prevented default, and although Mexico was able to weather the storm, the faltering economy served to further stimulate immigration north.

Many Mexicans who could not obtain visas crossed the border without them. Like the braceros, a large number of these newcomers to the United States labored in agriculture, but most worked in urban service, construction, or industrial jobs, undertaking tasks shunned by most American citizens. In 1977 a Los Angeles resident remarked, "You couldn't eat at a hotel in this town if a vacuum cleaner scooped up all the illegal aliens." A number of Americans viewed the influx of so many undocumented aliens with alarm, and they proposed that the federal government take action to stem the flow. They wanted tighter border controls and above all a law outlawing the employment of those without proper immigration documents. Congress hesitated, but after much debate and compromise the Immigration Reform and Control Act (IRCA) was passed in 1986. It outlawed the employment of illegal aliens but also granted an amnesty to many of those already here. Nearly three million people were able to take advantage of the amnesty. But Congress failed to provide effective controls to halt illegal immigration.

As a result, illegal immigration began to rise again in the 1990s. By the end of the decade, border patrol guards were catching more than one million people annually trying to enter the United States without documents. In 1996 Congress passed new legislation and gave INS additional funding to hire more agents and beef up walls and barriers along the border. How effective these measures would be was a question that could not answered by the legislation. One problem in the 1990s was that about half of the undocumented population was estimated not to have successfully crossed the border, but rather to have entered legally on visitor or student visas and then simply stayed on when the visas expired. It was nearly impossible to track such people down and deport them.

While undocumented aliens from Mexico had previously been single males with few skills and little education, the situation in Mexico deteriorated so drastically in the 1980s that border agents reported catching new types of illegal entrants: skilled workers and highly educated professionals. An immigration official in Washington, D.C. observed, "There is a perception on the border that there are more people with higher-level skills coming in. We seem to be running into more middle-class people and family units than we did before the big influx at . . . the start of their economic crisis."

The reference to family migration meant that more women were crossing the border. Mexico, unlike most other nations after World War II, sent more men than women to the United States, but by the 1990s the gender totals were about even. Some women followed or accompanied their husbands, but others came on their own. Like male undocumented aliens, women knew of the ethnic networks that led to housing and jobs. For Mexican women this often meant work as domestics or in the garment shops of California.

Both Mexicans and Mexican Americans were victimized and exploited. But why they endured such abuse for decades, with few protests until the 1960s, requires a deeper inquiry into their backgrounds. A majority of them in the Southwest were products of several centuries of intermixture between Spaniards and American Indians (there was also a "rica" class of landowners and ranchers), and they came from a culture of poverty. For generations, both in Mexico and in this country, they had been forced to assume the lowest position in the social order. The Roman Catholic Church, which in Mexico combined traditional doctrine with native folk practices, preached a certain fatalism about life, and the relationship of the rural poor to the major landowners, or *patrons*, reinforced these teachings. Education for the peons in Mexico prior to 1930 was practically nonexistent, and they came to regard it as a luxury for the upper classes. The immigrants brought such attitudes with them to the United States, and this, combined with the prejudices and inadequacies of schoolteachers and administrators ill prepared to handle Spanish-speaking children, prevented many Mexican children from exploiting educational opportunities in the ways that Jewish, German, Greek, Armenian, and Asian children had. Finally, it must be noted that many Mexican workers looked upon their years in the United States as a temporary expedient. They expected to return home; their sojourn north of the border more likely than not gave them an improved status in their native communities. As one Mexican newspaper explained it, in the United States these workers "learn many good things, to be temperate, to dress well, to earn good wages, to live properly, to eat properly, to speak English and much of modern agriculture. That is, they become cultured and when they return to Mexico, they progress rapidly."

The Mexican peasants who moved to the United States may have crossed an international boundary, but for the most part they continued to dwell in a land whose physical characteristics were familiar and among people who might easily have been their neighbors at home. The Mexican communities in the Southwest, for example, were so well developed that the newcomers did not have to relinquish their faith, their language, or their cultural ties to be accepted. Continued migrations sustained Mexican *colonias* in the United States and to a considerable extent retarded acculturation and assimilation.

In this country large farmers and industrialists welcomed the Mexicans for the labor they provided. Lack of familiarity with Mexican customs allowed the Americans to misinterpret good manners and respect for authority as docility, illiteracy as ignorance, and a lack of the Puritan work ethic as laziness. Moreover, the scarcity of good jobs and the fact that illegal entry compromised a migrant's position also kept Mexican resentment and anger from surfacing at the wrong moments. The Mexicans' willingness to work has sometimes been misrepresented in a paternalistic and prejudicial manner. A brochure to entice large employers to Tucson in 1977 stated, "Employers who have established plants in Tucson say that our Mexican Americans are easy to train, will follow instructions, are more loyal, and equal or exceed the productivity of workers in other parts of the country." The advertisement created controversy within the city; Mexican American inhabitants resented its tone as well as the stipulated characteristics.

That Mexicans are docile is belied by their history in the past century. In Mexico the revolution of 1910 was at least in part a peasant movement, and in the United States too there were enough incidents of labor strife to call for a reexamination of careless characterizations. Mexicans led strikes in the Texas Panhandle in 1883 and on the Pacific Railway in Los Angeles twenty years later. To protest labor conditions, thousands of Mexican workers walked away from sugar beet, onion, celery, berry, and citrus crops in California, Texas, Idaho, Colorado, Washington, and Michigan in the 1920s and 1930s. That these protests produced few permanent advances does not reflect defects in the Mexican character. Instead, it reflects the harshness of reprisals, the intense competition for jobs, the shifting nature of the migrant work force, the mechanization of agriculture, and the movement of the more prosperous and accomplished to urban areas where industrial jobs promised greater remuneration.

Mexican women were also involved in the trade union movement, and they joined *mutualista* (political organizations) to further their goals of providing a decent living for their families. Historian Vicki Ruiz reports that in 1939 two women were the main leaders in *El Congreso de Pueblos de Hablan Espanola* (the Spanish-speaking People's Congress), the first national Latino civil rights assembly. During the 1930s women activists joined the Cannery and Agricultural Workers Industrial Union, and they participated in strikes in cotton fields. They also organized a pecan shellers union and had some success in organizing canneries.

In our own era, about 10 percent of Mexicans are members of trade unions, a figure only slightly below the national average. They have joined the United Auto Workers, the United Steel Workers, and the Mine, Mill, and Smelter Workers; and within these unions they have sometimes formed Hispanic caucuses. However, the industrial unions have been in decline, and the Mine, Mill, and Smelter Workers was charged with being communist-led and ran into hard times during the McCarthy era (the 1950s). In the 1970s some unions, such as the International Ladies' Garment Workers' Union

(ILGWU), recognized the sweat shop conditions of many Mexican women in California and moved to organize them, even those without documents. It was difficult for the ILGWU to organize shops that paid low wages, demanded long hours, and, at times, maintained unsafe working conditions. In the 1970s one of the bitterest strikes was against Farah Manufacturing Company in El Paso. Most workers were Mexicans; 86 percent of them were women. Managers knew that they could find other Mexican women to take the place of strikers, and they resisted the union drive. After several years of conflict, Farah finally recognized the Amalgamated Clothing and Textile Workers as the representative of its employees.

Another problem that Mexicans as well as other minorities had in the United States was that Americans could or would not understand why any group was reluctant to part with its own heritage and embrace the values of the dominant culture. But Mexican peons struggled merely to provide the essentials of life for their families. Often they did not see the long-range benefits that might accrue to their children from a good education. Even when they did, they may have been shrewd enough to recognize that American education would lead their children away from family traditions. Even in rural Mexico in the 1930s schools were built faster than students could be found to occupy them. Peasants were not enthusiastic about educating their children, for they cherished a family life in which everyone had a prescribed role. The status quo provided too much comfort and security for them to sacrifice it for another culture whose values they had difficulty in comprehending. Given Mexican American uneasiness with acculturation and the continued influx of newcomers from the old country, it is not surprising that many Mexican American families speak Spanish at home. And while in the past few broke away from their cultural patterns, in the 1990s far more newcomers recognized the benefits of education for their children.

For those immigrants who sought to mix more with other Americans, societal prejudices until about the 1980s formed an almost insuperable barrier. Although discrimination existed throughout the American Southwest, it was not entirely uniform. For example, Mexicans were expected to live in their own *barrios*, and if they did find housing elsewhere it was usually in deteriorating neighborhoods. They were often blocked from using many public recreational facilities, could obtain mostly menial and relatively unskilled jobs, and in general were expected to accept a subordinate role in society. In New Mexico, however, there was a tradition of Hispanic participation in government, and upper-class Americans of Mexican background moved easily throughout society. In New Mexico also, those of Mexican descent, regardless of class, have been active in local politics, and their numbers (until recently almost half the population) have determined where and when they could hold office. In Colorado, Mexican *colonias* date back to the 1850s, and there too prejudice existed but was not intense. Nor was Arizona, despite its segregated schools and movie theaters, a particularly harsh place for Mexicans.

But in California and especially in Texas, bigotry toward Mexicans was extreme. In the Lone Star State, with its strong southern heritage, Mexicans encountered more overt discrimination than anywhere else in the country. Restaurants and merchants routinely refused to serve them; kindergarten teachers called their children "greasers"; churches held separate services "For Colored and Mexicans." One Texas farmer told an interviewer "You can't mix with a Mexican and hold his respect, it's like the nigger; as long as you keep him in his place he is all right." And during World War II, when the Mexican government, incensed at the treatment those of Mexican ancestry received in Texas, refused to allow braceros to work in the state, one Mexican American weekly noted: "The Nazis of Texas are not political partners of the Führer of Germany but indeed they are slaves to the same prejudices and superstitions."

It was also during World War II that two particularly heinous events involving Mexican Americans took place in Los Angeles. One, in 1942, involved the arrest and conviction of a gang of teenage boys for murder although the prosecution presented no evidence at the trial to justify their conviction. Existing community prejudices, combined with the unkempt and disheveled appearance of the youths (the prosecuting attorney instructed the sheriff to prevent them from bathing or changing their clothes during the first week of the trial) sufficed to bring forth a guilty verdict. Similar miscarriages of justice reflecting community prejudices have been rendered in other sections of the country toward other minority group members at different times, but few have been marked by such gross disregard of evidence. Unable to raise bail, the defendants were forced to spend two years in San Quentin prison before a California appeals court unanimously reversed the lower court's decision "for lack of evidence" and reprimanded the trial judge for his behavior during the proceedings.

The other event that won national attention and pitted Mexican Americans against Anglos took place in June 1943. The Zoot Suit Riots involved Mexican American youth sporting the then faddish zoot suits: baggy trousers with high waists and tight cuffs, long coats with wide shoulders and loose backs, and broad-brimmed flat hats. On the evening of June 3, 1943, a group of sailors was assaulted while walking in the Mexican *barrio*. The sailors claimed that their assailants were Mexicans. They reported the incident to the police, who returned to the area but could find no one to arrest. The following night 200 sailors took the law into their own hands, went into the Mexican district of Los Angeles, and beat up every zoot suiter they could find. One naval officer explained their mission: "We're out to do what the police have failed to do, we're going to clean up this situation." Not surprisingly, the Los Angeles police did nothing at the time to deter the servicemen from their course. For the next few nights sailors, soldiers, and marines paraded through the streets of Los Angeles indiscriminately attacking Mexicans in what *Time* magazine called "the ugliest brand of mob action since the coolie race riots of the 1870s." It took the intervention of the Mexican government with the U.S. Department of State to curb military leaves in the Los Angeles area, which put an end to this mob action. The Zoot Suit Riots led to the formation of the Los Angeles Commission on Human Rights in 1944, but the new organization did little to alter established prejudices.

In retrospect it is difficult to imagine positive effects from a miscarriage of justice or from a bloody riot; yet the two events focused attention on Mexican Americans in an urban setting. Most writing about Mexican Americans portrayed them as living in rural areas and as being exploited by money-hungry large-scale growers. Although this picture is not totally inaccurate, after World War II only the Mexican American minority, not the majority, was still tied to the land. In 1950 two thirds of Mexicans in the United States lived in urban areas; today about 90 percent live in cities.

Urban Mexican Americans came to resemble other immigrants and minorities in American history. The second and third generations began to break away from familiar traditions and place more emphasis on American values. The extended family was gradually replaced by the more typically American nuclear family, and work horizons expanded. During World War II, when opportunities developed in airplane plants and shipyards, urbanized Mexicans did not have to leave at harvest time to earn more money in the fields.

After the war opportunities continued to expand as the economy grew and discrimination declined. The growing popular disdain toward bigotry led to the enactment of civil rights laws and affirmation action programs. Professional, semiskilled, and skilled jobs opened up opportunities for advancement and assimilation for minorities. Enrollments in colleges and universities went up, as did the number of those who were becoming lawyers and health professionals. Even so, minorities were underrepresented in these elite occupations and on college campuses. The attack on affirmative action in the late 1990s led the University of California's campuses and professional schools to eliminate affirmative action programs, and the number of minority students dropped.

The education situation pointed to one of the key problems for Mexican immigrants: lack of skills. Latinos lagged behind European Americans and

Asians in educational attainment. In 1995 only 6.5 percent of Mexicans were college graduates, compared to 23.6 percent of the total population. Approximately three quarters of the adult immigrants had not finished high school (the average number of educational years was about 8); and of more than 6 million immigrants, only 120,000 (less than one percent) had college degrees. Moreover, while their children and grandchildren were proficient in English, half of the immigrants reported difficulty with the language.

Mexican immigrants also earned less than others. In 1996 their incomes were only about 60 percent of the national average of white Americans, and approximately 30 percent of their families lived below the government's standard for poverty. Studies done of the immigrants themselves indicated little improvement in status in the 1980s and 1990s, and their real wages dropped.

Although too many Mexican American families lived in poverty or struggled with low incomes, a growing number succeeded in business. María Elba Molina immigrated with her family to Arizona when she was eight years old. Through education and hard work she became a vice-president of Home Federal Savings and Loan in Tucson. Still dissatisfied, however, she began her own company, the J. Elba Corp. Inc., to sell products in the Hispanic community. "I decided I would incorporate my own firm, do what I had always wanted, which was to be on my own; I would try it," she recalled. She successfully sold not only to small clients but also to television stations and banking institutions.

Individual Mexican Americans have been successful in various areas of American life, winning the admiration of other Americans. In 1997, the magazine *Hispanic* singled out "Movers and Shakers," the twenty-five most "powerful Hispanics in Washington, D.C." They included Maria Echaveste, an assistant to President Bill Clinton; Xavier Becerra, chair of the Congressional Hispanic Caucus; Raul Yzaguirre, head of the National Council of La Raza; Aida Alvarez, head of the Small Business Administration; Anita Perez Ferguson, head of the National Women's Political Caucus; and Antonia Hernandez, president of the Mexican American Legal Defense and Educational Fund.

These rising leaders attested to growing Latino influence. In the late 1960s, when African Americans and American Indians were protesting, the Chicano movement took shape. The Chicanos wanted to retain their ethnic identity while raising the standard of living of all Mexican Americans. Although they cherished the traditional values of their culture, including respect and affection for the family, the cult of masculinity (*machismo*), and sense of obligation to others in the community, their demands for equal education, training, and job opportunities awakened state and federal legislatures to problems that needed attention.

Mexican American women were also an integral part of the protests. Women active in labor and civil rights groups participated in campus activism that emphasized Latino and women's studies programs in college and university curricula. In 1971 they held the first national Chicana conference, which put forth a feminist platform. At times they criticized Mexican American men for their attitudes and neglect of women's issues.

Reflecting the goals of this emerging movement in the 1960s were four prominent Mexican American leaders—César Chávez, Reies López Tijerina, Rudolpho (Corky) González, and José Angel Guitiérrez—committed to ending the existing inequalities. The best known of the four was César Chávez. Along with 600 Filipinos and Filipino organizer Larry Itliong, he led California's grape pickers on a five-year strike that resulted in higher wages and better working conditions. Chávez's union lost contracts and workers to the Teamsters Union in 1973 and 1974, only to win most of them back later when California passed a law permitting agricultural workers to unionize. Organization among Mexican American farm workers has been successful during a period of increased use of farm machinery, which has meant a loss of jobs in agriculture. Chávez was the first Chicano leader to achieve national prominence, and he became a symbol and a unifying force.

Since the 1960s many new organizations and groups have developed: the Brown Berets, the Mexican American Youth Organization (MAYO), the Mexican American Legal Defense and Educational Fund, and a Congress of Mexican American Unity representing 200 Chicano organizations, all dedicated to fostering the goals that the four leaders articulated so well. These groups are now sophisticated in using their political influence. One of the most important is a coalition of 26 Hispanic organizations founded in 1968 as the Southwest Council of La Raza and renamed the National Council of La Raza in 1973. The council's move to Washington, D.C., in 1970 reflected its national orientation.

Politicians have responded to the growing power of Hispanics. Whereas Richard Nixon appointed fewer than 10 Hispanics to presidential and policy positions in the federal government and Gerald Ford fewer than 25, by mid-1979 Jimmy Carter had appointed nearly 200 Latinos to important managerial and judicial posts. Presidents Ronald Reagan and George Bush, and the Republican Party generally, paid little attention to Latino concerns despite the 1988 appointment of Lauro F. Cavazos, the first Hispanic ever to serve in a president's cabinet, as Secretary of Education; but the administration of Bill Clinton was aware that Mexican Americans voted for his party, and he appointed several Latinos to cabinet and other important positions. Henry Cisneros became head of the Department of Housing and Urban Development; Bill Richardson (whose mother was Latino) UN ambassador; and Federico Pena head of the Department of Transportation and later the Department of Energy.

Below these national positions, a number of Latinos began to win election to state, county, and local offices as well as to Congress. Yet they remained underrepresented; in 1999 for example, in California where Latinos were 31 percent of the population, they held only 17 of the 80 seats in the state assembly and seven of the 40 senatorial seats. But their gains were impressive. In 1986 the National Association of Latino Elected and Appointed Officials reported that 3,202 Latinos were serving in public office. By 1994 the figure had increased to 5,459.

When Henry B. Gonzalez retired from Congress in 1996 he could look back and see much progress. He had been the first Latino congressman elected from Texas. When others joined him, he founded the Congressional Hispanic Caucus, which had a record high of 21 members in 1998. In Congress the Caucus worked with liberals on matters of concern to Latinos, such as welfare and education. In 1986 the Caucus worked effectively to ensure that the Immigration Reform and Control Act (IRCA) had a generous amnesty provision, and ten years later, even in a Republican-dominated Congress, it was able to join with others to weaken tough bills on immigration.

A sign of encouragement for the future of Latino politics is the surge in applications for citizenship, which is needed in order to vote. As immigrant bashing arose in the 1990s and Congress passed a bill denying certain benefits to immigrants, Mexican Americans and Latinos generally rushed to become American citizens. About a quarter of a million people naturalized in 1990, but in 1996 the figure jumped fourfold, and it leaped again in 1997. These new Latino voters overwhelmingly cast their ballots for Bill Clinton and the Democrats. In a sensational upset in Orange County, California in 1996, voters threw out archconservative Robert Dornan and replaced him with Lorreta Sanchez. That same year Cruz Bustamante became the first Latino speaker of the California assembly. When he won election as lieutenant governor in 1998, another Latino, Antonio Villaraigosa, replaced him. In Florida, even the solid Republican vote of Cubans fell off in 1996. Alarmed Republicans who had used harsh words about immigrants began to take another look in early 1997 and agreed to soften some provisions of the immigration restriction legislation passed the preceding year.

Becoming citizens and getting to the polls were important for political influence. But another issue facing Latinos was the fact that they represented a variety of cultures and nationalities, and their experiences and concerns were not always the same. On the East Coast the differences are especially noticeable among the three largest Latino groups: Puerto Ricans, Dominicans, and Cubans.

The United States acquired Puerto Rico from Spain at the end of the Spanish-American War in 1898, and in 1917 Puerto Ricans were granted American citizenship. Ever since, Puerto Ricans have been moving to the mainland. In 1910 the census recorded 1,500 of them; by 1930 there were 53,000. Like members of other groups, those who came were escaping from a land with too many people and too few jobs. The Great Depression and World War II cut the flow to the mainland, but beginning in 1945 it swelled to a torrent. Relatively cheap air transportation and an abundance of skilled and semiskilled jobs in New York City served as the magnets. As late as 1940 New York City had slightly more than 60,000 Puerto Ricans; in a decade the figure had quadrupled. Today there are over 2 million Puerto Ricans scattered throughout the continental United States, with a third in the New York area. In 1998, the other major centers for Puerto Ricans were Chicago with a colony of about 100,000 and Philadelphia with more than 30,000, but the official figures probably underestimate the actual totals. There were also Puerto Rican communities in Bridgeport, Connecticut; Rochester, New York; Dayton, Ohio; Boston, Massachusetts; Miami, Florida; Milwaukee, Wisconsin; and numerous cities in New Jersey.

By the mid-1970s the exodus from Puerto Rico had slowed and it appeared that the number of Puerto Ricans leaving the mainland was greater than those arriving. No one knew the exact figures but some experts suggested that the net flow back to Puerto Rico was around 200,000. The severe recession and inflation of that period accounted for much of the trend. Some Puerto Ricans found that the skills they picked up in New York City, Chicago, and other cities, including mastery of English, enabled them to get ahead in Puerto Rico. But those returning were not always welcome and were sometimes derided as "Newyoricans," a pejorative term meaning pushy, aggressive, and out of touch with life in Puerto Rico.

The Puerto Rican experience in New York and other major cities on the continent is probably closer to that of the European immigrants who landed on the East Coast and settled in urban areas than to that of the Mexicans in the West. Although there are Puerto Rican migrant workers who move up and down the East Coast according to the seasons, essentially they are an urban people with the problems of the city's poor.

In New York they replaced the European immigrants in lower-level factory jobs—especially the Jews and Italians in the garment district—and in the city's worst slums. Like the Europeans, they spoke a foreign language, but unlike them, they encountered a color problem. Many Puerto Ricans are the products of centuries of racial mixing between the island's white and black populations. Although higher status is accorded those of lighter complexions, darker skin does not have quite the impact in Puerto Rico that it has in the United States. On the mainland, though, Puerto Ricans learned that the darker their skin, the greater the difficulty in gaining acceptance and adjusting to the dominant culture. One social worker reported that in her dealings with Puerto Rican drug addicts, inevitably the darkest member of the family was the one affected. Piri Thomas, in his moving *Down These Mean Streets*, an autobiographical account of growing up in New York City's East Harlem ghetto, recalled his own difficulties as the darkest member of his family and how bitter he felt toward his father for passing along such pigmentation to him.

To read the social and economic statistics of Puerto Ricans in New York City and elsewhere is to recall the plight of minorities in the past. Although they gained in real incomes during the 1980s, the 1990 census revealed that 38 percent of their families, and more than half of the children, lived in poverty, double the rate for the city as a whole. A distressing number of families were headed by women. Most did not work but lived on welfare, which did not provide a decent standard of living. The proportion reporting a high school diploma had increased since 1980, but still lagged behind the general average. Twenty-three percent of New Yorkers had college degrees, but only six percent of Puerto Ricans.

In addition Puerto Ricans had a higher incidence of juvenile delinquency and drug addiction, and were particularly susceptible to ailments like tuberculosis and venereal diseases. There were also greater incidents of police brutality toward them. In a word, they have been plagued with the disabilities historically associated with lower-class, poorly educated immigrants. Until American society decides to be more humane and more concerned with these people their plight will be precarious at best.

Dominicans also settled in New York City in growing numbers. Because some entered illegally and many went back, the precise number living in the United States was not known, but from 1960 to 1996 over 700,000 migrated to the United States, with a substantial majority settling in New York City; in 1990 they constituted the largest foreign-born group in New York City. On the Upper West Side of Manhattan their community was known as the second largest "Dominican" city in the world. Because many were undocumented their employment opportunities were limited. Yet even among the legal immigrants, many lacked skills and education, and few spoke English fluently. For those coming from a rural background, the adjustments were especially difficult. Restaurants, hotels, and nonunion construction jobs provided their main employment. Some Dominican families had small grocery stores (*bodegas*). One Dominican noted that his store carried special products for customers; however, running such stores did not mean high profits, and several *bodega* owners were killed or badly injured when their businesses were robbed.

Scholars find that Dominican women favor America's more liberal society compared to the one at home where their roles are clearly proscribed. As wage earners for their families, they have a definite say in household issues, and they are less likely to return home. But life has not been kind to Dominican women in the United States. They find themselves employed in the garment shops and low-paid manual jobs, and almost half of Dominican households are headed by women. In addition to public aid and what they earn, they are assisted by groups such as the Union of Dominicans, an organization of professionals. Some second-generation Dominicans have improved their lot, and as they have naturalized they have become more politically sophisticated. They are now using their growing power to better their communities.

The third Latino group that has had a major impact on the East Coast, and the first immigrant group to change the complexion of a southern city in the twentieth century, is the Cubans, whose experience has been quite different from those of Puerto Ricans and Dominicans. Cubans came in several waves. The first began in 1959 and lasted until the Cuban Missile Crisis of 1962 brought it to a halt. Another exodus began in the fall of 1965 and lasted into the early 1970s. The third migration came in 1980 when over 120,000 landed in Key West, Florida. As a group the Cubans are considerably different from most other immigrants into this country. First, the bulk of them were political refugees who left their homes because of the policies inaugurated by Fidel Castro after he led a successful revolution against the regime of Fulgencio Batista in 1958. Second, many Cuban refugees came from the elite of their society. According to one study, in the first wave about 70 percent were professional, skilled, or white-collar workers; almost 40 percent had some college education; and 80 percent had yearly incomes above those earned by the average Cuban.

The exodus of 1980 was somewhat different. Social and economic problems in Cuba and the reports coming from the United States by visiting Cuban Americans in the late 1970s set the stage for the dramatic exodus. When Castro decided to permit the dissatisfied to leave, a vast flotilla of ships, large and small, set sail from Florida to pick up refugees in Cuba. Relatives and friends of the Cubans and those eager to make money out of providing transportation were involved in the movement, as were voluntary agencies helping the newcomers settle. The Carter administration was uncertain how to handle the situation, but for the most part permitted hundreds of boats to land their passengers. Using the camps inhabited by the Vietnamese refugees in the mid-1970s, the immigration authorities worked with voluntary agencies to settle the Cubans and reunite them with their families in the United States.

Since Miami, Florida is the city closest to Havana in both distance and culture, most Cuban refugees went there. They have made an impressive impact in the city since they left Cuba a generation or more ago and have moved up the economic ladder to achieve middle-class and upper middle-class status in this country faster than any other ethnic group since the Huguenots of colonial times.

The 900,000 or so Cubans in fact revitalized a sleepy southern town and transformed it into a major international hub. Miami is now regarded as the capital of Latin America because it attracts businesspeople and financiers from the entire Western Hemisphere. Argentine ranchers, Ecuadoran manufacturers, and Colombian drug peddlers find the city enticing and exciting. Nightclubs, resorts, and hotels abound. It is perhaps the most comfortable place in the country for Latin Americans because Spanish and English are both the languages of communication. Businesspeople who speak English only are at a severe competitive disadvantage. Enterprising Cubans have taken over or established thousands of businesses. Whereas in 1970 there were fewer than 1,000 establishments owned by Cubans, a decade later the figure hovered around 10,000—banks, construction companies, radio and television stations, and so forth. No significant area of business has been immune to the Hispanic presence. Miami now has more international and out-of-state banks than any other city in the country save New York. These banks and financial institutions attract money from every Latin American nation. In addition, an enterprising Cuban thought up the now established Trade Fair of the Americas, an annual event in which practically all Latin American nations participate.

Individual success stories about Cubans abound. Carlos Arboleya was chief auditor of Cuba's largest bank when he fled his native land. Beginning anew with little money, he worked as a clerk in a shoe factory before finding his place in banking again. By 1968 he had become president of the Fidelity Bank and a U.S. citizen. He later assumed the vice-chairmanship of the Barnett Bank of South Florida, which had assets of $3.5 billion. While banking was attractive to Cubans, so was Miami's garment industry, formerly run by Italians and Jews. "The Cubans really put some zing into this industry. Almost 100 percent of the small manufacturers are Cuban, almost 100 percent of the contractors, big and small, are Cuban and almost all the top management is Cuban," noted one businessman.

Another Cuban immigrant, Yvonne Santa Maria, had never held a job before leaving for Miami in 1963. She arrived with no funds. "No money. No jewels. We were not even allowed to take out phone numbers," she recalled. She worked in several of the city's banks, and at age 57 was president of the Ponce de Leon Federal Savings and Loan Association in Coral Gables, Florida. But no Cuban was as successful as Roberto Goizueta, who until his death in 1997 headed the Coca-Cola Company. Educated at Yale University, he began to work for the corporation in Havana in 1954. When he fled Cuba he had to start over, but rose rapidly to become the company's billionaire chairman and chief executive.

Many Cubans at first did not think of themselves as Americans, but looked instead to the day when Fidel Castro's government would be overthrown and they could return home. Some did return in the 1990s, but only as visitors. To be sure, some still agitated for strong American action to bring down Castro, and were angry when the Clinton administration moved in 1994 to head off another boat exodus from Cuba to the United States. But they subsequently made rapid economic progress, became American citizens, and began to be involved in American politics. In 1985, Miami elected Harvard-educated lawyer Xavier Suarez as its first Cuban American mayor. He defeated another Cuban, Raul Masvidal; both men were born in Cuba and had come to America twenty-five years earlier. The following year, Richard Martinez, another Latino, won the governorship of Florida. In 1988 Ileana Ros-Lehten became the first Cuban American woman elected to Congress, and a second Cuban American joined the Congressional Hispanic Caucus a few years later. As the older exiles died, the younger Cubans looked more to America and less to Cuba.

Mexicans, Puerto Ricans, Dominicans, and Cubans constituted the vast majority of Latinos coming to America in the last half century, but they were by no means the only ones. Like Cubans, some Central Americans emigrated because of political turmoil. The civil wars in Nicaragua, Guatemala, and El Salvador in the 1980s prompted many to leave. If they did not fear direct political persecution, they still experienced violence in their daily lives. Many could not obtain visas but came anyway, hoping for a better life in the United States. The U.S. government did not wish to give these people political asylum, although the anticommunist Nicaraguans had better success than the others in gaining this status. Those who had arrived illegally before 1982 were covered by the amnesty of the 1986 immigration statute. The status of others was precarious until late 1997, when Congress and the Clinton administration agreed upon a measure to allow Nicaraguans, Salvadorans, and Guatemalans to adjust their status and become resident aliens. Certain conditions applied, but this action gave these Central Americans a chance to be legal entrants to the United States. No one knew exactly how many people would be covered, but it was estimated that 300,000 would benefit from the measure.

Central Americans generally settled in areas that already housed other Latinos. The largest Nicaraguan community developed in the Miami area, the center of a growing population from South and Central America. In 1970

Cubans constituted 91 percent of the Latinos there, and even though their population grew, the figure had dropped to only 59 percent by 1990. Moreover, 200,000 new immigrants settled in Dade County (Miami) between 1990 and 1996. Nicaraguans joined not only Cubans but also people from Honduras, Peru, and Colombia. The parish of St. John Bosco Church was founded in 1963 to tend to the religious needs of Cuban Catholics, but in 1997 over two thirds of its members were Nicaraguans. The first Nicaraguans to come to the Miami area were the wealthy, who fled a left-wing government that took power in 1979. However, as conditions deteriorated in their homeland the middle and working classes also left. Like so many other Latino women, the Nicaraguan women became domestics or found employment in garment factories, replacing Cubans who found better opportunities elsewhere. The men worked in construction or at manual labor. Miami's Latinos did not always get along with one another. The latest newcomers were not as well off as the Cubans, who generally voted Republican and were strongly anti-Castro. In Little Havana in 1996 the banning from the Calle Ocho festival of a Puerto Rican singer suspected of communist sympathies angered Puerto Ricans. And when the president of the Latin Chamber of Commerce blamed newcomers for trash piling up in Little Havana, he drew protests from Nicaraguan groups.

Guatemalans and Salvadorans located in cities such as Miami, San Antonio, Chicago, San Diego, Houston, and San Francisco. Washington, D.C., also became a center for their settlement. Others could be found in smaller communities on Long Island or in Spring Valley, New York, doing a variety of manual jobs. Their major settlement was in southern California, especially Los Angeles.

While they had political motives for immigration, Central Americans closely resembled Mexicans in socioeconomic status. According to the 1990 census, only 3 percent of Salvadorans and 4 percent of Guatemalans had a college degree. The vast majority had not graduated from high school. Central American women were usually working for money, but in low-paid occupations. In Los Angeles over 80 percent of working Salvadoran and Guatemalan women were maids. The men also took low-paid jobs, and even though a high proportion of the women worked, two-earner families struggled to get ahead. One fourth of these families lived below the poverty line.

The situation was similar elsewhere. On Long Island, a network of Salvadorans helped their countrymen find jobs and housing. They cleaned houses, cut and trimmed lawns, or did other casual day labor. Men without their families shared housing and even beds with other Salvadorans. While they made little, they hoped to learn English and find better jobs. In the meantime, they provided a cheap labor force for other residents and still managed to send money home. Like Mexicans, in some communities they congregated at particular street corners to offer their labor for a day.

Immigration from South America also increased rapidly after 1960. The 1990 census revealed over one million South Americans living in the United States, the bulk of them recent immigrants. They represented a variety of nationalities. The largest group came from Colombia, with its major center being New York. In the 1950s political turmoil stimulated emigration and in the next two decades economic problems pushed others out. Like so many other immigrants the Colombians sought new opportunities; over half of the Colombian women, a percentage higher than the national average, went to work after they arrived in the United States. In New York City they earned a reputation as hard workers, which helped them get jobs but also opened them up to exploitation. Colombians tended to be conservative and many sent their children to Catholic parochial schools, which they believed had better discipline than public schools, despite the fact that they resented the non-Hispanic, and especially Irish-American, control of the Church. In recent years, however, the Catholic hierarchy in the Northeast has made special efforts to reach out to the Hispanics. Spanish-speaking priests have been appointed to head parishes and to preach in the language of the parishioners.

Colombians were better off than Central Americans, as were South Americans generally. Many were well-educated professionals or members of the middle class. One scholar studying Brazilians in New York City found that 31 percent were college graduates and that nearly half had attended college. These Portuguese-speaking immigrants, like so many others, nonetheless found a tough labor market in the city, and the women were reduced to cleaning other people's houses. A few even became "go-go" girls in bars, while some of the men were reduced to shining shoes to make a living. Because they were Portuguese-speaking they formed their own groups, joined Portuguese churches, and in typical New York City fashion, held an ethnic street fair.

The sharp increase in the Latino population was not welcomed by all Americans. While the newcomers were mostly praised for their (especially low wage) labor, they aroused anxiety about America's changing demography, a topic that will be explored in the epilogue.

Chapter 7

Pilgrims' Progress:
Ethnic Mobility in Modern America

THE GRIM LIVING CONDITIONS facing the different waves of immigrants also confronted their children and sometimes their grandchildren. Often, the newcomers moved slowly out of poverty and the ghettoes, and gains made by the second and third generations were lost. Yet the striking fact of American history is social mobility, an overall improvement in status and living conditions for the descendants of the millions who flocked to the United States. Progress was by no means even from group to group or from generation to generation.

Of the European immigrants, the Irish probably had the most difficult time, but a few made spectacular progress and became veritable personifications of the rags-to-riches story. Robert Joseph Cuddihy began as an office boy in Funk & Wagnalls publishing house in New York City at the age of sixteen. Working his way up, he became a wealthy and powerful publisher. Joseph P. Kennedy, the son of a Boston immigrant saloon keeper and father of President John F. Kennedy, made his fortune on Wall Street and in the motion picture business and later served as ambassador to Great Britain. John Buckley, the founder of one of America's leading conservative families, emigrated to America without much money. After a mixture of success and failure in Texas, his son, William F. Buckley, arrived in New York City nearly penniless in 1922 but soon thereafter became a millionaire. Peter McDonnell began his career as a bondsman in New York City and laid the foundation of a major Wall Street brokerage house.

But most of America's Irish moved up the social scale slowly. Working in unskilled occupations provided few opportunities for advancement. The growth of canals and railroads offered low-paying, backbreaking jobs that left the workers unemployed and practically destitute whenever and wherever each project ended. As a result, Irish settlements developed all over the country but usually at or near canal and railroad depots. The opening of textile mills in New England also created opportunities for those willing to work long and hard.

The Irish managed to improve their lot during the nineteenth century. By the 1870s in Boston they had already come to dominate the police and fire departments. Throughout the nation young Irish women staffed urban elementary schools. They constituted 25 percent of the teachers in Boston and New York City in the 1880s and a generation later gained a foothold in the teaching ranks of Buffalo, Chicago, and San Francisco. In the twentieth century Irish men and women used their connections to win more municipal jobs. Young Irish women continued to be important in urban schools while the men became police and firemen in cities other than Boston. In New York City, for example, by the 1930s they constituted 75 percent of the fire department and half of the police. They also constituted 25 percent of the sanitation workers. In the private sector women became clerks in telephone and insurance companies and waitresses in Schrafft's and Stouffer's restaurants. The Irish also dominated New York City's transit system and its Transport Workers Union. The most thrifty of the workers saved money to buy houses. This was possible in part because many persisted at one job and in one place year after year. The Irish also tended to marry late, thereby enabling young workers to save enough for down payments on modest homes. If these schemes for property accumulation proved insufficient, wives and children worked and contributed to the family coffers. Putting children to work added to the family's income, of course, but it also hurt the younger generation's chances for future mobility.

The Irish were successful in many businesses at a time when education was not as necessary as it would later become. The construction industry boomed as urban America grew. The Irish, using the influence of friends in city halls, became contractors and builders. By 1890 there were twice as many of them in these occupations compared to other immigrant groups. In Philadelphia Edward J. Lafferty constructed the city's waterworks, and James P. (Sunny Jim) McNichol, another Irish politician-contractor, helped build the city's subways, sewers, and water filtration plant.

During the twentieth century, and especially after World War II, the Irish progressed rapidly to middle- and upper middle-class status. They ran businesses, worked in banks and insurance companies, and became doctors, lawyers, professors, civil servants, and technicians. The occupational distribution of the American Irish in 1980 resembled that of the northern urban Anglo-Saxon Protestants. Among the white Catholics in America, the Irish usually had more education, better jobs, and higher incomes. Few could claim the fabulous wealth of America's most famous Irish family, the Kennedys, but not many were poor, either. The American Irish had at long last arrived.

To consider the Irish experience solely in terms of the move from shanties to suburban homes and from ditch diggers to lawyers is to form an incomplete picture. In two special vocational areas—the Roman Catholic Church and politics—the Irish had experiences that were unique, not because they were so lucrative but because the ethnic group valued these positions. To have a son become a lawyer or doctor was of course a sign of success, but the Irish also considered it important to give a son or a daughter to the Church.

That the Irish dominated the Catholic Church in America is not surprising. In Ireland the Church carried the faith and was a source of comfort in the face of English oppression. It served a similar function in America. The hostility of native Protestant Americans to the Irish and to Catholicism only made the Church more important, for it provided the embattled Irish immigrant with a bulwark of security.

Shortly after the Irish arrived in the 1840s, they became the dominant group in the American Catholic hierarchy. From Archbishop John Hughes of New York, to Minnesota's John Ireland, to Baltimore's James Cardinal Gibbons, the first American cardinal, and to New York City's Francis Cardinal Spellman, Terrence Cooke, and John O'Connor, the leading American Catholics have usually been of Irish origin. The Irish supported the parochial schools, sent their sons and daughters to do God's work, and gave what they could from their meager incomes for religious activities. When non-Irish Catholics, such as the Italians, arrived in large numbers, they often resented Irish control of the Church and demanded their own clergy and parishes. The Church disapproved of nationality or ethnic parishes in principle, but they existed among Germans, Poles, and French Canadians. In the twentieth century, Irish control of the Church hierarchy gradually lessened but never disappeared. In the 1990s the Irish constituted fewer than one fifth of the Catholics in the United States but about a third of the clergy and half of the hierarchy.

During the 1980s and 1990s the Roman Catholic Church experienced a shortage of priests and nuns; in part this was due to the fact that Irish Americans were achieving widespread success in other professions. Practically all regions of the nation contained parishes looking for clergy, and hospitals and schools looking for nuns as nurses and teachers. In 1998 California's Oakland Diocese had only 6 students at St. Patrick's Seminary in Menlo Park, compared to 24 twenty years earlier. The diocese itself had only 110 active priests to serve its half million Roman Catholics, a figure far below the national average. Nationally the number of priests had fallen from almost 60,000 in 1978 to 48,000 in 1998 even though the Catholic population had grown. Some parishes were being run by laypeople and by nuns who did everything except give the sacraments. Scholars noted that as the Irish, and Italians as well, chose other careers, the Church had to go abroad for clergy. One parishioner commented, "When I was young, most parents were delighted to have a son in the seminary. Today they want their kids to go to

Stanford or Harvard." Such shortages prompted considerable debate, but no change, in the Church's attitude toward married clergy and ordination of women.

Irish domination of urban politics was not so complete as of the Church, but it was impressive. New York City elected a Roman Catholic mayor in 1880, and Boston followed suit four years later. Before the end of the century Irish "bosses" dominated local politics in New York, Jersey City, Hoboken, Boston, Chicago, Buffalo, Albany, and Troy (New York); Pittsburgh, St. Paul, St. Louis, and Kansas City (Missouri); Omaha; New Orleans; and San Francisco. New York City's famed Tammany Hall passed into Irish hands when "Honest John" (his enemies called him "crooked as a ram's horn") Kelly succeeded Protestant boss William M. Tweed in 1874, and it remained under Irish control for the next eighty years. Bosses Frank Hague of Jersey City and Tom Pendergast of Kansas City, Missouri were legends in their day, as was Mayor Richard Daley of Chicago in his.

No Irish urban politician was so extraordinary as James Michael Curley of Boston. He served in local offices before becoming U.S. congressman, mayor of the city, and then governor of Massachusetts. Curley symbolized many aspects of the Irish style in politics. He maintained his contacts with the Church and the Irish community and was a skillful showman. He played upon the Irish resentment of Boston's Brahmins to build a personal following, and he provided jobs and social services for the poor. He also knew how to appeal to his followers: "My mother was obliged to work . . . as a scrubwoman toiling nights in office buildings downtown. I thought of her one night while leaving City Hall during my first term as Mayor. I told the scrubwomen cleaning the corridors to get up; 'The only time a woman should go down on her knees is when she is praying to Almighty God,' I said. Next morning I ordered longhandled mops and issued an order that scrubwomen were never again to get down on their knees in City Hall." Critics attacked Curley for corruption, but no matter—he won an election even while in jail.

The Irish reach for the presidency began in 1928 when Al Smith from the Lower East Side of New York City became a candidate. He rose swiftly through New York City's Democratic organization (Tammany Hall) and served as state legislator and governor before grasping for the big prize. Smith epitomized the Irish Catholic politician, a factor that worked both for and against him in 1928. He opposed Prohibition, attacked immigration restriction laws, and was a devout Catholic. As a result, he won the Catholic and immigrant vote in many places and reversed Democratic fortunes of the 1920s by capturing a dozen or so of the nation's largest cities. The Democratic presidential candidate amassed more popular votes than any of his predecessors ever had. (Part of the explanation for this, no doubt, was that a larger percentage of women voted in 1928 than had done so in 1920 or 1924.) Nevertheless, many Protestants feared that the Roman Catholic Church would exert a strong influence on a Catholic in the White House and voted Republican for the first time in their lives. Herbert Hoover won the election.

After Smith's defeat no Irish Catholic and no other member of an ethnic minority group made a bid for the presidency until John F. Kennedy's triumph in 1960. Keenly aware that politicos still regarded his Roman Catholic faith as a severe handicap, Kennedy faced the religious issue squarely. His victory in the West Virginia primary proved that he could win Protestant votes, and his smooth political machine achieved a first-ballot nomination at the Democratic convention. Yet the religious issue would not die, and Kennedy had to make several strong statements about his belief in the separation of church and state. In the election Kennedy lost some votes because of his Catholicism, but he ran strongly in the heavily Catholic Northeast and slipped into the presidency by the narrowest margin of any victorious candidate since Woodrow Wilson in 1916.

Kennedy's election, culminating a century of Irish political activity, was built on the earlier victories of Irish politicians in city wards. His religious commitments were public knowledge, as were his ties to the Irish community. Some even said an "Irish Mafia" had won him the nomination. A few Catholics went to the other extreme and insisted that Kennedy was not Catholic enough. Kennedy was clearly different from both Al Smith and James Curley. Born into a wealthy family, educated at Choate and Harvard, he was assimilated, cosmopolitan, and intellectual, and he did not seem particularly Irish—except for political purposes. Whether another type of Irish politician could have won in 1960 is debatable, but the old ward boss was a thing of the past by then. The Irish had arrived in politics as they had in business and in the Church.

Another Irish Democrat, New York's Senator Daniel Patrick Moynihan, later pointed out that on the day that Kennedy died the Speaker of the House of Representatives, the majority leader of the U.S. Senate, and the chairman of the Democratic National Committee were all Irish Catholic Democrats. Moynihan suggested that perhaps such Irish domination will not occur again, but Thomas (Tip) O'Neill, former Speaker of the House, was one of the most prominent Democrats to oppose President Ronald Reagan, also of Irish descent, during his tenure in the White House. Irish Catholic ancestry is obviously no longer a handicap for any candidate making a bid for the presidency.

The largest of the nineteenth-century immigrant groups, the Germans, generally rose faster than the Irish. They had certain advantages: they were not so poor when they arrived and they had more education. Unlike the

Irish, many Germans farmed successfully, but most lived in or later moved to cities. Those without skills or education took laboring jobs, but many became skilled workers in America's growing industries. They were also cabinet makers, bakers, tailors, bookbinders, and furniture makers, and often they were the leaders in craft unions. For example, the bakers' unions in the 1870s and 1880s were solidly German. Some German workers even veered off into radical politics.

German immigrants and their children did well in business and were a successful minority by the time of World War I. They brought with them their love of beer drinking and their beer-making skills, and they founded breweries that became virtually a German monopoly in the early twentieth century. St. Louis and Milwaukee are centers of the beer business, and names like Pabst, Miller, Schlitz, Schaefer, and Anheuser-Busch became household words in twentieth-century America. Germans also ran beer gardens, hotels, and restaurants like Mader's in Milwaukee and Luchow's in New York City. An observer said of the beer gardens: "The commencement of one of these establishments appears to be very simple. A German obtains a cellar, a cask of beer, a cheese, a loaf of bread, and some pretzels—puts out a sign and the business is started." Although breweries and beer gardens were the most notable German connections to the liquor business, a few Germans, such as Paul Krug, developed vineyards in California.

Germans were also successful in other areas of business. George Westinghouse, a poor farm boy from upstate New York, patented the air brake for trains and then founded a major corporation. Another inventor, Charles Steinmetz, who became known as the wizard of Schenectady, was the dynamic force behind the huge General Electric Company. Although Steinmetz had a European education, he arrived at Ellis Island from Germany without funds or a job. Indeed, he was almost deported. His mastery of electricity led him to fame and fortune. John A. Roebling, another innovator, put his ideas about steel cables to use in building suspension bridges. Roebling died while supervising the construction of his most famous, the Brooklyn Bridge.

Other Germans used their talents in the ethnic community as clergymen and editors of German periodicals and newspapers, which were numerous on the eve of World War I, or operated small businesses that catered to the German American community. A few branched out into politics, among them Robert Wagner of New York and the socialist Victor Berger of Milwaukee. These politicians, like the Irish, built their strength on the ethnic vote and service to ethnic communities. Germans had elected congressmen and senators regularly after the Civil War and governors in Illinois and Kentucky in the 1890s.

Germans also excelled in music. City orchestras in the nineteenth century were heavily German, and German singers were popular in America, as were German singing societies. Germans also made musical instruments. Steinway and Sons was the most famous of the German piano makers, but others such as Knabe, Weber, and Wurlitzer were well known too.

Although World War I was a shattering experience for many German Americans and caused many of their institutions to decline, it did not impede their socioeconomic progress. They prospered in practically every key area of American business, the professions—as doctors, lawyers, engineers—government, and science. They were well represented among the American corporate elite, and had high education levels and solid incomes. Not many were poor. So much were the descendants of German immigrants a part of American life that few Americans conceived of them as a distinct ethnic group. Nevertheless, President Richard Nixon's chief White House assistants from 1969 to 1973, H.R. Haldeman and John Ehrlichman, were known to a number of Washingtonians as the "German shepherds."

The Swedes have also prospered. The children and grandchildren of many of those who tilled the soil in the upper Midwest sought opportunities in burgeoning cities like Minneapolis and Chicago. In urban areas they became skilled workers and clerks and gradually moved into better jobs. As a group Swedes prospered about as much as Germans; in the twentieth century they were second only to the British in their proportion of skilled workers in America. A few even advanced into the business elite; Swedish-born Rudolph A. Peterson, for example, became president of the giant Bank of America in 1961. A minority remained farmers and prospered on the land.

Norwegians were similar to Swedes in their immigration patterns, migrating into the upper Midwest to become farmers and farm laborers. But Norwegians were also sailors and found jobs as seamen in American ports; they were especially important on the West Coast. Like the Swedes, they became increasingly urbanized after 1900, and many came to America with skills that they could use in the expanding industrial society. By the 1980s Norwegian Americans had done well and had generally moved into the middle class, with many becoming successful businessmen, skilled workers, and professionals. Of course, politics was open in areas where Norwegians and Swedes were numerous. In 1892 Knute Nelson, with the aid of his fellow Norwegians, won the governorship of Minnesota, and Swedish and Norwegian names have been prominent in the politics of Minnesota, Wisconsin, and the adjacent states ever since.

Finns in America were slower to move up the occupational ladder than their Swedish and Norwegian neighbors. Of the Protestant groups immigrating after 1880 the Finns were the least skilled, and this accounts for some of their difficulties in achieving occupational mobility. They generally settled in the Midwest but were not inclined to become farmers. They moved frequently in search of work and were especially numerous in the mining regions of the upper Midwest. They often worked in company towns, where few opportunities existed for those without skills. Finns also tried to found their own businesses but were not notably successful. Later generations finally moved out of the unskilled ranks and competed more successfully, but socioeconomically they usually lagged behind Swedes and Norwegians.

None of the immigrants coming in large numbers before 1890, not even the Irish, were so scorned as the Chinese. After they had been forced out of mines and had helped build the railroads and raise crops in California, the Chinese drifted to the cities in search of employment. A few were successful merchants, but most found urban life harsh and jobs limited. They worked as domestics, as cigar makers, or in other low-paying industries. Most important to the livelihood of Chinese Americans was the proverbial laundry, which developed largely because the Chinese could find little else to do. The shortage of women on the frontier left this domestic service, considered women's work, open to the Chinese. A laundry required little skill and practically no capital, only soap, a scrub board, an iron, an ironing board, and long hours of hard labor. Laundries were usually one-man or family enterprises. As the Chinese moved into the cities or to the East, they took their businesses with them. By 1880 over 7,000 Chinese made their livings in laundries in San Francisco alone, and in 1920 the U.S. Census Bureau reported that nearly a third of employed Chinese were engaged in laundry work.

Restaurants and groceries were also important to the Chinese community. The restaurants originated in the mining camps along the railroads, where the Chinese preferred their own food. The railroad bosses agreed that letting the Chinese cook their own meals was cheaper than furnishing an American diet. The Chinese discovered that others liked their cuisine too; chop suey and chow mein became staples on their menus. Restaurants required some capital, hence they were not as numerous as laundries. But like the laundries, they were often family businesses and served as outlets for entrepreneurs blocked from other jobs. Groceries, the third main type of Chinese small business, were not so important as restaurants and laundries. Nevertheless, enterprising businessmen found them outlets for their skills and energies. In the South and West, Chinese groceries thrived, and a few later expanded into supermarkets.

Until World War II the Chinese American community had many service workers, small proprietors, and operatives, and few professional and technical workers. But a strong family system, a commitment to education, and hard work changed patterns after 1945. Declining prejudice, especially during World War II when America was an ally of China, also helped. Prior to the war Chinese Americans serving in the U.S. Navy had been delegated to work as messmen and stewards, but during the war they were admitted as apprentice seamen. Shipyards, aircraft factories, and other defense industries experiencing labor shortages began to employ workers of Chinese ancestry. These were modest changes, but they marked the beginning of improved employment opportunities.

The Chinese American community of the 1990s was different from that of a century before. By 1960 many Chinese had moved into the middle class. They shunned jobs in laundries and other undesirable forms of employment in favor of technical and professional occupations. Particularly in mathematics and science the Chinese made a name for themselves; several won Nobel Prizes, among them Chen Ning Yang and Yzyng Dao Lee. Veneration for learning and scholarship was revealed by the fact that by the 1960s proportionately more Chinese than Caucasians had completed college.

In business, while laundries were declining, restaurants thrived, and Chinese Americans found new opportunities in finance, trade, architecture, and computing. Perhaps most well-known of the Chinese immigrants was I.M. Pei, who achieved an international reputation as an architect. Pei arrived in the United States in 1935 to study engineering at the Massachusetts Institute of Technology. He later switched to architecture and decided to remain in the United States, becoming an American citizen in 1954. He was asked to design major projects, including the John Hancock Building in Boston and the East Wing of the National Gallery in Washington, D.C. A similar story of fame and success could be told of An Wang, founder of the Massachusetts computing firm that bears his name.

Chinese women, like American women generally, have moved into the professional and managerial labor market, and some have become successful in spite of discrimination against their sex. One of San Francisco's most well-known restaurants was run by Cecilia Chiang, who entered the United States in 1958. She said, "I have confidence. I love people, I love food, and about Chinese food, I think I know better than all the people I know." While running restaurants was a traditional Chinese occupation, it was unusual for women. By 1986 Chiang owned four restaurants in California. Since 1983 another enterprising Chinese American woman, Connie Chung, has been a high-paid and leading television news personality.

As the twentieth century drew to a close, Chinese Americans generally earned more than most other Americans, including many people of European origin, and they were well represented in professional occupations. In universities they stood out in science and computer departments; at the University of California at Berkeley, one of the nation's premier institutions, Chinese American Chang-Lin Tien was named chancellor in 1990. Asians made up 4 percent of the faculties of American universities in the 1990s, which was about the same proportion of Asians in the population. In California, Asians were 10 percent of the population but constituted one third of the state's undergraduates and 20 percent of the university faculty. Their academic success put them in a difficult situation. Long the victims of racism, Asians discovered during California's debate over affirmative action that if class rank and SAT (Scholastic Aptitude Test) scores were the bases of admission, they would benefit from a nonethnic admissions policy.

It is important to remember that Chinese Americans, and Asians generally, have done well because of education, strict family values, and a culture in which both parents encourage high aspirations. Chinese Americans, however, complain that American businesses have glass ceilings that keep them from the top jobs. And many of the latest newcomers lack proficiency in English and do not have the skills for economic success. As discussed, the Indochinese refugees have had an especially difficult time in adjusting to their new homes; in the late 1990s a large number of families were still living in poverty or on welfare.

With a small population on which to build a political base, politics was not a common way up the social ladder; but in Hawaii, with its large Chinese population, the chances were better. Hiram Fong made his political career there. He began as deputy attorney for the city and county of Honolulu, then moved into the legislature, and finally ended in the U.S. Senate. Fong's career in some ways symbolizes the rise of Chinese Americans. Born into a large and poor family, he began as a farm laborer. But he was an enterprising young man and worked his way through the University of Hawaii and Harvard Law School. He became a successful lawyer and businessman before he launched his political career.

Outside of Hawaii it was more difficult for Chinese Americans, and Asians generally, to win elective office before the 1980s. When the people of Delaware choose Shien Biau Woo lieutenant governor in 1984 he won national recognition. In 1985 Los Angeles elected its first Chinese American to the City Council, and Mayor Dianne Feinstein of San Francisco appointed a Chinese American to the Board of Supervisors. Elsewhere a few other victories were scored, but none compared to the election in 1996 of Gary Locke as governor of Washington. Locke won by a lopsided vote even though Asians in that state constituted only 4 percent of the population. A graduate of Yale University, Locke had served as a county executive and had been in the state legislature for ten years.

Of the millions of immigrants coming after 1880, no other group experienced such startling success as the Jews. Sephardic and Ashkenazi Jews who came in the colonial period were already solidly middle class when the central European Jews (most of whom were German) arrived before the Civil War. Many in this earlier wave had been traders in Germany, and they took up peddling and storekeeping in the New World. Spreading out over the nation, they made rapid progress in commerce and trade. The Lehmans and Seligmans achieved prominence in finance and banking while Benjamin Altman and Adam Gimbel became major department-store owners. A study made in 1889 of 18,000 gainfully employed Jews, most of whom were from German-speaking ares, found that approximately one third were retailers; 15 percent were bankers; 17 percent were accountants, bookkeepers, clerks, and copyists; and 12 percent were salesmen, commercial travelers, and agents.

The bulk of eastern European Jews, coming after 1880, was poor, but they too succeeded in America in the twentieth century. In 1980 family incomes of America's Jews were higher than those of any other ethnic group, including the elite white Protestant Episcopalians. And their educational levels were also high. Almost 90 percent of Jews of college age were attending institutions of higher education in the 1970s, and a high proportion were in graduate and professional schools.

Of the first generation from eastern Europe, a majority worked in the garment industry and in trade, with only a few in the professions. Jews were involved in the formation—and in their early years made up most of the members—of both the International Ladies' Garment Workers' Union and the Amalgamated Clothing Workers Union, founded in 1910 and 1914, respectively. Children of these union members more often than not went to college and sought higher-status occupations. Anti-Semitism in the professions, including discriminatory quotas in medical schools, made it harder to achieve professional mobility, but they accomplished it nonetheless. Statistics of the late 1960s indicated that about half of all gainfully employed adult Jews were professionals, more than double the figure for Protestants and Catholics. And by the early 1970s yearly incomes for a majority of Jewish families whose heads were typically between 30 and 59 years of age averaged over $16,000, compared to a national average for all families of under $11,000. In the 1990s scholars estimated that Jews earned almost 50 percent more than non-Jews.

Second-generation Jews usually chose professions in which they could be independently employed and not subject to the bigotry of prejudiced employers. As a result many became physicians, lawyers, accountants, pharmacists, and dentists. In the 1930s and even in the 1960s, Jews made up more than half of New York City's dentists, physicians, and lawyers. The third generation of Jews still found law and medicine attractive, but the decline of discriminatory hiring practices in the business and academic worlds opened opportunities not available to their parents and grandparents.

On Wall Street, large investment houses, law firms, and major banks rarely hired Jews, Italians, and other people of southern and eastern European origins unless the firms were Jewish themselves. In the 1970s and 1980s, however, the need for talent was great, a more tolerant atmosphere developed, and the sharp division between Jewish and Gentile investment houses began to blur. In 1987 the top executive of the nation's fourth largest bank—the Manufacturers Trust Company—was Edward Miller, the son of Lithuanian immigrants. Miller had not gone to an Ivy League school, but had attended Brooklyn College in New York City. In 1983 another Jewish banker, Boris S. Berkovitch, became vice-chairman of a firm run by old-stock Americans, Morgan Guaranty Trust Company. A study completed in 1986 revealed that 58 percent of the nation's 4,350 senior executives just below the chief executive level were Protestant, but seven years before the figure had been 68 percent. The percentage of Jews had grown from 5.6 percent to 7.4 percent in the same period. An examination of Chicago's top business leaders revealed similar findings. Among those under age 40, non-Protestants made even larger gains. By the end of the twentieth century American Jews had succeeded in many fields. *Forbes* magazine estimated that over 30 percent of the richest Americans were Jews. During the presidency of Bill Clinton, two New York Jews served in politically sensitive positions that affected the nation's—and the world's—economic policies. One was Alan Greenspan, appointed as Chairman of the Board of Governors of the Federal Reserve System by President Ronald Reagan in 1987; the other was Robert Rubin, chosen Secretary of the Treasury in 1994.

The career of Henry Kissinger in both academia and politics is indicative of the rise of American Jews. Kissinger excelled as a professor at Harvard, a university that for several decades limited the number of Jewish students it would admit. He later served as the first Jewish Secretary of State under Presidents Richard M. Nixon and Gerald R. Ford. The State Department itself was another outpost that had long had a reputation for anti-Semitism. As for elective offices, Jews increasingly won seats in the House of Representatives and in the Senate. At one time in the 1990s, ten senators were Jewish.

In academia Harold Shapiro earned a Ph.D. at Princeton and taught at the University of Michigan before turning his hand to administration. In 1987 he accepted the presidency of Princeton University, the first Jew to do so. Princeton had been the symbol of white Protestantism, and until the 1960s had restricted its Jewish enrollment. Upon hearing of Shapiro's appointment, a member of the Hillel Foundation said, "This shows that Princeton has come a long way. If you had asked Jewish students at Princeton in the 1960s if they could picture Princeton with a Jewish president, I'm sure they would have said no." Harvard, Yale, Dartmouth, and Columbia universities also appointed men of Jewish heritage in the 1980s and 1990s. In 1945 the president of Dartmouth had publicly declared that his college was "a Christian college founded for the Christianization of its students." But less than four decades later a Jew became president of Dartmouth. College presidents were only one sign of Jewish presence in higher education; Jewish professors were prominent in the nation's leading colleges, universities, and professional schools.

Like all American women, Jewish women have had an uphill battle to achieve what they could in business, politics, the arts, and academia. Perhaps more than any other affected group, Jewish women benefited from the Civil Rights Act of 1964. Coming from the same socioeconomic backgrounds as their brothers and with similar educations through college, once the discriminatory barriers came down they were available and had the necessary skills to take advantage of equal opportunities in society. They entered law and medical schools in record numbers, and moved into the stock market, investment banking, and other endeavors from which they had been barred by restrictive academic and corporate gender policies. Ruth Bader Ginsberg became the first Jewish woman appointed to the Supreme Court in 1993; both Gerda Lerner and Linda Kerber were chosen to be president of the Organization of American Historians; and Bella Abzug became the first woman to win election to the House of Representatives on a women's rights platform in the early 1970s.

Other successful Jewish women could be found in the arts. Barbra Streisand, of Hollywood fame, came to prominence on the New York stage in 1963, the same year that Betty Friedan published her classic commentary on the expectations for middle-class women in *The Feminine Mystique*. Wendy Wasserstein, like Lillian Hellman in a previous era, won high praise for her plays and one of them, *The Heidi Chronicles*, received a Pulitzer Prize.

Although individual Jews can be found in almost every line of business and professional endeavor, as a group the eastern Europeans, their children, and their grandchildren have made their greatest impact in the clothing, entertainment, and intellectual worlds of American society. By the earliest years of the twentieth century the manufacture of ready-to-wear clothing was in the hands of Jewish owners; in 1950 more than 85 percent of American-made clothes were manufactured in Jewish-owned shops. In the late

1980s, Michael Dell started his now world-famous computer business, and in 1998 he became the richest man in Texas.

In the entertainment field both the theater and the movies provided avenues of mobility for Jewish actors, actresses, writers, tunesmiths, directors, and producers. Two Jews of Russian ancestry, David Sarnoff and William Paley, developed what one financial publication called "perhaps the world's two greatest broadcasting empires," the Radio Corporation of America (now part of General Electric) and the Columbia Broadcasting System (CBS), respectively. In the intellectual community leading journals such as *Commentary*, since 1945, and *The New York Review of Books*, since the 1960s, have relied on Jewish sponsors and/or editors. Authors like Norman Mailer, Philip Roth, Saul Bellow, Bernard Malamud, and Meyer Levin have been among the major figures in American literature in the post-World War II era. And in academia prominent scholars like historian Oscar Handlin, social scientist Seymour Martin Lipset, and economist and Nobel Prize winner Milton Friedman won international recognition. Artist Ben Shahn, discoverer of the polio vaccine Jonas Salk, filmmakers Stanley Kubrick and Steven Spielberg, violinist Yehudi Menuhin, conductor and composer Leonard Bernstein, and former Supreme Court Justice and ambassador to the United Nations Arthur Goldberg are only a few of the Jews of eastern European descent who have distinguished themselves in American society. Not all Jews are as prominent and accomplished as the aforementioned group, but it is worth noting that no twentieth-century European minority has risen as fast, socially and economically, as have the descendants of Jews who arrived from eastern Europe at the turn of the century.

The remarkable success of Jews was undoubtedly the consequence of hard work, skill, and an arduous struggle in an expanding economy. Their traditional respect for learning facilitated advancement because education was an important vehicle for social mobility. To what extent American public schools really served immigrants is a subject of debate and in need of study, but in the case of Jewish immigrants they were of great advantage. Parents pushed their children to achieve, and they themselves, eager for an education, attended public evening schools. As journalist Abraham Cahan, chronicler of the Lower East Side of New York City, put it, "The ghetto rang with a clamor for knowledge."

In addition to their respect for education, Jews brought with them urban living experiences and skills that could be used in commercial and industrial America. Though Jews faced tensions and problems common to all immigrant groups, their families were relatively stable, providing a sense of security as well as a springboard for their children. The older German-Jewish community, another extraordinarily accomplished group, with its many welfare agencies, was sometimes suspicious of and hostile to the greenhorns from eastern Europe with their different dress, language, and ideas; but on the whole was a source of strength to newcomers. Inadvertently, anti-Semitism united and strengthened the entire Jewish community and prompted many of the more successful to help their less fortunate kin.

Also to be reckoned with in analyzing Jewish immigrants' success are the intangibles, such as the culture of the group, which cannot be precisely measured. Certainly, there was a clash between Protestantism and Judaism, but in many ways there was agreement over key values. Jews found it easier than did some others to accept the American stress upon individual achievement and mobility. Differences over religion did not lead to the rejection of these broader American values. On the contrary, more than one analyst has observed how readily Jewish Americans accepted the Protestant ethic of hard work and material accomplishment.

Perhaps the reasons for Jewish emigration also had something to do with their success in the United States. Like so many others, they came in search of a better life, but unlike many others, they could not go back to the Old World. The pogroms that had driven them away in the early part of the twentieth century and the Holocaust of the 1940s dimmed most hopes of returning. Because of religious persecution in Europe, Jews came with a determination to make America truly the Promised Land.

As we have seen, Italians had a somewhat different experience. They were probably poorer than the Jews and, coming from a rural background, were unfamiliar with city life. A large number were interested only in collecting a bit of cash and then returning to Italy. For many Italians success meant bringing something home, not achieving status in the United States. Often they moved from job to job and finally back to Italy. Consequently, they did not experience the rapid social mobility that Jews did, but they gradually prospered nonetheless.

Although most Italians lived in cities, a few succeeded on the land. On both the East and West Coasts Italians became skillful truck farmers and supplied growing urban areas with food. The di Giorgio orchards eventually covered 40,000 acres in California. More famous in that state were the wineries, like Italian-Swiss Colony and Gallo Brothers. In 1971 the Gallo Winery had revenues of a quarter of a billion dollars. Along with German wines, Italian American wines became the best known in American stores. A few Italians also became successful in the South, raising cotton, sugar cane, and other crops.

Like all other ethnic groups, Italians have their notable success stories. Among northern Italians the career of Amadeo P. Giannini, founder of the Bank of America, is outstanding. Giannini began as a banker for immigrants but expanded his operations in the early twentieth century. When the San Francisco earthquake struck in 1906, he rescued his bank's gold, hidden in a produce wagon, and was quickly ready to open for business again. Expanding from San Francisco's North Beach Italian colony, he branched out and made his bank a major factor in the state's growing economy. He saw the future in branch banking and expanded from real estate to industrial financing. When he retired in 1945, Bank of America had become the largest private bank in the world, with $5.5 billion in deposits and over 3 million depositors.

Other Italians ran groceries and opened restaurants. Some were importers of products such as olive oil, macaroni, and ravioli; others were producers of ethnic goods in demand by Italian Americans and later by other Americans as well. One such family ethnic enterprise was begun by Joseph Pellegrino. As a boy he arrived in America from Sicily with $13. After shining shoes and buying and selling cooking oils for a living, he went into the pasta business. He eventually took over the Prince Company and made it the largest pasta maker in America, employing 1,000 people in the 1980s.

For most, however, success came gradually and not spectacularly. Beginning as garment workers in New York City, day laborers or miners in Pennsylvania, or in other unskilled or semiskilled jobs, Italian Americans found the path upward difficult. Although some individuals made giant leaps, the second generation improved itself over the first modestly, becoming construction workers and foremen, small businessmen, and lesser white-collar workers rather than unskilled laborers, factory workers, and miners. After World War II the third generation made greater progress. As job opportunities expanded with the decline of prejudice, some Italian Americans even found new chances in large businesses, finance, and the professions. In the early 1970s the presidents of Ford Motor Company and Chrysler Corporation were John Riccardo and Lee A. Iacocca, both of Italian descent. When Riccardo left the failing Chrysler Corporation, Iacocca replaced him to have a try at putting the company on its feet. His dynamic leadership and the revival of Chrysler made Iacocca something of a folk hero and made his autobiography, *Iacocca*, a best-seller in the mid-1980s.

The rise of these two men in business was both symbolic and representative of the upward mobility of ethnic Americans into the nation's business elite. As banks and corporations began to hire Jews, they hired men and women of Italian, Hungarian, and other ancestries as well. In 1985 Anthony P. Terracciano, the grandson of Italian immigrants, became vice-chairman of New York City's Chase Manhattan Bank, the same position that Peter C. Palmieri had obtained at Irving Trust Company the year before.

It is not difficult to explain the reasons these opportunities became available in the formerly restricted field of investment banking. A *New York*

Times article in June 1986 pinpointed the need for change: "Deregulation has forced large commercial banks to engage in new activities that require skilled, aggressive executives. To fill the posts, the banks are tossing aside old barriers and converting their upper managements increasingly into meritocracies. As Barry M. Allen, first vice-president of the Bank of Boston, put it: 'We can't afford to keep out any talented person.'" Therefore old school ties, family connections, and a "gentleman's C" in college grades were less important factors in the banking world. And ethnic names, which had once been the kiss of death, became irrelevant except when policies concerning affirmative action were involved.

Changed values after the end of World War II had incredible ramifications. Until 1945 most Italian Americans who attended college were of northern Italian descent. Even so, the general education level of Italian Americans was lower than the average for other whites. In the 1950s, for instance, fewer than 5 percent of native-born Italian Americans were completing college, a figure well below the national average. Yet Italians began to catch up in college attendance after 1960. For those with education, prestige jobs were open and with them the possibility of higher incomes. In general, Italian Americans were achieving middle-class status, not the equal of Jews or even the Irish, but ahead of recent immigrant groups like the Puerto Ricans (who are of course American citizens by birth) and Mexicans. Italian incomes were above the national median according to the 1990 census, and as they increasingly attended college and professional schools they found employment in the nation's law firms, as physicians, and in universities. In the 1990s L. Jay Oliva became the first Italian American to be appointed president of New York University, succeeding John Brademus, of Greek ancestry, who had held that position in the 1980s.

Settling in large numbers in urban areas and being Catholic opened other possibilities to Italians for broader participation and achievement, in particular with regard to the Catholic Church and politics. However, the Irish controlled the Church and played a large role in urban politics. Not until after World War II did Italian Americans begin to break into the hierarchy of American Catholicism. In 1967 the grandson of an Italian immigrant became bishop of the diocese embracing Mississippi, and a year later another Italian American became bishop of Brooklyn, the largest diocese in the United States. Although Italians were moving up in the Church by the 1990s, they were still underrepresented in the hierarchy.

Once Italians began to register and vote in American elections, they began to rise politically. But in this area too their move upward was slow. Before World War II the most successful Italian American politician was congressman and later mayor of New York Fiorello La Guardia. La Guardia was something of an anomaly. He was Protestant, not Catholic; he had a Jewish mother; and he could speak several languages. He also tried to appeal to many groups, not merely to Italian Americans. San Francisco with its large Italian population also had an Italian mayor in the 1930s, but not until after the war did Italian Americans make significant political breakthroughs. In 1946 in Rhode Island, John O. Pastore became the first man of Italian background to be elected governor of a state. Rhode Island later sent Pastore to the U.S. Senate, the first Italian American elected to the upper house of Congress. Increasingly, in the 1950s and 1960s Italians were elected to important political offices as congressmen, state legislators, and mayors of big cities. In the 1970s Connecticut voters twice elected Ella Grasso governor of the state; this was the highest political office ever held by an Italian American woman. In 1982 in neighboring New York, Mario Cuomo became the first Italian American to be elected governor of the Empire State, and he was reelected twice. He was succeeded as governor by George Pataki, of Hungarian ancestry. Italians remained active and visible in the state, however. Alphonse D'Amato was one of the two U.S. Senators from New York, serving his state in the 1980s and 1990s; in 1984 New York Congresswoman Geraldine Ferraro was both the first woman and the first person of Italian ancestry chosen to run for Vice-President of the United States on the Democratic ticket. Another Italian American, Rudolph Giuliani, won his second term as mayor of New York in 1997.

For a long time Italians had received negative publicity because some of them had participated in organized criminal activities. In the 1950s Senator Estes Kefauver of Tennessee conducted hearings about crime in America and paraded Italian American gangsters before his Senate committee and a national television audience. Kefauver said that the Mafia, controlled by Italian Americans and Italians in Italy, was "the shadowy international organization that lurks behind much of organized criminal activity." The charge that Italians in America were involved with the Mafia was not new. As early as 1891 the New York *Tribune* had insisted that "in large cities throughout the country, Italians of criminal antecedents and propensities are more or less closely affiliated for the purpose of requiring injuries and gratifying animosities by secret vengeances. These organizations in common speech and belief are connected with the *Mafia*, and that designation fairly indicates their character and motives. Through their agency the most infernal crimes have been committed and have gone unpunished."

Certainly some Italian Americans have been involved in organized crime. As Humbert Nelli, historian of Italians in Chicago, put it:

> Crime, one means of economic advancement independent of education, social background or political connections, provided for all classes of

Italians opportunities for quick and substantial monetary gain and sometimes for social and political advancement as well. Within the colony bankers and padroni, blackhanders and other lawbreakers all realized small but important profits by swindling or terrorizing compatriots. The "syndicate," a business operation reaping vast profits from the American community, offered almost limitless opportunities for promotion within its hierarchy. Thus for some, crime offered means of advancement within the ethnic community and for others, opportunities outside it.

How many or what percentage of Italians and their children engaged in such work is impossible to determine. Popular accounts and later stereotypes about the Black Hand, the Mafia, and members of *La Cosa Nostra* emphasized unduly this type of activity among Italians and Italian Americans.

However, Italian Americans have not monopolized organized crime. Historians and sociologists remind us that various other ethnic groups have been associated with criminal activity. In the nineteenth century the Irish were notorious in New York City's Five Points district, and crime has always been a part of ghetto life in this country; as the ethnic occupants of the slums change, so do the names on the police arrest lists. One study of the top underworld figures in Chicago in 1930 estimated that 30 percent were of Italian background, 29 percent of Irish background, and 20 percent of Jewish background. While Al Capone was famous in the Chicago rackets of the 1920s, men like Arnold Rothstein and Meyer Lansky were prominent in New York City.

It should also be kept in mind the extent to which criminal activities were an avenue of social mobility. In previous eras, old-stock Americans have held powerful positions in American industry, banking, insurance, and commerce. With few exceptions they have always been loath to allow immigrants or their children opportunities for advancement to the middle and upper levels of management. Crime, like entertainment and sports, was a way out of the ghetto and a means of achieving material success. Reluctantly, some chose it; for others the choice was not so reluctant.

Another point that must be made is that while certain activities are legally considered crimes, not everyone in the country regards them as wrong. Swedes and some pietistic Protestant immigrants may have shared the old-stock white Protestant aversion to gambling and drinking, but others did not think it so terrible to gamble or to supply liquor to thirsty throats during Prohibition. Besides, it was the so-called respectable citizens' patronage of illegal liquor suppliers that made Prohibition a failure. President Warren G. Harding drank during his tenure in the White House, and it was rumored that he and his cronies supported private bootleggers. As Chicago gangster

Al Capone asked in the 1920s: "What's Al Capone done, then? He supplied a legitimate demand. Some call it bootlegging. Some call it racketeering. I call it a business. They say I violate the prohibition law. Who doesn't?"

If crime has been a path upward for older immigrants, there is evidence that more recent migrants to the city will follow a similar pattern as their predecessors move into more respectable occupations. Recent research has indicated that African Americans, Russians, Colombians, and Jamaicans were already moving to take over organized crime as other minorities had done before them. Or as one Italian American said, "I guess it's their turn now."

Even though only a few Italian Americans have been associated with crime, they have left a lasting impression. The revelations of the Kefauver committee and best-selling books and movies like *The Godfather* have produced a sense of shame and indignation at the stereotype of the Italian criminal. In 1972 Frank Sinatra complained in *The New York Times* that "there is a form of bigotry abroad in this land which allows otherwise decent people . . . to believe the most scurrilous tales if they are connected to an Italian-American name."

The experiences and paths of mobility of other ethnic groups that were part of the great surge from southern and eastern Europe at the end of the nineteenth and the beginning of the twentieth centuries have varied from those of the Italians, and to a considerable extent from those of one another. Greeks were apt to be entrepreneurs—restauranteurs, theater owners, food processors—or professionals, such as doctors, lawyers, and teachers. The career of Alexander Pantages was typical of wealthy ethnic minorities. He came from a middle-class background but made his fortune in the entertainment world. After emigrating to the United States and working at odd jobs, he made money in gold in the Yukon and then made a fortune in the movie-house business, owning at one time a chain of eighty theaters. The Skouras brothers also owned a large number of movie houses, and Spyros Skouras became president of a major Hollywood organization, Twentieth Century-Fox. Although the careers of Pantages and the Skourases were exceptional, most Greek Americans were ensconced in the upper middle class by the 1980s.

Slavic peoples also began largely as unskilled workers in industrial America, but the second and third generations did not improve their positions as fast as some others of European descent. The working-class districts of American cities were often centers of Polish, Hungarian, and Russian life, of neat and well-kept houses, not prosperous but substantial. Like the Irish before them, the Slavs prized home ownership and invested their savings in their homes and neighborhoods. Disproportionately members of the working class, their offspring were mainly trade unionists and blue-collar workers. A survey of Slavs in Connecticut in the 1960s showed, for example, that 40 percent belonged to unions. Slavic Americans generally had incomes lower than those of the Irish or Jews or white Protestants, and their educational levels were also low. They had often found schools—important for mobility—inhospitable, and many dropped out before completing high school.

Although just reaching the middle-income level in the 1950s and 1960s, many Slavs were nonetheless continuing their educations, moving up the economic ladder, and finding better jobs. One scholar has concluded that throughout the 1920s and 1930s college attendance for Polish American men increased but lagged considerably behind the national norm. By the 1950s, he argues, Polish American males were just as likely to attend college as other white males, and a decade later Polish American women reached the national average for white women. Among Slovaks, Slovenes, and Croatians, the pace was just a bit slower than that of Poles.

These upward trends were confirmed by a study the United States Commission on Civil Rights published in 1986. From census and other data the commission found that Americans of southern and eastern European descent had achieved educational and earning parity with other whites of European background, meaning Germans, British, Irish, and Scandinavians. The commission noted that when millions from southern and eastern Europe arrived after 1880, they generally had about four fewer years of schooling than other white Americans and earned considerably less in their unskilled jobs. The third generation coming of age in post-World War II America had caught up with and even surpassed other whites. They had better jobs than their immigrant ancestors, earned more, and were well educated. The study found both men and women from southern and eastern Europe to have equaled their white counterparts from other areas of Europe.

Of course the success of Jews, whose ancestors hailed from Poland, Russia, and Rumania and who earned relatively high incomes and were quite well educated, would in part explain the results of the study, but even non-Jewish descendants of immigrants from eastern Europe did well. At the bottom of the income scale, the commission discovered proportionately fewer people of southern and eastern European descent living below the poverty line. The commission concluded:

> The results reveal that along virtually every dimension, Americans of southern and eastern European ancestry have generally succeeded as well or better than other Americans. This does not imply that many individuals of eastern or southern European heritage have not suffered from prejudice; it only suggests that for the groups as a whole, there is

no overt indication of current and widespread discrimination against them in the labor market—that is, the excellence of group-specific differences that cannot be explained by standard economic variables such as those accounted for in this report.

However, this assessment does not mean that the children and grandchildren of southern and eastern European immigrants were uniformly successful. Sometimes children did not do as well as their parents. Many second-generation Jewish businessmen were dismayed that their professionally trained children earned less money than they did. Moreover, in all groups there were poor people. Finally, it is important to keep in mind that the top positions in American society did not open up for many minority group members until the 1970s, and most key posts in leading law firms, businesses, and banks are still filled by old-stock Americans. The trend toward a more open executive suite was evident, but only in recent decades have members of most minority groups been hired solely on the basis of talent and ability.

Just as Irish, Germans, and, later, Italians did, the descendants of Slavs, Greeks, and other eastern Europeans became active in political affairs. In the early 1930s Anton Cermak became the first Czech mayor of Chicago, but most breakthroughs occurred later. Like so many other immigrants, Czechs were slow to become involved in politics; but the second and third generations began to assert themselves more effectively. In 1958 the Polish American press reported that thirteen Americans of Polish background had been elected to Congress, and Poles were important politically in cities like Chicago, Cleveland, Milwaukee, and Buffalo. In 1968 Edmund Muskie of Maine became the first American of Polish extraction to run for vice-president, the same year that Spiro T. Agnew, governor of Maryland and the first politically prominent Greek American, was elected to that office. Six years later voters of Massachusetts chose a Greek American, Michael S. Dukakis, as governor. In 1986 he won his third term by the biggest margin of any Massachusetts governor in the twentieth century. After that victory, Dukakis, who speaks Greek, Spanish, and Korean in addition to his native tongue, English, ran unsuccessfully against George Bush for the presidency in 1988. Besides Dukakis, the other most prominent Greek American political leader in the 1980s was U.S. Senator Paul Sarbanes of Maryland. In 1986, voters of that same state sent Barbara Mikulski, a Polish American woman, to the Senate. President Jimmy Carter also elevated Polish Americans to high posts. He chose Muskie for Secretary of State and Zbigniew Brzezinski for National Security Adviser.

While the descendants of southern and eastern European immigrants were making their marks both economically and politically, so were the descendants of the one Asian group—Japanese Americans—that had come during the same period as the eastern Europeans. Yet of the immigrants arriving in large numbers between 1880 and 1920, no other group experienced such intense prejudice as these Asians. Moreover, only the Japanese had to endure the shock of being placed in virtual concentration camps during World War II. Those interned on the West Coast lost nearly everything they owned, including their stakes in agricultural and small businesses. Beginning from scratch after the war, they rapidly improved their position. The key to much of their success was education. By 1950 the Japanese had a higher educational level than whites, with a considerable segment going to college. In the 1990s nearly 90 percent of third-generation Japanese Americans were attending some college or university, double the national rate and well above the 58 percent figure for second-generation Japanese Americans. Their attainments, combined with lessening prejudice, led to better jobs and higher incomes. Japanese Americans as a group tend to concentrate in prestige white-collar positions with higher than average incomes.

Many examples can be cited of the changing fortunes of Japanese Americans. S. Stephen Nakashima was interned with his family during World War II. He graduated from Berkeley in 1948 but could not find a job as an accountant; companies at that time refused to hire Japanese Americans. He went to Berkeley's Boalt Hall School of Law and upon graduation built a successful law practice. In 1989 Governor George Deukmejian (the first Armenian to become governor of an American state) appointed him to the California Board of Regents supervising public higher education, where he was joined by another Asian, Chinese American David Lee. Now successful, Nakashima found himself opposing the university's affirmative action program, saying that it discriminated against whites and Asians.

Even political life beckoned after the war for Japanese Americans. The *Issei* (the first generation) were ineligible for citizenship and hence excluded from politics. But members of the native-born second generation (*Nisei*), who were automatically citizens, grew into a potent political force. Sharp increases in the number of registered voters were translated into electoral victories. In 1968 both members of the House of Representatives from Hawaii as well as Democratic Senator Daniel Inouye were of Japanese ancestry. By 1980 another Japanese American, Spark Matsunaga, had joined Inouye in the Senate. Japanese Americans were also well represented in the Hawaiian legislature, the civil service, and business organizations. California, the state that had fostered so much hostility toward Japanese immigrants and their children, in 1976 elected S.I. Hayakawa, a Japanese American, to the U.S. Senate.

In 1997, the new Congress included seven people of Asian and Pacific Island ethnicity. Japanese Americans were the most prominent, but unlike other Asian groups they were predominately American born and hence U.S. citizens. As noted earlier in the case of the Chinese, it took time for newcomers to become assimilated and familiar with American politics. In the 1990s Asians formed new groups such as the Asian Pacific Americans for a New Los Angeles and the Asian Pacific Planning Council to push for their own agenda. As they began to enter politics, more Asians were elected to office. The first Korean American elected was Jay Kim, who won a seat in the House of Representatives in 1992 from California's wealthy Orange County. Kim, a conservative Republican, represented the interests of his affluent European American constituents.

As noted, many Chinese Americans were beginning to make their marks, as were Vietnamese, Asian Indians, Koreans, and Filipinos. In fact, the striking accomplishments of Asians were among the highlights of America's postwar ethnic experience. Newspapers, magazines, and television and radio stations carried features in the 1980s such as "What Sends Asians to the Head of the Class?"; "A Look at Success of Young Asians"; "Asians: The Model Minority"; or "The Triumph of Asian Americans."

Asian Americans scored well on academic tests and were well represented in the nation's top schools. More than one professor was known to remark that the way to increase the nation's Scholastic Aptitude Test (SAT) scores in math was to increase Asian immigration. In 1986, Asian Americans made up about 2 percent of the nation's population but accounted for 19 percent of Massachusetts Institute of Technology's undergraduates and 8 percent of Harvard's undergraduates. In the top music schools in the 1990s they were also disproportionately represented in the enrollment figures. "We have twenty-four Kims alone. It's incredible," reported Osegnam Fuschi of the admissions department of the Juilliard School of Music. Yehudi Menuhin, the celebrated violinist, called Asians "the Jews of the future," and predicted their achievements would equal those of eastern European Jewish descendants such as Jascha Heifetz, Vladimir Horowitz, and Arthur Rubinstein, among other great musicians.

Much evidence existed to support the impression that Asian Americans and new Asian immigrants, men as well as women, were prospering. Each year after 1980 the list of winners of the annual Westinghouse Science Talent Search competition contained a disproportionate number of Asian names. In 1987 David Kuo of New York City became the third member of his remarkable family to be named a Westinghouse Science Talent Search winner. The 1993 list of forty finalists included George Lee and Constance Chan from California; H Van Nguyen from Florida; Ravi Shanker Kamath from Kansas; Ken Sandor Wang from Maryland; Youngju Ryu, Erwin Lin, and

Willis Huang from New York; and Mahesh Kalyana Mahjanthappa from Colorado. Academic achievements resulted in improved incomes and better jobs. Asians generally were better educated than other Americans, and were more apt to be professionals; thus they earned more money, a fact revealed by the 1990 census which reported that median incomes for Japanese, Chinese, and Asian Indian families were above those of white families, and Koreans were about at the same level as the median. Moreover, a smaller proportion of Asians lived below the government's poverty line.

Asian Americans still confronted discrimination, and violence was not unknown in the 1990s. The Civil Rights Commission reported a rise in incidents of violence after 1980. For women there was also resistance from their own families and communities to their achieving success outside of the family. To be sure, CBS's Connie Chung was highly visible, as were important scholars such as Sucheng Chan. Gay Wong, a professor of education at California State University at Los Angeles, remarked in 1994, "You see families here now in the United States with American-born children, and the sons are still the inheritors of the property. You see in-laws baby-sitting the son's children, not the daughter's children." Another professor added, "Even though they may not be taught in a conscious way, the socialization we undergo is such that we might feel guilty or ashamed if we don't fulfill those roles."

While Asian success was often praised it is important to remember that whites with similar educations did better financially than Asians, and that the nation's Chinatowns housed many working-class and poor Chinese. While individual success stories can be found among Vietnamese, Cambodians, and Laotians, many of their families struggled to make ends meet. Such class and ethnic divisions made it clear that Asian Americans constituted many groups with diverse cultures, education, and incomes.

Asians did not stand out in athletics, but many men from other ethnic groups did. Athletics, in fact, might be compared to entertainment as one of the great levelers of American society for men. For women, achievement came only in tennis and golf until the 1990s when other professional sports, such as basketball, began to open. Sports have therefore been a way for many members of ethnic groups to escape working-class lives. Famed nineteenth-century boxers like John L. Sullivan and James Corbett were Irish, and Notre Dame's great football team of the 1930s, coached by Knute Rockne, was known as the fighting Irish. Gertrude Ederle, the first woman to swim the English Channel, was of German descent. In baseball other Germans found fame and sometimes fortune. Lou Gehrig, Honus Wagner, Rube Wadell, and the greatest German American player of all, Babe Ruth, born George Herman Erhardt in Baltimore, were idols in their day. Irish, English, and Germans dominated baseball until the 1920s, when Polish and Italian players began to rise. The DiMaggio brothers were the most famous of the Italian baseball players. Stan Musial, Ed Lopat, and Ted Kluszewski were of Polish ancestry. In our own day, African Americans and Hispanics are finding the world of professional athletics one arena in which they can compete and be judged strictly on the basis of their talents and accomplishments.

Because baseball is popular in the Caribbean and throughout Latin America, it is no surprise that many Latinos play after coming to the United States. Dominican Juan Marichal was a star pitcher for a number of years, and his countryman Manny Ramirez stood out for Cleveland in the late 1990s. Another Hispanic, Puerto Rican Orlando Cepeda, won the National League's most valuable player award in 1967. In 1996, Texas Ranger Juan Gonzalez won the American League's most valuable player award. Then in 1997 the Boston Red Sox signed Pedro Martinez to a $75 million, multiyear contract, which made him the highest-paid player in baseball—until Mike Piazza of the New York Mets dethroned him in 1998 by putting his signature on a contract worth $90 million. By the end of the decade Hispanics constituted approximately 20 percent of major league rosters, even though they were only 10 percent of the population. Players came from Mexico, Nicaragua, Panama, Columbia, Venezuela, Puerto Rico, and the Dominican Republic. In the 1990s Joe Cubas aided Cuban ballplayers in defecting from Castro's communist state. He managed to negotiate a lucrative contract for Livan Hernandez of the Florida Marlins in 1996, and Hernandez received the most valuable player award for his performance in the 1997 World Series.

Latin Americans also entered other sports. Boxing was a big attraction, and on occasion some played football. *Hispanic* magazine counted fourteen Latinos in the National Football League in 1997. Perhaps the most successful was Daniel Villanueva, a field goal kicker for the Dallas Cowboys and Los Angeles Rams. After his retirement, he became general manager of KMEX, a Spanish-language TV station in Los Angeles. He expanded his community and business interests and was reportedly the second wealthiest Mexican American, with a net worth of $86 million. Only Texas oilman Antonio R. Sanchez, Jr., was reportedly worth more.

Of course achievement in athletics was related to the background of the players. Ice hockey, a cold-weather sport, was not particularly well known in Latin America or among large numbers of Mexican Americans. Thus people of Canadian or Scandinavian background were more apt to be hockey players, just as blacks have excelled in basketball and football due to greater opportunities to participate in those sports.

Obviously, most of the descendants of immigrants could not be outstanding athletes and had to take the more usual paths—white-collar and professional positions—to middle-class security. Better jobs provided higher incomes and a route out of the ghettoes. At first the move was to better neighborhoods in the city, but since the end of World War II the trek has been increasingly to the suburbs. In New York City in the late 1920s fewer than 10 percent of Jews still lived on the famed Lower East Side. The completion of the subways stimulated the exodus to the upper reaches of Manhattan and the Bronx and across the East River into Brooklyn and Queens. In Chicago the original Italian districts declined in the 1920s. The subsequent depression and post-World War II housing shortage curtailed movement, but the affluence of the 1950s rejuvenated it. The growth of suburbia in the 1950s and 1960s can be attributed largely to the exodus from the city of the children and grandchildren of the Irish, Italians, Poles, Jews, and Scandinavians who shared in the nation's growing prosperity. So great was the trend that by 1970 the census showed more people, overwhelmingly white, living in suburban America than in central cities. In many cases the pattern of movement went far beyond neighboring greenbelts. Sunshine and job opportunities drew people to the South and the West. Florida and California in particular more than doubled their populations in the decades after World War II, and the growth in job opportunities in regional centers such as Washington, D.C., and Houston, Texas also resulted in mushrooming populations. California and Texas, aided by immigration, are now the most populous states in the nation.

However, old ethnic neighborhoods did not disappear completely. Slavs and Italians, less affluent and strongly attached to their homes and old family neighborhoods, were the last to leave, and many simply remained where they were. As a result there are still ethnic enclaves of Italians in New York City and Newark, New Jersey, and Slavic neighborhoods in Philadelphia, Detroit, Milwaukee, Cleveland, Baltimore, Pittsburgh, and Buffalo. Moreover, refugee arrivals since 1945 have strengthened some of the old ethnic neighborhoods. Just as the descendants of the original Chinese were moving out of the Chinatowns in America, renewed immigration in the 1980s and 1990s once again swelled the neighborhoods' populations. Similarly, refugee Hasidic Jews reinforced the Jewish population of Brooklyn when they settled in the Williamsburg, Crown Heights, and Borough Park sections.

Yet the general trend was clear. The older and more prosperous immigrants' descendants measured their success by their movement. Many of the recent Asian immigrants did likewise. They too headed for the suburbs to live in more substantial housing and to send their children to better schools. In the process they left behind less affluent blacks, Mexican Americans, Puerto Ricans, and other Latin Americans. This was particularly noticeable in major metropolises. New York City, the symbol of the nation's ethnic diversity and the port of entry for so many newcomers, was becoming less

Irish, Jewish, and Italian and more black, Asian, and Hispanic. The borough of Queens, formerly a step up for the second and third generations, now houses immigrant colonies of Maltese, Greeks, Croatians, West Indians, Armenians, Koreans, Thais, Vietnamese, Cambodians, Laotians, Filipinos, and Japanese.

Two major differences between most of these more recent settlers and immigrants of earlier generations are that the newer arrivals are generally better educated and of a higher social status than turn-of-the-century immigrants, and their presence is not resented as much as was their predecessors'. A New York City population analyst observed in the summer of 1980: "The Asians are generally perceived by their neighbors as a stabilizing influence." They open stores, encourage their children in school, and apparently have the same goals and values as middle-class Americans.

However, Hispanics are not always viewed so favorably. Despite their achievements in sports, the new Latinos' chances of climbing the ladder of success have been limited. As noted, the Cubans have done much better than Mexicans and Central Americans. For other post-1945 immigrants, evidence is already mounting of a pattern of mobility. Scholarly studies show that those who arrived in the 1940s and 1950s are making more money than many native-born Americans of similar characteristics.

It is too soon to chart the progress of Asians and peoples from the Caribbean, Middle East, and Africa arriving in the post-1965 waves, yet some evidence is available. Many take jobs initially in lines of work below their training and find an inadequate knowledge of English to be a barrier. Professionals have at times encountered difficulties in obtaining licenses to practice their skills. Nevertheless, some are already demonstrating an entrepreneurial spirit, and with more time in the United States they move ahead. As one journalist put it in 1997, "Immigrant families are the building blocks. . . . They repopulate desolate communities. . . . Immigrant families save better than American-born families do, educate their children better and raise their living standards faster than the native born." While these observations hide some failures and the many differences among immigrants, they point to the continuing belief that America is the land of opportunity.

Chapter 8

Whither Ethnic America?
Assimilation into American Life

THE MASSIVE FLOW of immigrants after the 1840s bewildered old-stock Americans. They could not agree on how newcomers could best be absorbed into the mainstream of American life. Proponents of the melting pot had one theory, Americanizers had another, and advocates of pluralism had yet a third point of view. Americans eventually agreed on one thing: immigration had to be controlled both in social composition and in numbers. Although they were willing to allow more immigrants after World War II and do away with the national origins systems in 1965, general restrictions remained.

But what of the immigrants themselves? Did they and their descendants maintain separate subcultures, blend with old Americans to form a new type, or assimilate into the larger society? As we have seen, people who arrived in the colonial era eventually lost their distinct national heritages and became part of the common American culture. There were exceptions, of course, such as the Amish, who still live apart from the rest of society in their religious communities. But the Amish number only about 130,000 today. Little remains of the original Scots-Irish, Welsh, German, or Huguenot societies of early America. Immigrants coming in large numbers between 1840 and 1890 from northern and western Europe have largely assimilated. Immigrants coming after 1880 and now producing a fourth generation have assimilated, although some Jews, Italians, Poles, Chinese, Japanese, and others still retain aspects of their traditional heritages. In fact, in the wake of the civil rights movement of the 1960s, there was a renewal of ethnic self-consciousness, which was subsequently reinforced by waves of immigrant Italians, Irish, Greeks, Portuguese, Croatians, and Russian Jews from Europe; Hispanics from the Western Hemisphere; and Asians. The most recent newcomers are of course still largely unassimilated. The U.S. Supreme Court's 1974 ruling in *Lau v. Nichols*, which requires public schools to teach children in a language that they can understand, may inhibit the pace of future assimilation— or, paradoxically, it may hasten change by educating those who had been turned off by English-only schools. Bilingualism remains one of the most hotly debated topics about ethnicity in the 1990s, and it is not clear whether it has hindered or helped the process of assimilation.

Over the years, for some groups external events have forced wrenching and radical change. German Americans, for example, opposed American involvement on the side of the Allied powers against Germany after World War I broke out in Europe in 1914. When the United States finally entered the conflagration on the Allied side in 1917, German Americans were torn. Issues were not clear-cut in spite of the shrill cries about German militarism, stories of atrocities, and alleged threats to American interests. Moreover, when the United States entered the war against Germany, German Americans were faced with the reality of fighting a nation in which many of their relatives and friends lived. Despite the acute agony caused by their situation, German American soldiers fought as valorously as other Americans.

Yet American entry into the war forced all dissidents into an untenable position. The slightest indication of doubt or disagreement about the righteousness of the cause led to accusations of disloyalty and traitorous behavior. Superpatriots were especially critical of German Americans, the Irish, pacifists, and radicals. Some German Americans and some radicals, such as Socialist Party leader Eugene Debs, continued to oppose the war once the United States joined in. Two sons of a prominent German Philadelphia brewing family, Erwin R. and Grover Cleveland Bergdoll, refused to serve in the military because "we do not fight our own kind." One of the two was apprehended and sentenced to a federal prison; the other fled to Germany. Upon his return to the United States he too was imprisoned.

After the war some German Americans were bitter, but most accepted the outcome. When Hitler's armies marched in the 1930s, few German Americans had supported them. American Nazi organizations in the 1930s, with small memberships, had a few German immigrant members, but second and third generations turned their backs on Nazism. Antiwar sentiments were voiced in German areas of the Midwest in the 1930s, but when World War II came, descendants of German immigrants supported the United States without reservation. About 30 percent of American soldiers fighting in Western Europe in 1944–1945 were German in origin.

The American Irish were also reluctant belligerents during World War I. Why, Irish American leaders asked, should the Irish fight on the side of Great Britain when she had refused to free Ireland? It was a valid question, especially for President Woodrow Wilson, who professed to make the war a crusade for democracy and the self-determination of nations. But the answer was relatively simple: as in the past, soldiers fought for their own country no matter what their personal preferences might be. Only a handful of Irish in America resisted the war effort, although others grumbled about Allied powers. The omission of Irish independence from the peace treaty irked the Irish and caused some to desert the Democratic Party; but this was a political matter, hardly an issue of citizenship or disloyalty. Ireland achieved independence in 1922. Thus the Irish question was largely dead by World War II, although some Irish were not overly sympathetic to Great Britain at any time.

The crisis for Italian Americans, a newer immigrant group, came later. They had reservations about American foreign policy during the 1930s because of the growing friction between the United States and Italy. During the 1920s and 1930s, many of them, as well as many other Americans, admired Mussolini, but some bitterly opposed him and the advent of fascism in Italy. The difficulty for antifascists was that they seemed to be "un-Italian" if they attacked *Il Duce*. An Italian American said: "Whatever you fellows may think of Mussolini, you've got to admit one thing: he has done more to get respect for the Italian people than anybody else. The Italians get a lot more respect now than when I started going to school. And you can thank Mussolini for that." The Italian attack on Ethiopia in 1935 aggravated divisions. Some Italian Americans turned away from the Democratic Party of Franklin Roosevelt because he condemned Italy's actions, as some of the Irish had done when another Democratic president, Woodrow Wilson, did not insist on Irish independence.

The menace of fascism and the coming of the war in Europe doomed such sentiment, however. Although some Italian Americans were uneasy about going to war against Italy, they supported the United States once it was involved. Owners of bars that had pictures of Mussolini hanging quickly took them down and put up portraits of President Franklin D. Roosevelt. Even those segments of the Italian American press that had praised Mussolini and fascism in Italy proclaimed their loyalty to America, and Columbus Day celebrations became rallies to support the war and buy government war bonds. A half million Italian Americans served in the military during the war. To be sure, some in the federal government distrusted the Italy-born generation, which numbered about 600,000, and they were put under travel restrictions. These were lifted on Columbus Day, 1942. Ten thousand German, Bulgarian, Hungarian, Romanian, and Czech aliens were interned, along with several hundred Italian immigrants, even though there was no evidence that Italians were connected with espionage and sabotage.

The most excruciating test of loyalty faced by an ethnic group was that of Japanese Americans during World War II, discussed in chapter 4. When the government interned West Coast Japanese in 1942, it did not distinguish between those who were citizens (*Nisei*) and their parents (*Issei*), who were born in Japan and ineligible for American citizenship. At first the army refused to draft Nisei and did not allow them to enlist. The government insisted upon testing their patriotism further by making them answer a series of questions. The camp experience and the questionnaire divided many; a few Japanese were classified as disloyal to the United States and segregated at the Tule Lake, California center. Several thousand of the "disloyal" asked to be returned to Japan after the war, and some even renounced their American citizenship. Yet it was the familiar story. Most of the 110,000 interned Japanese Americans professed their allegiance to the United States, and when given the opportunity, the Nisei joined the army. About 33,000 Japanese Americans served, roughly half from the Hawaiian Islands and half from the mainland.

Japanese Americans fighting during World War II as members of the 442nd Regimental Combat Team became the most highly decorated soldiers of the war. In addition to thousands of medals for heroism, they received 9,486 Purple Hearts for their battle wounds. In the 1980s some of the unit's veterans wanted more recognition for their service. The president of the unit's veterans' association told the *Los Angeles Times* in 1986, "Our mission today is to get our story retold. . . . We don't want our children and our grandchildren, or the rest of the world to forget what we fought for." Another veteran summed up the unit's patriotism, "All we've ever wanted is for people to know that we are Americans first and foremost and nothing else."

Since World War II there have been no major wars to divide ethnic attachments in America. Groups like the Irish and Italians have strong loyalties to Eire or Italy, but most of the immigrants' descendants have become too thoroughly Americanized to be as troubled as their forebears were during World War I. (The exception of the Jews and Israel will be discussed later.)

The longer groups have lived in the United States, the more they have relinquished their Old World cultures. Immigrants retained their native languages or became bilingual. Their children and grandchildren gradually lost the old languages and spoke only English. Typically, when the government searched among second-generation Japanese Americans in the camps during World War II for possible interpreters, it found that not many Nisei could speak and understand Japanese well, and fewer still could read and write it. In 1974 a middle-aged Czech woman had this to say about a declining Czech community in New Jersey.

> The old Czechs are dying and moving away. Our parents are the ones
> who were very active. The people of my age still had their parents
> around. They remember the customs, and that is something you can't
> forget. But you can't pass memories on to your children. The younger
> generation marry people who are not Czech and don't keep up the lan-

guage with their children. I go to see a friend of mine who's 83, and I talk Czech with her. If I didn't I'd forget the language.

Institutions depending on foreign languages began to disappear as the immigrants' descendants could not use them. The German-language press was thriving on the eve of World War I and was the most important of the foreign-language presses, accounting for about 40 percent of their circulation. The war shattered the German-language press and hurt the standing of the language generally; it was driven off the newsstands and out of the schools. In 1910 there were 70 German dailies in America; in 1960 only 6 remained. Other major foreign-language newspapers also declined, especially Yiddish, Italian, and Scandinavian ones. Italian dailies decreased in number from 12 earlier in the century to 5 in 1960; French dailies decreased in number from 9 to 1 during the same period. From a high of 142 daily newspapers in 1910, the foreign-language press has less than half that quantity today, and the number and circulation of weeklies have also dropped. A 1940 census counted 1,092 ethnic periodicals in 39 languages; the 1996 *Editor and Publisher Yearbook* counted fewer than 500, and many of these were read by the post-World War II newcomers.

The changes in one of the most famous foreign-language papers illustrate the decline. In 1997 the *Jewish Forward* observed its hundredth birthday. At its peak in the 1920s this Yiddish daily newspaper had a circulation of 250,000. By the time its centennial came, it was a weekly of only 40,000, published in three languages. The Yiddish edition numbered 10,000 and catered mainly to an elderly audience. The Russian edition printed 4,000 copies. But the largest, the English edition, begun in 1990, had a circulation of 25,000.

The new immigrants from Asia, Europe, and Latin America began to publish new foreign-language newspapers to serve their growing populations. Hence Korean newspapers appeared in Los Angeles and circulation of Spanish newspapers increased greatly as the Mexican American population of that city grew. In New York City, no fewer than four Chinese and three Spanish daily newspapers were being published after 1990. No doubt if the present immigration trends continue, new foreign-language papers will appear, and some of the older ones catering to the latest newcomers will expand. But in general, the older foreign-language press is on a steep decline in this country.

The loss of Old World culture can also be seen in the declining use of foreign languages in one of the most important immigrant institutions, the church. The Danish Lutheran churches are a case in point. As the young learned English, churches began to abandon Danish, first in the Sunday schools in the 1920s, then in youth work, and finally in the services a decade later. Most of the books and periodicals published by Danish Lutherans in the late nineteenth century were in Danish, and as late as 1940 the annual reports for the United Evangelical Lutheran Church were about half in Danish, but the use of the language was discontinued after that.

The decline of foreign languages in churches was indicative of the growing Americanization and loss of ethnicity in American religion in the twentieth century. Lutheranism, which was originally divided mainly along ethnic or nationality lines such as Swedish, Danish, German, and Norwegian, is a good example of this process. In 1967 the United Evangelical Lutheran Church, of Danish background, merged with two other synods, one German and the other Norwegian in origin, and became the American Lutheran Church. Two years later another Danish Lutheran church, the American Evangelical Lutheran Church, joined with German, Swedish, and Finnish synods to become the Lutheran Church in America. These various Lutheran groups were no longer using their old languages or recruiting ministers from the Old World, and since they already were cooperating in religious activities, they reached the inevitable conclusion: merge into an American Lutheranism. Mergers went a step further in 1987 when the American Lutheran Church and the Lutheran Church in America joined with the Association of Evangelical Lutheran Churches, originally of German origin, to become the 5.3 million-member Evangelical Lutheran Church in America.

The same Americanization process happened in Catholicism. In the late nineteenth century a burning issue in American Catholicism was the nationality parish supported ardently by, among others, German, French Canadian, and Polish Catholics. The Church disapproved of nationality parishes in principle although it continued to allow them in practice. In the twentieth century, however, the nationality issue gradually became less important and so did the issue of national parishes.

The Germans illustrate this change. In the 1890s German Catholics were most insistent upon having their own priests and organizations and fostered the slogan "Language Saves Faith." The largest of these organizations was the *Central Verein*, founded in 1855. It reached a peak membership of 125,000 on the eve of World War I and was especially strong in New York, Pennsylvania, and the Midwest. Second-generation German Catholics, however, were already losing interest in an ethnic church when the war began. Twenty-three German Catholic publications were discontinued between 1917 and 1923; and in those that remained, English became prevalent during the 1920s. Membership in the Central Verein declined to 86,000 in 1930 and less than half that a decade later. The journal of the Verein, *Central Blatt and Social Justice*, printed more of its material in English (it discontinued

German sections entirely in 1946) and changed its name to *Social Justice* in 1940 but continued to lose readers; by the late 1960s, circulation barely reached 2,000.

As churches lost their national identities, so too did many of the other immigrant organizations. Social clubs, benefit societies, welfare organizations, and the like lost much of their membership and vitality as old immigrant neighborhoods decayed. They are strongest today among Poles and Italians. The largest of the nationality organizations was the *Deutsch-Amerikanische National Bund* or National German American Alliance, which was organized in 1901 to promote German culture in America and the political interests of German Americans. At its peak before World War I it claimed a membership of about two million. In addition to promoting German language and culture, it was an agent of assimilation, for it urged German immigrants to become citizens and insisted its primary loyalty was to the United States, not Germany. The Alliance opposed American entry on the side of England in World War I, came under attack during the war, and had to disband in 1918. It was not only the war that killed it, however. Third-generation German Americans were not as interested in German culture as their parents and grandparents had been. In common with members of other minority groups they were moving out of ethnic neighborhoods, especially after World War I, and joining assimilationist organizations. Another example of organizational decline is the fate of Japanese American groups which, without substantial immigration, were losing membership in the 1990s. The major support unit for the Nisei was the Japanese American Citizens League. It played an important role in winning an apology from the United States government for the internment camps of World War II and a small monetary compensation for those interned. But in 1995 the League claimed only 25,000 members, mostly elderly, down from 31,719 in 1977.

Parents attempted to maintain old ways by sending their children to ethnic or religious schools. This was true of Scandinavians, Germans, East European Jews, Greeks, and Chinese. Yet many of these schools have gradually dropped language teaching and have had difficulty attracting students. During the school crises of the 1960s and early 1970s, many parents removed their children from public schools to prevent racial integration, and as a result enrollments in some ethnic schools—Jewish day schools, for example—rose. These schools continue to thrive; however, the main reason for their growth is a commitment on the part of the children's parents to revive traditional values and commit themselves to perpetuating Jewish heritage.

The largest parochial school system in the United States is run by the Catholic Church. Only a minority of Catholics attend these institutions despite the growth spurt in the 1950s and early 1960s. Financial troubles have

beset parochial schools, however, and since the late 1960s a number have
had to close. Those remaining in cities often cater to new immigrants and
African Americans, some of whom are not Catholic.

As the descendants of immigrants improved their incomes, jobs, and education, they moved to new neighborhoods in cities and to mushrooming suburbs. There they absorbed the values of the mass culture preached by the
media and in the schools and came into social contact with a broad range of
other people. These contacts led to intermarriage among nationality and religious groups. The importance of this cannot be overstated. The family is
the primary social unit in our society, and as families mix, so do other institutions. In other words, intermarriage is the ultimate form of assimilation.

For the first generation, on the contrary, marriage outside the ethnic group
was rare. Many of the immigrants, who were disproportionately male, even
returned to the motherland to find spouses. Marriage within the group provided security and acceptance; outside of it, disgrace and ostracism. When the
children of orthodox Jews chose Gentile mates, for example, their parents
sometimes mourned their children as though they had died. Roman Catholics were considered to be living in sin when they chose Protestant spouses
and married outside the Catholic Church. Many states barred Asians from
marrying Caucasians. When individuals ventured outside their nationality
groups, they usually stayed within the same religious group, so that Irish
Catholics married English or German Catholics (but rarely Italian Catholics)
and German Jews married East European Jews.

Data on intermarriage is not plentiful, but studies indicate that rates of intermarriage have increased. One important analysis of trends in New Haven,
Connecticut, from 1870 to 1940 revealed that 91 percent married within the
nationality group in 1870, 65 percent in 1930, and 63 percent in 1940. Thus
the investigator found a decreasing tendency to marry within national groups
but still a high tendency to marry within religions; in effect, national background faded while religion remained important. Eighty percent of Protestants, 84 percent of Catholics, and 94 percent of Jews married within their respective faiths in 1940. The author drew the conclusion that instead of a
single melting pot developing in American society, there was a triple melting
pot—Protestant, Catholic, and Jewish groups—and intermarriage occurred
within these religious groups. Other scholars confirmed this as the direction
of assimilation in America.

More recent data suggests that the triple-melting-pot thesis is outdated. In
Iowa, the only state that kept religious records in the 1950s, over 40 percent
of Jewish marriages were interfaith. A study of Jewish marriages in Washington, D.C. in the 1960s indicated that only one percent of the first, 10 percent of the second, and 18 percent of the third generation married Gentiles.

Alarmed by the growing rate of outmarriages among Jews, the Council of Jewish Federations and Welfare Funds conducted a national survey of the period 1966–1972. Findings indicated that 31 percent of all Jews who married during that period chose non-Jewish mates. In the middle of the 1980s rabbis estimated that perhaps 20 to 35 percent of Jews in the East, but well over 50 percent of those in parts of the West, were doing so. And in the 1990s some estimated that the interfaith marriage rate in cities like Phoenix and Denver exceeded 70 percent. Sectional discrepancies may be accounted for by noting that in more traditional and heavily populated areas, Jewish roots ran deep, there were greater opportunities to meet others of a similar background, and perhaps family and community pressures existed, while in the western cities many Jews were newcomers with fewer ties to tradition or to coreligionists.

The Jewish outmarriage rate causes considerable alarm among those Jews who worry about "continuity"—the current buzzword. Even though there has been a resurgence of Orthodoxy among Jews since the early 1970s, the Orthodox constitute less than 10 percent of the Jewish population. In 1974 Atlanta rabbis organized Jewish Compu-Date, a computer dating service for the city's widely dispersed Jewish singles. One rabbi explained its purpose: "We started Compu-Date . . . to preserve Judaism and our heritage; it is important that Jews meet and marry one another." In 1995 the Connecticut *Jewish Ledger* announced that it would continue its practice of not mentioning Jewish-non-Jewish marriages in its pages.

Among Catholics in the 1960s about one in three married someone raised as a non-Catholic. Irish and Germans were more apt to marry outside their nationality and religious group than French Canadians, Poles, or Italians. Only about 40 percent of Irish and Germans married other Irish or Germans during the 1960s, while the rate for Italians, Poles, and French Canadians was about 60 percent. Among the newest Catholic Americans from Mexico and Puerto Rico, early studies indicate little intermarriage with non-Catholics. Data for recent decades, though, show an uptrend.

Recognizing this increase, the Roman Catholic Church modified some of its teachings in the mid-1960s. No longer were those who married outside the faith excommunicated. Non-Catholic clergy were also permitted to be present at ceremonies involving interfaith marriages and to give blessings after the exchanges of vows. In 1973 an Eastern Rite Catholic professor of religious studies and pastor of a Ukrainian Catholic church gave a statement more sympathetic to the drift of public opinion: "The danger from increasing interfaith marriages is not that Catholics will join some other churches or religions—which would not be bad at all—but that they will become indifferent and estranged from religion in general."

Among Protestants, despite variations, the trend has also been toward increased incidence and acceptance of intermarriage. Among Scandinavians, for example, the Swedes, like others, originally opposed marriage outside the group but were more inclined to them than the Norwegians. Most of the outmarriages among Swedes occurred first with other Scandinavians or with Germans, but those of the fourth generation have chosen partners from a wide assortment of faiths and nationalities.

Mixed marriages among those of Asian and European ancestries have also been common, especially marriages between Europeans and Japanese Americans. But first the law had to change. States began to abolish bans on interracial marriages during the 1950s and 1960s, and in the Supreme Court decision in *Loving v. Virginia* (1967), the justices declared that such bans were unconstitutional. In the 1990s most Japanese American women married non-Japanese partners. How the children of such marriages will identify themselves is not clear. In 1993 one young boy put it, "I'm half Italian, half Japanese and all American." His mother was born in Italy, the niece of a monsignor in the Roman Catholic Church, and his father was born in Japan of a Buddhist family. Similar trends are taking place among other Asians and Latino Americans. But there is a crucial difference. The constant stream of new immigrants reinforces existing communities even as assimilation happens.

The twentieth-century development of a public school system has been another key factor in breaking down ethnicity. Immigrants' descendants were, and are, being instructed in Anglo-American values. After World War II most Americans attended, and roughly three quarters graduated from, the nation's high schools. In the post-World War II era colleges and universities expanded rapidly, and by the 1990s nearly half the college-age population could be found in institutions of higher learning. If elementary and high schools are often homogeneous, institutions of higher education are less so and expose students to diverse ideologies and ethnic strains. Away from the watchful eyes of parents, youth seem more willing to learn about different people. No wonder ethnic leaders are concerned about intermarriage on college campuses!

Along with the expansion of education came the development of mass media in American culture. The printed word was important before World War I in the form of newspapers and journals, but after 1920 came radio and movies and then, after World War II, television. Of course, many minorities operated presses and ran radio and TV stations, but they could not compete with the dominant corporations. Major networks had huge advertising budgets, and national programs beamed identical messages into most American homes. Regardless of ethnic background, children are exposed to this mass culture of nationally available products, common heroes, and similar values.

By and large, descendants of immigrants have absorbed this common culture. The core values of American society—like beliefs in success and individual achievement—have been accepted. National standards in dress and taste have also been observed. Musicians, movie stars, and athletes are almost universally acknowledged heroes and models. Even certain observances of religious holidays are becoming part of the national culture. In New York City, for example, public schools and many businesses close on some Jewish holidays, not just on Christmas Day. This is true in other cities as well. And on the holiest days of the Jewish New Year, stock markets throughout the world have fewer trades than on other business days.

Well-educated members of mobile ethnic groups tend to lose their ethnicity. Business and professional people, especially the more highly educated, have joined organizations with mixed memberships. Upward mobility has also been accompanied by horizontal mobility, with large numbers of descendants of immigrants moving out of old neighborhoods and into the growing suburbs. In suburbia, where social divisions commonly follow class and racial lines, it has been more difficult to maintain ethnicity. Common interests, such as education and zoning, bring people together.

One minority, the Franco-Americans, long known for retention of their culture, illustrates many of the pressures for assimilation. As noted, French Canadian communities in New England since the nineteenth century have been kept vital by sustained migration and contact with Canada. In recent decades that migration has decreased. But as long as French Canadians lived and worked in textile and shoe factories in isolated New England towns, they could easily maintain the values of family, church, and local community. Since 1960, as they have moved from mills to better-paying jobs in service industries, their attachment to the old culture has lessened. English has been a necessity in these new jobs and French strictly a secondary language.

The religious revival that was said to have followed World War II, especially in the suburbs, was in part an attempt to create a bulwark of security and ethnicity in new surroundings. Church suppers and youth programs provided social entry for families until they could put down new roots. But also important was the development of contacts among religious groups. This led to increased toleration, which in turn opened new paths for social mobility and assimilation. Moreover, modern Judaism, Protestantism, and Catholicism have grown together ritually and theologically, thus further reducing differences and conflicts. The modernization movement, especially in American Catholicism, brought changes in practices and beliefs, and a decline in church attendance after 1970. In 1978, with polls revealing that 80 percent of Roman Catholics approved of intermarriages with Protestants, it was not surprising to find that liberal beliefs about controversial matters such as birth control

and abortion were shared by Catholics, Protestants, and Jews of the same social and economic backgrounds. At the same time, however, Roman
Catholics were still prominent in groups opposed to the Equal Rights Amendment and to women's right to choose abortion. There they were joined by conservative Protestants and Orthodox Jews.

In the late 1960s, just when European minorities seemed well on the way
toward assimilation, ethnicity became chic in American life and politics.
Whereas folk customs and costumes used to be an embarrassment to ethnic
children, except on festival days, suddenly there were cries for ethnic studies programs on college campuses, proclamations of ethnic heritage days in
cities, formations of new ethnic organizations, and political assertions that
the melting pot would and should not work. Michael Novak, author of *The
Rise of the Unmeltable Ethnics* (1972), national columnist, and editor of
several newsletters devoted to ethnic affairs, was a particularly eloquent
spokesman for the descendants of southern and eastern European Catholic
immigrants; so too was Roman Catholic priest, novelist, and sociologist Andrew Greeley.

Many communities and colleges responded with special events and programs. Czechs in Nebraska started the tradition of a two-day Czech festival
in Wilbur every August. A Sheridan, Wyoming radio station began airing a
weekly two-hour "Polka Party" to honor the Polish heritage of many of its
residents; this reputedly became one of the station's most popular shows. A
host of people from Wisconsin's "Little Norway" began putting on an annual
production of *Song of Norway*, a former Broadway musical based on the
works of Edvard Grieg. In 1975 it was done in Norwegian for members of the
State Historical Society meeting in Oshkosh. The performers took pride in
the fact that they had memorized all the foreign words for the show. In Kearney, New Jersey, which began to attract many Scottish workers in the late
nineteenth century, town residents celebrated Scottish poet Robert Burns's
birthday for one week each year.

College campuses around the nation also developed ethnic programs,
among them Puerto Rican studies, Jewish studies, African American studies,
Basque studies, and Mexican American studies. At Louisiana State University the foreign language department introduced a new course in the Cajun
language. The Louisiana Cajuns, descendants of several thousand Acadians
who came to southern Louisiana from Canada in the 1750s, had traditionally
maintained their French-derivative language and culture by the spoken word;
now they have not only a course but also a textbook, first published in 1977.

Not to be outdone by communities and campuses, politicians, who have
usually been aware of ethnic differences only when counting votes, began to
take notice. In 1972 the U.S. Congress, as part of the Elementary and Sec-

ondary Education Act, established and allocated funds for an Ethnic Heritage Program and a National Advisory Council on Ethnic Heritage Studies.To some degree, politicians responded in this fashion because of the renewed assertiveness of individual ethnics who found the spirit of the times conducive to new crusades. Meir Kahane's Jewish Defense League (1968), although representing only a small minority of Jews, made headlines because of its demonstrations. Kahane lashed out against assimilation and preached a militant brand of Jewish nationalism. Arrested for his activities in the United States, he went to Israel, where his militancy also brought him into confrontation with the law.

Some Italians also showed a renewed concern with ethnicity. Joseph Columbo's Italian American Civil Rights League, founded in 1970, countered alleged insults to Italian Americans and staged marches in New York City. Italian Americans vehemently protested the alleged prejudicial treatment that the media and law enforcement officials displayed. They resented, for example, television programs in which the underworld figure's name always ended with a vowel. They also railed against alleged discrimination by the Federal Bureau of Investigation (FBI), which they claimed unfairly portrayed Italian Americans as criminals. During the summer of 1971, groups of Italian Americans paraded in front of FBI headquarters in New York City chanting

> Hi-di-hi
> Hi-di-ho
> The FBI
> Has got to go!

New manifestations of ethnicity were sharp reminders that Americanization was taking generations to achieve. Old groups like the Amish and new groups like the Hasidic Jews, who chose to remain in secluded enclaves, were at the far end of the spectrum of ethnicity in America. The Amish live as farmers, apart from other Americans. They do not allow carriers of modern culture, such as television or radios, in their homes, and their children drop out of school as soon as state laws permits them to do so. Unlike the Amish, Hasidic Jews of New York City, numbering 100,000 or so, are an urban group; they live close together in several neighborhoods. There they can control social activities and their children's education. They own their own stores, employing other Hasidic Jews, and sell computers, cameras, and a variety of electric appliances.

At the other end were older groups that had thoroughly blended into Anglo-American culture; in between stood the progeny of the millions who came after 1880. Descendants of these immigrants had lost much of the Old

World culture but still had some common bonds of religion, customs, political interest, and family and group life that held them together.

To understand ethnicity it is important to remember that each ethnic group brought with it a unique lifestyle. Roles of family members, expectations of spouses and children, and attitudes toward education and religion often determined how quickly and how well various minorities were absorbed into American society. Members of groups whose economic and educational aspirations were low, and who therefore lacked mobility, were least likely to be assimilated. Many Slavs, Italians, and Hispanics fell into this category. Unfortunately, for most people in the immigrant generation the promises of American life remained unfulfilled. Their offspring, though, did have greater opportunities. By the 1960s militant members of still-depressed minorities demanded that the benefits of American life become theirs—and quickly.

For this and other reasons there was a resurgence of ethnicity in the 1960s. The black civil rights and black nationalist movements emphasized a quest for identity, and some ethnic groups sought to emulate their pressure-group tactics. Mexican Americans, American Indians, and Italians were among the most prominent of the groups that demonstrated for greater opportunities and respect in American society. They did not feel part of WASP America, and they wanted both recognition and celebration of their own backgrounds. The editor of a Polish American weekly in New Jersey, for example, announced in 1970 the formation of I'm-Proud-to-Be-Polish clubs. Seven years later a Polish American woman marketed a Polish coloring book. About culture she said, "You have to start with the young. It can't be done later in life."

Social scientists are quick to remind us that ethnic voting behavior was and is important in American politics and often transcends class or regional lines. Politicians are clearly aware of ethnic trends in voting and regularly appear at the appropriate parades or events to eat pizza, bagels, or chop suey. Orville Freeman, who served as governor of Minnesota and then as Secretary of Agriculture during the Kennedy and Johnson administrations, attributed his defeat for reelection as governor in 1960 to the fact that his grandfather had changed the family name from Johnson, a name that strikes a responsive chord among Scandinavians in Minnesota.

Ethnic politics is usually most intense at the city level, where political parties strive for ethnically balanced tickets. In New York City the three major elective posts—mayor, president of the city council, and comptroller—usually went to people of Irish, Italian, and Jewish backgrounds when their votes were most influential. An Irish name is no longer politically significant, and the city's Italians seem to have moved toward the Republican and Conservative parties. Blacks, Asians, and Latinos are now the ethnic groups, besides the Jews, to whom New York City Democrats make appeals. In Buffalo a Polish name is an asset; in Milwaukee a German name is favored; and in parts of the Southwest a Hispanic name attracts votes. In Baltimore Barbara Mikulski, now a U.S. Senator, came to prominence in the 1960s as a spokeswoman for the Slavs of her city.

National political parties are also aware of the relationship between ethnic factors and voting. Democrats had a temporary nationalities division in 1936 and made it permanent in 1948. As blacks, Poles, Italians, and Jews became more important, the party courted their votes aggressively. John F. Kennedy brought Cleveland's Mayor Anthony Celebreze into his cabinet as Secretary of Health, Education, and Welfare in 1962, and political pundits surmised that the president did so with one eye on the Italian vote. A year later the Democratic Party made its newly named All American Council a more elaborate organization.

The Republican Party responded more slowly to the new immigrant minorities, but in 1968 Richard Nixon made an attempt to capture votes from some of the white ethnic groups with promises and appeals to these people and appointments of their members to office. His final choice for a vice-presidential running mate was reputedly between John Volpe, of Italian background, and Spiro Agnew, of Greek ancestry. He chose Agnew, but placed Volpe in his cabinet as Secretary of Transportation. Republicans also set up a nationalities division under the direction of Laszlo Pasztor, a Hungarian freedom fighter from the 1956 uprising. In 1971 the division, now called the National Republican Heritage Groups (Nationalities) Council, became a permanent part of the Republican Party. Its goals were "to attract the more than 40 million Americans of ethnic background to all levels of GOP activity; and to formalize the already substantial support among ethnic Americans for President Nixon's domestic and foreign policies." In 1997 and 1998, alarmed by Latino leaders' accusations that Republicans were hostile to newcomers from south of the border, Republican leaders softened their attacks on immigrants.

The largest celebration of ethnicity occurred in the summer of 1986 when the Statue of Liberty was rededicated. Amid a huge extravaganza in New York City's harbor, the nation heard numerous speeches about the blessings of immigration. Politicians were quick to identify with the nation's immigrant history and to join with organizations giving out medals to representatives of America's many ethnic groups.

The ethnic revival movements seemed to appeal most to those who believed that intellectuals, the government, and white elite groups (usually of old stock) were giving favors to blacks at their expense. Such supporters did not share in the bounties of upper middle-class America, but they had respect for the institutions of society and the traditional values of family solidarity, hard work, and patriotism. The inflation of ethnic awareness that began in the late 1960s aggravated their frustrations with ethnic as well as youthful protest groups of almost every variety, and they vented their anger against the most downtrodden minorities in society, especially Hispanics and blacks. They wanted politicians to be tough with criminals, demonstrators, and rioters. They were especially concerned about busing their children into different neighborhoods to promote integrated schools. The anti-integration movement sponsored by Alabama's Governor George Wallace's bid for the presidency in the 1960s appealed to this resentment, as did Frank Rizzo's law-and-order campaign for mayor of Philadelphia in 1971. Rizzo concentrated his efforts in white working-class neighborhoods. A police officer by occupation, he said that if elected he would not permit riots, marches, and demonstrations. He was elected, and his tenure in office was characterized by conflicts with Philadelphia's black population over affirmative action programs, charges of police brutality, and other racial issues.

After 1970 confrontations occurred not only in politics but also in the courts. Controversies arose over busing as well as quotas, affirmative action programs, and bilingualism, pitting white ethnic groups against blacks and Hispanics over jobs and coveted places in law and medical schools. The Bakke case in California in the late 1970s was one example. Alan Bakke, of Norwegian descent, sued for admission to University of California's medical school at the Davis campus on grounds that he had been denied admission even though he was more qualified than some blacks who had been admitted. His case, which he eventually won, was supported by some Jewish groups that had traditionally backed the civil rights movement. In 1980 Puerto Ricans and blacks found themselves opposed by Jewish, Italian, and Irish police—both men and women—in a court fight over hiring procedures in the New York City police department. In the 1990s in Texas several whites brought court cases against the state's law school alleging discrimination. California abolished its affirmative action program in higher education in 1996 and attempted to cut its bilingual programs in schools in 1998.

Not all ethnic political and legal fights were manifestations of white backlash. The Calumet Community Congress of Indiana, formed in 1970, tried to bring white ethnic groups and blacks together to deal with common problems. In Detroit, where many blacks and descendants of Poles lived, leaders of both groups organized the Black-Polish Conference in 1968 to work for their common interests. In 1971 the American Jewish Committee formed the National Project on Ethnic America to bridge the gap between whites and blacks. Its director said:

We have a black problem and we have a white reaction to it. You can't solve the one without solving the other. Civil rights gains have been stalemated in many parts of the North and Midwest because the groups who are resisting have been left out. . . . The task is to push whites off a strictly negative anti-black agenda. We have to make them conscious of their own realities. A new breed of ethnic leaders has to be developed who are as visible as the demagogues trying to exploit ethnic fears.

It was not the black movement alone that heightened awareness of ethnicity. The question of values after the 1960s also raised issues. Many descendants of the post-1880 European immigrants had been ardent proponents of American nationalism as professions of their loyalty. They were especially hostile to the Soviet Union and its policies of oppression in eastern Europe. They were perplexed and confused by the war in Vietnam and the divisiveness that it prompted. Appeals to loyalty touched them and their conception of America, and when they came under attack, they were somewhat bitter about the privileges accorded sons and daughters of the affluent, such as exemption from the draft for college students. In the confusion of the 1960s they, like so many other Americans, looked for security and a source of identity, and many found it in ethnicity. Ethnic identity was an answer for much of the alienation of the times.

The persistence of prejudice also serves to reinforce ethnicity. Although ethnic and racial prejudice declined after the 1940s, it has not been eradicated and probably never will be. Perhaps the outstanding reminder is its strength in the WASP country clubs and social clubs, which continue to be the bastions of corporate and economic power. Although Jews, Japanese, and other minorities find opportunities practically equal elsewhere, they cannot gain access to some private clubs. In the late 1980s civil rights laws and court decisions begin to challenge the restrictions of private clubs. The existence of prejudice reflects the frustrations of the descendants of earlier immigrants who are unwilling to tolerate differences in others.

On occasion prejudice becomes blatant. In 1979, letters to "Dear Abby," a syndicated columnist in newspapers from coast to coast, ran 200:1 against admitting into this country the Asian boat people, who were adrift at sea. Three correspondents exhibited the vilest character and the most incredible misunderstanding. A West Virginian asked, "Are we going to let overbreeding Asiatics take over our country? We should help them only if they agreed to be sterilized!" A waiter from El Paso wrote, "Let the Chinese go where they can get raw fish, rice, ride bicycles, live 20 in a room and smoke opium!" An Indiana resident expressed the belief that the Vietnamese "are bringing more diseases with them than we have cures for. I think it's a Communist plot to destroy this country!" These letter writers were especially vicious but not entirely unrepresentative of public opinion. Surveys indicated that most Americans were opposed to taking in refugees from Indochina. When Cubans began arriving in the spring of 1980, polls again revealed that substantial majorities of the population were opposed to letting them in. In May 1980 the Gallup organization reported that almost 35 percent of those questioned thought Cubans should be allowed to resettle in this country; 56 percent opposed the idea.

In 1980, reflecting a conservative and dangerous trend, both Republicans (in Michigan) and Democrats (in California) nominated avowed members of the Ku Klux Klan for seats in Congress. At the same time a right-wing group known as the Moral Majority claimed, without proof, that it had 60 million American followers. Its program called for the reintroduction of prayer in public schools, opposition to the Equal Rights Amendment, and denial of women's individual rights to decide on abortion. The Moral Majority, which has evolved into the Christian Coalition in the 1990s, contends that the United States is a *Christian* country that should be run by and for those who professed fundamentalist Christian values.

The bigotry and self-righteousness of some Americans also help to explain why a number of ethnic Americans still show great concern over occurrences overseas. Some believe that events in this country might force them to find havens elsewhere. Thus the civil war in Ireland from 1969 to 1998 was followed by many Irish Americans. American Greeks keep their eye on this country's policies toward Greece and Turkey, and Arabs are often deeply involved with the troubles in the Middle East because many of them are refugees who fled the constant fighting and violence there. Lebanese especially have tried to keep ties to their ravished land. In addition, like other ethnic groups, Arab Americans are sensitive to how they are portrayed in the media and American culture generally. They objected to, among other things, a record album that included a song, "Killing an Arab." Because they are divided into Christians and Muslims and come from several Middle Eastern countries, Arab Americans sometimes have different views. As a result they have not been effective in marshaling public opinion to support their concerns.

Following the 1967 Arab-Israeli war, Helen Haje, the daughter of Lebanese immigrants, helped organize the National Association of Arab Americans to bring them together and to work with other groups to improve the image of her fellow ethnics. One of the groups she reached out to was the Arab-American Anti-Discrimination Committee, which labored to convince the American public that Arabs were being blamed for all violence in the Middle East.

The director of the Arab-American Anti-Discrimination Committee stated in 1986, "It is a time of anti-Arab hysteria. Every time there is a terrorist attack any place in the world, we feel the repercussions in our neighborhoods."

After the Gulf War in 1991, about 25,000 Iraqi refugees came to the United States. They became alarmed at American threats to bomb Iraq in 1998. Many claimed that, although they had no sympathy for the Saddam Hussein regime, they could see no good in bombing their native land. Even the U.S. economic sanctions, which they claimed were hurting the people and not the present regime, were too harsh. The casualties of a bombing, one man insisted, "will only be the children of Iraq."

American Jews are no less interested in Middle Eastern affairs. The overwhelming majority have favored a friendly American policy toward Israel ever since that nation was created in 1948. The succession of conflicts between Arabs and Jews in the Middle East, such as the Suez adventure in 1956, the Six-Day War in 1967, the Yom Kippur War in 1973, and the Gulf War in 1991 involving Iraq drew lavish financial and moral support for Israelis from Jews throughout the world. The emotional tie of American Jews to all other Jews, which is strengthened by the memory of pogroms and of genocide in World War II, cannot be exaggerated. Most Jews share a deep conviction that Israel must survive and that all efforts must be made to ensure that survival. In addition to financial and moral support, therefore, American Jews have communicated their views to their political representatives in Washington. One significant foreign policy accomplishment, in fact, to which President Jimmy Carter pointed with pride in 1980, was the Camp David accords, in which the Israeli and Egyptian presidents agreed to terms that all three of them hoped would lead to peace in the Middle East. But that accomplished little more than cessation of Egyptian-Israeli hostilities. Then, in 1993, at Oslo, Norway, there were further agreements designed to promote a speedy peace in the Middle East. President Bill Clinton brought the leaders of the Israelis and Palestinians together in 1998 and forced them to negotiate additional concessions.

These issues keep ethnicity alive and blunt the pressures for complete Americanization and assimilation. But what of the future? Will religion remain important or will the nation become increasingly secular? Will national origins be the key issue? Will new Asian arrivals significantly affect the direction of our country in the twenty-first century? Will Hispanics add a distinctive Latin flavor to our culture? Will all newcomers follow the path of immigrants before them and blend into a uniquely American culture?

The agonies contemporary immigrants endure during the Americanization process were poignantly discussed in a 1987 article by Fakhruddin Ahmed, a

Rhodes Scholar from Bangladesh living in New York City. Movement into the mainstream of life in the United States, which took previous immigrant groups perhaps two or three generations, has been accelerated by American occupational, educational, and cultural activities. Ahmed pointed out how his career opportunities in this country kept his family in America and how dreams of returning home faded as the years passed. Unlike in his homeland, where parents decided the course of family action, in America

> The children will decide the issue. They will not like to hear about returning to an impoverished country. To the consternation of the parents, the children, who will not have experienced a second country, will start growing up like American kids. At school they may be subjected to blatant and subtle forms of racism. This they will try to counter by aiming to be superachievers.
>
> Parents will tell the kids they should not forget their heritage, stressing, for example, that they should speak Bengali at home and that if they are born to a Moslem family they should pray five times a day and refrain from eating pork or sipping alcoholic drinks. To that the children, who will probably understand Bengali but not speak it, may respond: "Spanish would be more relevant to us!"
>
> The coup de grace will usually be delivered by the adolescent daughter wanting to go out on a date. Parents will explain in great detail why it is not allowed in their culture and will insist that she meet, under strict supervision, only with Bangladeshi boys. Sometimes the girl will relent, on condition that it is a Bangladeshi boy born and brought up in the United States. More often, after her 18th birthday, the daughter will politely but firmly inform her parents that according to U.S. law they cannot interfere in her personal life and that, to avoid further conflict over the boyfriend, she is going to move in with him.
>
> The parents will be devastated. Doubts and questions flood in. The decision to stay begins to haunt them.

Many other immigrant parents have similar experiences today, or have had them in the past, and wonder whether the opportunities in America have been worth sacrificing traditional cultures. American society always seems to be, or to have been, too powerful a magnet for most people born in this country to resist. Fortunately or unfortunately, the goals of today's most vocal minority groups coincide with the demands of a majority of other Americans. Those who favor the retention of an ethnic way of life must ask what they can offer that would retard their children's absorption into the mainstream of American society. The forces undermining ethnicity—suburbanization, mass education, social mobility, growing tolerance, and an

American culture—are strong determinants that no large group in the past has been able to withstand indefinitely. It does not appear likely, therefore, that any minority culture, except for small and dedicated groups like the Amish in Pennsylvania and the Hutterites in the western part of the Dakotas and eastern Montana, can sustain its own cultural heritage for more than three or four generations.

Epilogue

A New Immigration Debate

THE RISE IN IMMIGRATION and its changing composition after 1970 renewed the ambivalence and even hostility that Americans felt toward immigrants. In 1997 Hispanics constituted 11 percent of the population, blacks 12 percent, Asians 4 percent, and whites 73 percent. Hispanics and Asians had been considerably fewer in 1940; indeed, Hispanics constituted only 6.4 percent of the population as late as 1980 and Asians only 1.5 percent. Moreover, given the rate of immigration, averaging about one million annually in the 1990s, and high birth rates among Latinos, projections suggested that by 2050 Hispanics would rise to 25 percent of the population and Asians to 8 percent. Blacks were predicted to grow only to 14 percent, while whites would shrink to a bare majority of the United States population. Sounding much like Theodore Roosevelt during World War I, Patrick J. Buchanan, the national politician most concerned publicly about immigration and the nation's demography, warned in 1994 that the United States was heading for social fragmentation: "If America is to survive as 'one nation, one people,' we need to call a timeout on immigration to assimilate the tens of millions who have lately arrived. . . . We need soon to bring down the curtain on this idea of hyphenated Americanism."

The sluggish economy of the late 1980s and early 1990s, especially in California, helped fuel Americans' fears about the economic effects of immigration. Yet the initial impetus for a new immigration debate and movement to restrict the number of newcomers came from environmentalists, who were dissatisfied that groups like the Sierra Club and Zero Population Growth did not take positions favoring cuts in the migrant flow. They believed that too many people were coming to America and that the country's natural resources could not sustain a population growing at such a rate. When they could not move the mainstream population and environmental organizations, they formed their own groups, the most notable being the Federation for American Immigration Reform (FAIR), which came into existence in 1979. FAIR had about 70,000 members at the end of the 1990s and offices in both Washington and Los Angeles. It also produced a cable TV program and lobbied Congress to change immigration laws. FAIR was followed by similar groups, such as the Carrying Capacity Network (CCN), Californians for Population Stabilization (CAPS), and Population-Environment Balance (Balance). Another restrictionist group, the American Immigration Control Foundation (AICF), was organized in 1983. While occasionally referring to the nation's resources, it concentrated on social issues. In the 1990s local restrictionist organizations appeared in California, Florida, Texas, Washington, Arizona, and Chicago. They paid attention to environmental issues, but they also expressed other fears about immigration.

The older nativist organizations, such as the American Legion and the Daughters of the American Revolution, played little role in renewed debates, as did the eugenicists. Recognizing that public racism had fallen into disrepute, the new restrictionists did not use racist arguments, which had been so common at the turn of the century, against recent immigrants. Moreover, the themes of anti-Catholicism and anti-Semitism were rarely heard, and religion as an issue was muted. Although perhaps 5 percent of the new immigrants were Muslims, restrictionists did not call much attention to this fact.

The new arguments for immigration restriction centered on environmental concerns, economics, faults of the present system, and assimilation issues. Those wanting greater restriction insisted that the nation was growing too large and farms were disappearing; they foresaw shortages of water, farmland, and other resources. Too many people meant too many automobiles on the highways and in cities and too much pollution. Americans have certainly been worried about the environment, and Congress has responded with laws to clean up the nation's water sources and air. But legislators have expressed little interest in the relationship between population driven by immigration and the environment. Thus the new nativists have pointed to other issues. They see a poorly run Immigration and Naturalization Service (INS), a porous border between the United States and Mexico, an asylum system being abused, the entrance of immigrant criminals and terrorists, and a Congress unwilling to allocate funds for an efficient system of immigration regulation. Many of these complaints have to do with undocumented immigration. On this issue the restrictionists have much public support; a spokesperson for the National Council of La Raza, who did not believe that legal immigration was too high, remarked, "We are all against illegal immigration." In 1986 Congress passed the Immigration Reform and Control Act (IRCA), which outlawed the employment of undocumented immigrants, but the act has not proven effective in controlling illegal immigration. Congress responded again in 1996 and enacted more controls; it also increased funds for border patrols. As for the other complaints about the immigration system, in the 1990s legislators tightened the rules for asylum and prompted the INS to deport more alien criminals.

Yet illegal immigration was not the sole problem for those wanting immigration reduced. After all, said FAIR, the tide of legal immigration was much higher than the illegal flow. Academics like Vernon Briggs, Jr. of Cornell University insisted that the new mass immigration had an adverse impact on the earnings of low-wage Americans, especially blacks who had not finished high school. Another economist, Donald Huddle, wrote that immigrants were using America's welfare programs without paying their fair share of the cost; the United States spent billions of dollars on them each year. These attacks were echoed by members of CCN, Balance, CAPS, and FAIR, but they did not go unanswered. The pro-immigration lobby, led by the National Immigration Forum, insisted that immigrants were benefiting the United States and that the nation should continue to welcome them. Economic studies were sometimes inconclusive; as a result they provided ammunition for both sides in the debate. Even a 1998 study published by the National Research Council, carried out by a group of distinguished economists for the National Academy of Sciences, did not end the dispute. In fact, both sides claimed that the report supported their view. Two Harvard economists, who were on the Council's panel of experts, felt compelled to set the record straight in an Op Ed article for *The New York Times*. The study, they insisted, demonstrated that immigration had both positive and negative economic impact and that people using the study to demonstrate only the good effects were failing to look at the whole picture. "Overall," they concluded, "the academy report is not a one-sided pro-immigration tract."

In 1994 California became the center of the economics-of-immigration debate. In that year local organizations sponsored Proposition 187, which denied government services to illegal aliens and required officials to report their names to the INS. Most benefits for illegal aliens had already been banned, but the most controversial aspect of the proposition prevented the education of illegal aliens. The Supreme Court had already held that such prohibitions were unconstitutional, but California voters ignored this decision when they approved Proposition 187 by a vote of 59 percent to 41 percent. However, a federal judge enjoined it from being put into law because of the prior Supreme Court decision. In 1998 the judge repeated her decision, and Proposition 187 was virtually dead.

Besides emphasizing economic issues, many new restrictionists insisted that the new immigrants had values so different from those of native-born European Americans that the nation was heading for social fragmentation and conflict. These critics were especially alarmed by Hispanics arriving in large numbers. They talked of an immigration invasion or disaster and wished immigration would return to the low numbers of the 1950s, with Europeans dominating the flow. If changes were not made, the United States would continue on its "Path to National Suicide." They also attacked bilingual education programs and bilingual ballots, which they said retarded the process of assimilation. Others argued that language was the glue for American civilization, and they wanted to make English the nation's official language. US English, organized by Dr. John Tanton, who was also prominent in founding FAIR, was formed in 1983 to achieve this goal. Twenty-three states adopted laws or propositions saying English was their official language, but these were mainly symbolic gestures and Congress generally ignored the issue. Of course, not all supporters of US English were restrictionists. Newt Gingrich of Georgia, the Speaker of the House of Representatives in the mid-1990s, supported an amendment to the Constitution making English the official language, but he also opposed cuts in immigration.

Buoyed by the vote on Proposition 187, the Republican congressional victories in the 1994 elections, and public opinion polls indicating doubts about immigration, those who wanted substantial cuts in immigration looked to Congress in early 1995 to make changes. Yet they immediately confronted problems. Although Republicans indicated more willingness to reduce immigration than did Democrats, many Republican members approved of current immigration numbers. Some were probusiness and wanted to be able to import laborers, both low-wage unskilled migrants and those with high-tech educations. Other Republicans were unwilling to cut immigration because most newcomers entered under the family preferences of the current system, and these legislators believed that such immigrants had strong family values. Still other politicians did not want additional rules and regulations to burden employers.

Many Democrats agreed with these arguments. In addition, they represented the groups that had used the current system to come to America; obviously cuts were undesirable to these legislators and organizations. The fact that many Democrats and Republicans agreed that cuts were not necessary shows what strange bedfellows the politics of immigration has thrown together. The American Civil Liberties Union worked with the National Rifle Association, both opposing proposals for national identity cards. Advocates of a "loose border" brought together Hispanic groups and the *Wall Street Journal*, which on two occasions came out for an amendment to the constitution saying that "there shall be no borders." The Christian Coalition joined them, saying that family unification was good for America. Low-income blacks probably felt the adverse impact of immigration more than any other group, but African American legislators in Congress worked with the Hispanic Caucus on many issues, including immigration. In this case both groups opposed cuts.

Congress finally passed two laws affecting immigration in late summer 1996. The legislators did not reduce the numbers allowed entry, but instead placed tougher restrictions on asylum and illegal immigration. The INS was given additional agents and funding, but in general, anti-immigration forces experienced defeat. Dan Stein, the head of FAIR, explained in an open letter to the American people: "Your hopes of reining in uncontrolled immigration were dashed this spring—Congress gutted the long-anticipated Immigration Reform Bill . . . in the end, Congress sold out to the special interests."

More serious for immigrants, current and future, were the 1996 cuts in welfare. Congress eliminated Supplementary Security Income and food stamps for immigrants and gave states more control over what benefits immigrants might receive. Congressional opponents of welfare change and President Bill Clinton immediately worked to undo these cuts, insisting that they were too harsh. In addition, Republican governors suddenly realized that their states would be pressured to pick up the tab when the federal government was no longer willing to support immigrants. As a result, in 1998 Congress restored some benefits and states moved to fill gaps for those immigrants who had entered before the original legislation had passed in 1996.

There was another way for immigrants to remain eligible for federal programs: to become citizens. The Clinton administration had already been encouraging immigrants to identify more closely with the United States by applying for citizenship; then Proposition 187 and congressional proposals and cuts alarmed many newcomers. In 1990 only 250,000 of the newer immigrants had become citizens, but by 1996 the figure was over one million, with projections for still greater numbers ahead. In an effort to meet the demand for citizenship, the INS was overwhelmed and occasionally checked records haphazardly, thereby allowing individuals with criminal pasts to qualify. A number of private agencies aiding the INS proved to be poorly run. Republicans in Congress were annoyed by reports of loose regulations and careless practices, and some pointed to the fact that new Hispanic citizens voted overwhelmingly for Clinton and the Democrats. Moreover, critics of the speeded-up citizenship process said, the beneficiaries did not really accept American values; rather, the new citizens simply wanted to be eligible for federal welfare programs. Responding to this criticism, in 1998 INS began to tighten procedures.

The defeat of more radical proposals and the booming economy of the late 1990s combined to dash the hopes of those who wanted substantial changes in immigration policy. They still looked to the future and insisted that America must reduce the number of newcomers. While their "reforms" were temporarily sidetracked, immigration debates waxed and waned. The 1996 laws were merely the latest round; in the future there would no doubt be similar debates. In a nation with a long history of immigration—with 65 million people having come since 1820—this topic could not remain permanently on the back burner.

How Americans define themselves is in part an immigration issue; the demographic changes the nation was experiencing as the twenty-first century dawned were part of an ongoing process. In the past, anti-immigrationists raised alarms about the changes around them, and most of their worries turned out to be groundless. There is little evidence that the newest immigrants will not assimilate. To be sure, the European component of the population was shrinking, but with so much ethnic and racial mixing occurring, who could predict what the amalgam of Americans would be in the middle of the next century? In any case, the great diversity of the American people makes it a more cosmopolitan and vibrant nation—a place of such sparkle, energy, and creativity that it remains, warts and all, the country to which so many still want to emigrate.

Bibliographic Essay

THE FIRST POINT of departure for those interested in reading further should be Elliott Robert Barkan, ed., *A Nation of Peoples: A Sourcebook on America's Multicultural Heritage* (Westport, CT: Greenwood, 1999). It includes twenty-seven original essays on different ethnic groups in the United States and reflects the latest scholarship. Also worthwhile is Stephan Thernstrom, ed., *Harvard Encyclopedia of American Ethnic Groups* (Cambridge: Harvard University Press, 1980). It is at once scholarly and informative, covering every ethnic group from Acadians to Zoroastrians. It has maps, charts, statistics, and topical coverage as well. Moreover, many of the state and local historical journals, especially those in the Midwest and the West, have published numerous articles on the ethnic heritage of the people within their states.

There are several texts on ethnics. Maldwyn Allen Jones, *American Immigration** (2nd edition; Chicago: University of Chicago Press, 1990), is good through the nineteenth century. Roger Daniels, *Coming to America** (New York: HarperCollins, 1990) is broader in scope and extremely sympathetic in its treatment of Asian minorities. An older and somewhat biased factual account that pays too little attention to Asian and Latin American immigrants is Carl Wittke, *We Who Built America** (2nd edition; Cleveland: Press of Western Reserve University, 1964). Jay Dolan's *The American Catholic Experience* (Garden City, NY: Doubleday and Co., 1985) gives broad insights into the lives of a variety of people, especially the Irish. One work on immigration to urban America is John Bodnar, *The Transplanted: A History of Immigrants in Urban America** (Bloomington: Indiana University Press, 1985). For immigrants in New York City, the home of so many American newcomers, see Frederick M. Binder and David M. Reimers, *All the Nations Under Heaven: An Ethnic and Racial History of New York City** (New York: Columbia University Press, 1995). Elliott Barkan surveys recent immigration in *And Still They Come: Immigrants in American Society, 1920 to the 1990s** (Wheeling, IL: Harlan Davidson, 1996).

The literature on immigrant women has flourished in recent years, but the reader should begin with Donna Gabaccia, *From the Other Side: Women,*

*Titles available in paperback.

Gender, and Immigrant Life in the U.S. (Bloomington: Indiana University Press, 1994). Also worth going through is Maxine Schwartz Seller, *Immigrant Women* (2nd edition; Albany: State University of New York Press, 1994).

For the colonial era the reader might start with Bernard Bailyn's *Voyages to the West* (New York: Knopf, 1986), then use some of the following studies, most of which include bibliographic suggestions. Another vivid account of early English migration is David Fischer, *Albion's Seed: Four British Folkways in America* (New York: Oxford University Press, 1989). James G. Leyburn, *The Scotch-Irish: A Social History* (Chapel Hill: University of North Carolina Press, 1962) and Aaron Spencer Fogelman, *Hopeful Journeys: German Immigration, Settlement, and Political Culture in Colonial America, 1717–1775* (Philadelphia: University of Pennsylvania Press, 1996) are good on two important non-English groups. For the Scots, consult David Dobson, *Scottish Emigration to Colonial America, 1607–1785* (Athens: University of Georgia Press, 1994) and Ned C. Landsman, *Scotland and Its First American Colony, 1683–1765* (Princeton: Princeton University Press, 1985). For the Huguenots, John Butler, *The Huguenots in America* (Cambridge: Harvard University Press, 1983) is superior, but an earlier work is Arthur Henry Hirsch, *The Huguenots of Colonial South Carolina* (Durham: Duke University Press, 1928). For immigration policies in colonial America, see Marilyn C. Baseler, *"Asylum for Mankind": America, 1607–1800* (Ithaca: Cornell University Press, 1998).

Additional information about the Germans after 1789 can be found in John A. Hawgood, *The Tragedy of German America* (New York: Putnam, 1940); Stanley Nadel, *Little Germany: Ethnicity, Religion, and Class in New York City, 1845–1880* (Urbana: University of Illinois Press, 1990); Dorothee Schneider, *Trade Unions and Community: The German Working Class in New York City* (Urbana: University of Illinois Press, 1994); Bruce Levine, *The Spirit of 1848: German Immigrants, Labor Conflict, and the Coming of the Civil War* (Urbana: University of Illinois Press, 1992); Walter Struve, *Germans of Texas: Commerce, Migration and Culture in the Days of the Lone Star Republic* (Austin: University of Texas Press, 1996); and Kathleen Neils Conzen, *Immigrant Milwaukee, 1836–1860: Accommodation and Community in a Frontier City* (Cambridge: Harvard University Press, 1976). For German women see Linda S. Pickle, *Contented Among Strangers: Rural German-Speaking Women and Their Families in the Nineteenth-Century Midwest* (Urbana: University of Illinois Press, 1996). For the crisis of German Americans during World War I, see Frederick Luebke, *Bonds of Loyalty: German Americans and World War I* (De Kalb: Northern Illinois University Press, 1974).

Two outstanding works on the Irish in America are Kerby A. Miller, *Emi-*

*grants and Exiles: Ireland and the Irish Exodus to North America** (New York: Oxford University Press, 1985) and Hasia Diner, *Erin's Daughters in America** (Baltimore: Johns Hopkins University Press, 1983). Oscar Handlin, *Boston's Immigrants* (revised and enlarged edition; New York: Atheneum, 1968), may be the best chronicle of the Irish in Boston. For the first few decades of the nation's history consult David A. Wilson, *United Irishmen, United States: Immigrant Radicals in the Early Republic* (Ithaca: Cornell University Press, 1998). A good local study of Irish immigrants is David M. Emmons, *The Butte Irish: Class and Ethnicity in an American Mining Town, 1875–1925* (Urbana: University of Illinois Press, 1989). For the Irish in Boston politics see Thomas H. O'Connor, *The Boston Irish: A Political History* (Boston: Northeastern University Press, 1995).

Theodore Blegen, *Norwegian Migration to America* (Northfield, MN: Norwegian American Historical Association, 1940) and Jon Gjerde, *From Peasants to Farmers: The Migration from Balestrand, Norway to the Upper Middle West** (Cambridge, England: Cambridge University Press, 1985) are both first-rate analyses. Jon Gerdje has written another fine book, *The Minds of the West: Ethnocultural Evolution in the Rural Middle West, 1830–1917* (Chapel Hill: University of North Carolina Press, 1997). For urban Norwegians see Odd S. Lovoll, *A Century of Urban Life: The Norwegians in Chicago Before 1930* (Urbana: The Norwegian American Historical Society, 1988). David Mauk, *The Colony That Rose from the Sea* (Urbana: University of Illinois Press and the Norwegian American Historician Society, 1997) deals with Norwegians in Brooklyn, New York. For Swedes see Robert C. Ostergren, *A Community Transplanted: The Trans-Atlantic Experience of a Swedish Immigrant Settlement in the Upper Middle West, 1835–1915** (Madison: University of Wisconsin Press, 1988).

Since the 1960s Italians have benefited from renewed historical interest. Alexander DeConde, *Half Bitter, Half Sweet* (New York: Scribners, 1971); Richard Gambino, *Blood of My Blood** (New York: Doubleday, 1974); and John W. Briggs, *An Italian Passage: Immigrants to Three American Cities, 1890–1930* (New Haven: Yale University Press, 1978), are readable and insightful surveys. Three more specialized monographs include Donna R. Gabaccia, *From Italy to Elizabeth Street* (Albany: State University of New York Press, 1983); Deanna Paoli Gumina, *The Italians of San Francisco, 1850–1930* (New York: Center for Migration Studies, 1978); and Dino Cinel, *From Italy to San Francisco* (Stanford: Stanford University Press, 1982). Virginia Yans-McLaughlin, *Family and Community: Italian Immigrants in Buffalo, 1880–1930** (Ithaca: Cornell University Press, 1977) pays particular attention to the experience of women and children. An excellent study of Italians in Tampa, Florida is Gary R. Mormino and George E. Pozzetta, *The Immigrant World of Ybor City: Italians and the Neighbors in Tampa, 1885–1985** (Urbana: University of Illinois Press, 1987). For Italian women see Miriam Cohen, *Workshop to Office: Two Generations of Italian Women in New York City, 1900–1950** (Ithaca: Cornell University Press, 1993). Josef J. Barton, *Peasants and Strangers: Italians, Rumanians, and Slovaks in an American City, 1890–1950* (Cambridge: Harvard University Press, 1974) covers Italians from a comparative perspective.

There is an excellent five-volume history of American Jews edited by Henry A. Feingold and published by Johns Hopkins University Press in 1992. The volumes are Eli Faber, *A Time for Planting: The First Migration, 1654–1829**; Hasia Diner, *A Time for Gathering: The Second Migration, 1820–1880**; Gerald Sorin, *A Time for Building: The Third Migration, 1880–1920**; Henry L. Feingold, *A Time for Searching, 1920–1945**; and Edward S. Shapiro, *A Time for Healing: American Jewry Since World War II**. Howard M. Sachar, *A History of the Jews in America* (New York: Knopf, 1992) is a seminal history, as is Gerald Sorin's shorter synopsis, *Tradition Transformed: The Jewish Experience in America* (Baltimore: Johns Hopkins University Press, 1997). For an excellent study of Jews in a small city see Ewa Morawska, *Insecure Prosperity: Small-Town Jews in Industrial America, 1890–1940* (Princeton: Princeton University Press, 1996). For New York City see Daniel Soyer, *Jewish Immigrant Associations and American Identity in New York, 1880–1939* (Cambridge: Harvard University Press, 1997). Jewish migration to Los Angeles and Miami after World War II is covered in Deborah Dash Moore, *To the Golden Cities: Pursuing the American Jewish Dream in Miami and L.A.* (New York: The Free Press, 1994). One history of American anti-Semitism is Leonard Dinnerstein, *Antisemitism in America** (New York: Oxford University Press, 1994).

Paula Hyman and Deborah Dash Moore have put together a marvelous collection, *Jewish Women in America: A Historical Encyclopedia* (two volumes; New York: Routledge, 1998). An excellent book on Jewish women is Susan A. Glenn, *Daughters of the Shtetl: Life and Labor in the Immigrant Generation** (Ithaca: Cornell University Press, 1990). Another work on Jewish women is Sydney S. Weinberg, *World of Our Mothers** (Chapel Hill: University of North Carolina Press, 1988).

The east central European Slavs have found a brilliant historian to analyze their culture and experiences both in Europe and America—Ewa Morawska. Her study of Slavs in Johnstown, Pennsylvania, *For Bread with Butter* (Cambridge, England: Cambridge University Press, 1985), is much broader in its insights than the subject might suggest and certainly ranks with Oscar Handlin's *Boston's Immigrants* as one of the best works ever written about American ethnic groups.

For other books on immigrants from central and eastern Europe, see John

J. Bukowczyk, *And My Children Did Not Know Me: A History of Polish-Americans** (Bloomington: Indiana University Press, 1987) and Dominic A. Pacyga, *Polish Immigrants and Industrial Chicago: Workers on the South Side, 1880–1922* (Columbus: Ohio State University Press, 1991). See also Theodore Saloutos, *The Greeks in the United States* (Cambridge: Harvard University Press, 1965); Charles C. Moskos, Jr., *Greek Americans: Struggles and Success** (Englewood Cliffs, N.J.: Prentice-Hall, 1980). Other works covering eastern Europeans are June Alexander, *The Immigrant Church and Community: Pittsburgh's Slovak Catholics and Lutherans, 1880–1915* (Pittsburgh: University of Pittsburgh Press, 1987) and John Bodnar's excellent *Immigration and Industrialization: Ethnicity in an American Mill Town, 1870–1940* (Pittsburgh: University of Pittsburgh Press, 1977).

Treatments of other groups include William A. Douglass and Jon Bilbao, *Amerikanuak: The Basques in the New World* (Reno: University of Nevada Press, 1975); Alix Naff, *Becoming American: The Early Arab Immigrant Experience* (Carbondale: Southern Illinois University Press, 1985); and Gregory Orfalea, *Before the Flames: A Quest for the History of Arab Americans* (Austin: University of Texas Press, 1988). Caribbean immigrants are covered in Irma Watkins-Owens, *Blood Relations: Caribbean Immigrants and the Harlem Community, 1900–1930** (Bloomington: Indiana University Press, 1996); Ransford W. Palmer, *Pilgrims from the Sun: West Indian Migration to America** (New York: Twayne, 1995); Winston James, *Holding Aloft the Banner of Ethiopia: Carribean Radicalism in Early Twentieth-Century America* (London: Verso, 1998); and Philip Kasinitz, *Caribbean New York: Black Immigrants and the Politics of Race** (Ithaca: Cornell University Press, 1992). Black immigrants are also the subject of Marilyn Halter, *Between Race and Ethnicity: Cape Verdean American Immigrants, 1860–1965** (Urbana: University of Illinois Press, 1993) and Michael Laguerre, *American Odyssey: Haitians in New York City** (Ithaca: Cornell University Press, 1984). For the latest newcomers to New York City and Los Angeles, see Roger Waldinger, *Still the Promised City? African-Americans and New Immigrants in Post-Industrial New York* (Cambridge: Harvard University Press, 1996) and Roger Waldinger and Mehdi Bozorgmehr, eds., *Ethnic Los Angeles** (New York: Russell Sage, 1996). Jacques Ducharme, *The Shadows of the Trees: The Story of French-Canadians in New England* (New York: Harper & Row, 1943) is dated. New studies are needed.

Writing about Asian Americans has been growing in recent years. The most readable introduction is Ronald Takaki, *Strangers from a Different Shore: A History of Asian Americans** (Boston: Little, Brown and Co., 1989), but see also Sucheng Chan, *Asian Americans: An Interpretive History** (Boston: Twayne, 1991); Roger Daniels, *Asian America: Chinese and Japanese in the*

United States Since 1850 (Seattle: University of Washington Press, 1988); and Jack Chen, *The Chinese of America: From the Beginnings to the Present** (New York: Harper and Row, 1981). A penetrating study of a suburban Chinese community is John Horton, *The Politics of Diversity: Immigration, Resistance, and Change in Monterey Park, California** (Philadelphia: Temple University Press, 1995). Urban Chinese are discussed in *Chinatown No More: Taiwan Immigrants in Contemporary New York** (Ithaca: Cornell University Press, 1992). For Chinese laundrymen see Renqui Yu, *To Save China, to Save Ourselves: The Chinese Hand Laundry Alliance of New York** (Philadelphia: Temple University Press, 1993). For undocumented Chinese immigrants see Peter Kwong, *Forbidden Workers: Illegal Chinese Immigrants and American Labor* (New York: The New Press, 1997).

Asian women are treated in Ellie Berthiaume Shukert and Barbara Schibetta, *War Brides of World War II* (Novato, CA: Presidio Press, 1998); Judy Yung, *Unbound Feet: A Social History of Chinese Women in San Francisco** (Berkeley: University of California Press, 1995); Huping Ling, *Surviving on the Gold Mountain: A History of Chinese American Women and Their Lives* (New York: State University Press of New York, 1998); and Nancy Brown Diggs, *Steel Butterflies: Japanese Women and the American Experience* (New York: State University Press of New York, 1998).

Other groups of Asians are dealt with in Paul James Rutledge, *The Vietnamese Experience in America* (Bloomington: Indiana University Press, 1992) and Valerie O'Connor, *The Indochina Refugee Dilemma* (Baton Rouge: Louisiana State University Press, 1990). Koreans are covered in Illsoo Kim, *New Urban Immigrants: The Korean Community in New York City* (Princeton: Princeton University Press, 1981); Nancy Abelman and John Lie, *Blue Dreams: Korean Americans and the Los Angeles Riots* (Cambridge: Harvard University Press, 1995); and Kyeyoung Park, *The Korean Dream: Immigrants and Small Business in New York City* (Ithaca: Cornell University Press, 1997). For Asian Indians see Parmatma Sara, *The Asian Indian Experience in the United States* (Cambridge, MA: Schenkman Books, Inc., 1985); Arthur and Usha M. Helweg, *An Indian Success Story: East Indians in America* (Philadelphia: Temple University Press, 1990); and Joan Jensen, *Passage from India: Asian Indian Immigrants in North America* (New Haven: Yale University Press, 1988). For the Japanese see John Modell, *The Economics and Politics of Racial Accommodation: The Japanese of Los Angeles, 1900–1942* (Urbana: University of Illinois Press, 1977) and Paul Spicard, *Japanese Americans: The Formation and Transformation of an Ethnic Group* (New York: Twayne, 1996). For anti-Japanese sentiment see two books by Roger Daniels, *The Politics of Prejudice** (New York: Atheneum, 1968) and *Prisoners Without Trial: Japanese Americans in World War II** (New York: Hill and Wang, 1993).

The easiest introduction to Mexican American history is through two quite readable surveys: Carey McWilliams, *North from Mexico** (New York: Greenwood Press, 1968) and Matt S. Meier and Feliciano Ribera, *Mexican Americans/American Mexicans: From Conquistadors to Chicanos** (New York: Hill and Wang, 1993). Monographs like Mark Reisler, *By the Sweat of Their Brow: Mexican Immigrant Labor in the United States, 1900–1940** (Westport, CT: Greenwood Press, 1976); Abraham Hoffman, *Unwanted Mexican Americans in the Great Depression: Repatriation Pressures, 1929–1939* (Tucson: University of Arizona Press, 1974); Albert Camarillo, *Chicanos in a Changing Society: From Mexican Pueblos to American Barrios in Santa Barbara and Southern California, 1848–1930** (Cambridge: Harvard University Press, 1979); and Juan Ramon Garcia, *Operation Wetback* (Westport, CT: Greenwood Press, 1980), are excellent. Garcia's most recent book is *Mexicans in the Midwest* (Tucson: University of Arizona Press, 1996). Thomas Muller and Thomas J. Espenshade, *The Fourth Wave: California's Newest Immigrants** (Washington, DC: The Urban Institute, 1985) and Silvia Pedraza-Bailey, *Political and Economic Migrants in America* (Austin: University of Texas Press, 1985) discuss Mexicans and Cubans in the United States. Additional works on Mexicans are Peter Skerry, *Mexican Americans: The Ambivalent Minority** (New York: The Free Press, 1993); George Sanchez, *Becoming Mexican American: Ethnicity, Culture and Identity in Chicano Los Angeles, 1900–1945** (New York: Oxford University Press, 1993); Douglas Monroy, *Thrown Among Strangers: The Making of Mexican Culture in Frontier California* (Berkeley: University of California Press, 1991); and David G. Gutierrez, *Walls and Mirrors: Mexican Americans, Mexican Immigrants, and the Politics of Ethnicity** (Berkeley: University of California Press, 1995). A fascinating book is Karen Isaksen Leonard, *Making Ethnic Choices: California's Punjabi Mexican Americans* (Philadelphia: Temple University Press, 1992).

For Mexican American women see Sarah Deutsch, *No Separate Refuge: Culture, Class, and Gender on an Anglo-Hispanic Frontier in the American Southwest, 1880–1940** (New York: Oxford University Press, 1987) and two books by Vicki Ruiz: *Cannery Women, Cannery Lives: Mexican American Women, Unionization, and the California Food Processing Industry, 1939–1950** (Albuquerque: University of New Mexico Press, 1987) and *From Out of the Shadows: Mexican Women in Twentieth-Century America* (New York: Oxford University Press, 1997).

For Cubans see James S. Olson and Judith E. Olson, *Cuban-Americans: From Trauma to Triumph* (New York: Twayne Publishers, 1995); Maria Cristina Garcia, *Havana USA: Cuban Exiles and Cuban Americans in South Florida, 1959–1994* (Berkeley: University of California Press, 1996); Silvia Pedraza, *Political and Economic Migrants in America* (Austin: University of

214   Bibliographic Essay

Texas Press, 1985); and Robert Masud-Piloto, *From Welcomed Exiles to Illegal Immigrants: Cuban Migration to the United States, 1959–1995* (Lanham, MD: Rowman & Littlefield, 1996). Cubans and other Hispanics in Miami are covered in Alejandro Portes and Alex Stepick, *City on the Edge: The Transformation of Miami** (Berkeley: University of California Press, 1993). Central Americans are treated in Sarah J. Mahler, *America Dreaming: Immigrant Life on the Margins** (Princeton: Princeton University Press, 1995). Virginia Sanchez Korrol, *From Colonia to Community: The History of Puerto Ricans in New York City* (Berkeley: University of California Press, 1994) covers Puerto Ricans. Sherri Grasmuck and Patricia Pessar, *Between Two Islands: Dominican International Migration** (Berkeley: University of California Press, 1991) focuses on Dominicans in the United States.

For nativism and immigration restriction the standard work is John Higham, *Strangers in the Land: Patterns of American Nativism, 1860–1925** (New Brunswick: Rutgers University Press, 1988). Attitudes toward immigrants and disease are covered in Alan Kraut, *Silent Travelers: Germs, Genes, and the "Immigrant Menace"** (New York: Basic Books, 1994). Nineteenth-century nativism is treated in Tyler Anbinder, *Nativism and the Slavery: The Northern Know-Nothings and the Politics of the 1850s** (New York: Oxford University Press, 1992) and Dale T. Knobel, *"America for the Americans": The Nativist Movement in the United States* (New York: Twayne, 1996). Also for the early nineteenth century see Ray A. Billington, *The Protestant Crusade, 1800–1860** (Chicago: Quadrangle Press, 1964). A general treatment is David Bennett, *The Party of Fear: From Nativist Movements to the New Right in American History** (Chapel Hill: University of North Carolina Press, 1988). The latest movement to restrict immigration is covered in David M. Reimers, *Unwelcome Strangers: American Identity and the Turn Against Immigration** (New York: Columbia University Press, 1998).

Robert Divine, *American Immigration Policy, 1924–1952* (New Haven: Yale University Press, 1957) is a good summary, but his analysis of the displaced persons act is contradicted by Leonard Dinnerstein, *America and the Survivors of the Holocaust: The Evolution of a United States Displaced Persons Policy 1945–1950** (New York: Columbia University Press, 1982). Post-World War II immigration to the United States is dealt with in considerable detail in David M. Reimers, *Still the Golden Door: The Third World Comes to America** (2nd edition; New York: Columbia University Press, 1992). Post-World War II refugee policy is discussed in Gil Loescher and John A. Scanlan, *Calculated Kindness: Refugees and America's Half-Open Door, 1945–Present* (New York: The Free Press, 1986).

A great deal about ethnic mobility can be found in the works on various groups already noted. In addition, Niles Carpenter, *Immigrants and Their Children 1920* (Washington, DC: Government Printing Office, 1927) and Edward Hutchinson, *Immigrants and Their Children 1850–1950* (New York: Wiley, 1956), both based on census data, are informative.

These collections of essays give a good deal of insight into ethnic families and their values: *Ethnic Families in America**, edited by Charles H. Mindel and Robert W. Haberstein (New York: Elsevier, 1976) and *Ethnic Chicago**, edited by Peter D'A. Jones and Melvin C. Holli (Grand Rapids, MI: Erdmans, 1981). Two books by Stephan Thernstrom are useful: *The Other Bostonians: Poverty and Progress in the American Metropolis 1880–1970** (Cambridge: Harvard University Press, 1973) and *Poverty and Progress: Social Mobility in a Nineteenth-Century American City** (Cambridge: Harvard University Press, 1964). Guillermina Jasso and Mark R. Rosenzweig, *The New Chosen People: Immigrants in the United States* (New York: Russell Sage, 1990) contains a wealth of information about assimilation and the economics of immigration, as do Alejandro Portes and Ruben G. Rumbaut, *Immigrant America: A Portrait** (2nd edition; Berkeley: University of California Press, 1995) and Ivan Light and Carolyn Rosenstein, *Race, Ethnicity, and Entrepreneurship in Urban America** (New York: Aldine de Gruyter, 1995). Patterns of immigration, mobility, and assimilation in the twentieth century are discussed in Reed Ueda, *Postwar Immigrant America: A Social History** (New York: St. Martins, 1994). Additional information on these subjects can be found in John Isbister, *The Immigration Debate** (West Hartford, CT: The Kumarian Press, 1996) and Thomas Espenshade, ed., *Keys to Successful Immigration** (Washington, DC: The Urban Institute, 1997).

On the subject of assimilation, Milton Gordon, *Assimilation in American Life: The Role of Race, Religion, and National Origins** (New York: Oxford University Press, 1964) is a good beginning. Although Gordon's conclusions are open to criticism, his work is basic. Andrew Greeley, *Why Can't They Be Like Us?** (New York: Dutton, 1972) is lively and worth reading, as is Nathan Glazer and Daniel Moynihan, *Beyond the Melting Pot: The Negroes, Puerto Ricans, Jews, Italians, and Irish of New York City** (2nd edition; Cambridge: Harvard University Press, 1970). Judith R. Kramer, *The American Minority Community* (New York: Crowell, 1970) is less stimulating but rewarding. A profitable study on white Protestants is Charles Anderson, *White Protestant Americans: From National Origins to Religious Group** (Englewood Cliffs, NJ: Prentice-Hall, 1970). Yonathan Shapiro, *Leadership of the American Zionist Organization, 1897–1930* (Urbana: University of Illinois Press, 1971) is about the Jews; Harold J. Abramson, *Ethnic Diversity in Catholic America* (New York: Wiley, 1973) is about the Catholics. Perry Wood, *The White Ethnic Movement and Ethnics Politics* (New York: Praeger, 1973) is good on the ethnic revival movements of the early 1970s. A provocative but not totally convincing argument against assimilation is presented by Michael Novak in *The Rise of the Unmeltable Ethnics** (New York: Macmillan, 1972).

A broad and suggestive introduction to ethnicity and assimilation is Lawrence Fuchs, *The American Kaleidoscope: Race, Ethnicity, and the Civic Culture** (Hanover: Wesleyan University Press, 1990). See also Stanley Lieberson and Mary C. Waters, *From Many Strands: Ethnic and Racial Groups in Contemporary America* (New York: Russell Sage, 1988). A new book on ethnic food and assimilation is Donna R. Gabaccia, *We Are What We Eat: Ethnic Food and the Making of Americans* (Cambridge: Harvard University Press, 1998).

Appendix

Table A.1 Immigration to the United States by Country for Decades 1820–1995

Country	1820	1821–1830	1831–1840	1841–1850	1851–1860	1861–1870
All countries	8,385	143,439	599,125	1,713,251	2,598,214	2,314,824
Europe	7,690	98,797	495,681	1,597,442	2,452,577	2,065,141
Austria-Hungary	—	—	—	—	—	7,800
Austria	NA	NA	NA	453,649	32,868	3,563
Hungary	NA	NA	NA	442,693	30,680	7,861
Belgium	1	27	22	5,074	4,738	6,734
Denmark	20	169	1,063	539	3,749	17,094
France	371	8,497	45,575	77,262	76,358	35,986
Germany	968	6,761	152,454	434,626	951,667	787,468
Great Britain (former UK)	2,410	25,079	75,810	267,044	423,974	606,896
England	1,782	14,055	7,611	32,092	247,125	222,277
Scotland	268	2,912	2,667	3,712	38,331	38,769
Wales	—	170	185	1,261	6,319	4,313
Northern Ireland	NA	NA	NA	NA	NA	NA
Not specified	360	7,942	65,347	229,979	132,199	341,537
Greece	—	20	49	16	31	72
Ireland	3,614	50,724	207,381	780,719	914,119	435,778
Italy	30	409	2,253	1,870	9,231	11,725
Netherlands	49	1,078	1,412	8,251	10,789	9,102
Norway–Sweden	3	91	1,201	13,903	20,931	109,298
Norway	NA	NA	NA	NA	NA	71,631
Sweden	NA	NA	NA	NA	NA	37,667
Poland	5	16	369	105	1,164	2,027
Portugal	35	145	829	550	1,055	2,658
Romania	—	—	—	—	—	—
Spain	139	2,477	2,125	2,209	9,298	6,697
Switzerland	31	3,226	4,821	4,644	25,011	23,286
U.S.S.R.	14	75	277	551	457	2,512
Yugoslavia	—	—	—	—	—	—
Other Europe	—	3	40	79	5	8
Asia	6	30	55	141	41,538	64,759
China	1	2	8	35	41,397	64,301
India	1	8	39	36	43	69
Israel	—	—	—	—	—	—
Japan	—	—	—	—	—	186
Turkey	1	20	7	59	83	131
Other Asia	3	—	1	11	15	72
America	387	11,564	33,424	62,469	74,720	166,607
Canada & Newfoundland	209	2,277	13,624	41,723	59,309	153,878
Mexico	1	4,817	6,599	3,271	3,078	2,191
Caribbean	164	3,834	12,301	13,528	10,660	9,046
Central America	2	105	44	368	449	95
South America	11	531	856	3,579	1,224	1,397
Other America	—	—	—	—	—	—
Africa	1	16	54	55	210	312
Australia & New Zealand	—	—	—	—	—	36
Pacific Islands (U.S. adm.)	—	—	—	—	—	—
Other	301	33,032	69,911	53,144	29,169	17,969

Notes: From 1820–1867, figures represent alien passengers arrived; from 1868–1891 and 1895–1897, immigrant aliens arrived; from 1892–1894 and 1898 to the present time, immigrant aliens admitted. Data for the years prior to 1906 relate to country whence alien came; data from 1906–1979 and 1984 are for country of last permanent residence; and data for 1980–1983 refer to country of birth. Because of changes in boundaries and changes in lists of countries, data for certain countries are not comparable throughout.

The periods covered are as follows: from 1820–1831 and 1843–1849, the fiscal years ended on September 30 of the respective year—fiscal year 1843 covers 9 months. From 1832–1842 and 1850–1867, fiscal years ended on December 31 of the respective year—fiscal years 1832 and 1850 cover 15 months. For 1868, the period ended on June 30 and covers 6 months. Fiscal years 1868–1976 ended on June 30 of the respective year. The transition quarter (TQ) for 1976 covers the 3-month period, July–September 1976.

SOURCE: U.S. IMMIGRATION AND NATURALIZATION SERVICE.

1871–1880	1881–1890	1891–1900	1901–1910	1911–1920	1921–1930	1931–1940
2,812,191	5,246,613	3,687,564	8,795,386	5,735,811	4,107,209	528,431
2,271,925	4,735,484	3,555,352	8,056,040	4,321,887	2,463,194	347,552
72,969	353,719	592,707	2,145,266	896,342	63,548	11,424
24,860	67,106	20,621	9,478	18,340	3,511	2,895
3,469	36,637	5,401	6,550	6,545	944	1,039
7,221	20,177	18,167	41,635	33,746	15,846	4,817
31,771	88,132	50,231	65,285	41,983	32,430	2,559
72,206	50,464	30,770	73,379	61,897	49,610	12,623
718,182	1,452,970	505,152	341,498	143,945	412,202	114,058
548,043	807,357	271,538	525,950	341,408	340,780	31,572
437,706	644,680	216,726	388,017	249,944	157,420	21,756
87,564	149,869	44,188	120,469	78,357	159,781	6,887
6,631	12,640	10,557	17,464	13,107	13,012	735
NA	NA	NA	NA	NA	10,567	2,194
16,142	168	67	—	—	—	—
210	2,308	15,979	167,519	184,201	51,084	9,119
436,871	655,482	388,416	339,065	146,181	210,024	10,973
55,759	307,309	651,893	2,045,877	1,109,524	455,315	68,028
16,541	53,701	26,758	48,262	43,718	26,948	7,150
211,245	568,362	321,281	440,039	161,469	165,780	8,700
95,323	391,776	226,266	249,534	95,074	97,249	3,960
115,922	176,586	95,015	190,505	66,395	68,531	4,740
12,970	51,806	96,720	—	4,813	227,734	17,026
14,082	16,978	27,508	69,149	89,732	29,994	3,329
11	6,348	12,750	53,008	13,311	67,646	3,871
5,266	4,419	8,731	27,935	68,611	28,958	3,258
28,293	81,988	31,179	34,922	23,091	29,676	5,512
39,284	213,282	505,290	1,597,306	921,201	61,742	1,356
—	—	—	—	1,888	49,064	5,835
1,001	682	122	665	8,111	22,983	2,361
124,180	69,942	74,862	323,543	247,236	112,059	16,081
123,201	61,711	14,799	20,605	21,278	29,907	4,928
163	269	68	4,713	2,082	1,886	496
—	—	—	—	—	—	—
149	2,270	25,942	129,797	83,837	33,462	1,948
404	3,782	30,425	157,369	134,066	33,824	1,065
243	1,910	3,628	11,059	5,973	12,980	7,644
404,044	426,967	38,972	361,888	1,143,671	1,516,716	160,037
383,640	393,304	3,311	179,226	742,185	924,515	108,527
5,162	1,913	971	49,642	219,004	459,287	22,319
13,957	29,042	33,066	107,548	123,424	74,899	15,502
157	404	549	8,192	17,159	15,769	5,861
1,128	2,304	1,075	17,280	41,899	42,215	7,803
—	—	—	—	—	31	25
358	857	350	7,368	8,443	6,286	1,750
9,886	7,017	2,740	11,975	12,348	8,299	2,231
1,028	5,557	1,225	1,049	1,079	427	780
790	789	14,063	33,523	1,147	228	—

Table A.1   Immigration to the United States by Country
for Decades 1820–1995 *(continued)*

Country	1941–1950	1951–1960	1961–1970	1971–1980	1981–90
All countries	1,035,039	2,515,479	3,321,677	4,493,314	7,338,062
Europe	621,124	1,325,727	1,123,492	800,368	761,550
Austria-Hungary	28,329	103,743	26,022	16,028	24,885
Austria	1,880	1,314	1,340	641,425	
Hungary	1,034	809	850	544,512	
Belgium	12,189	18,575	9,192	5,329	7,066
Denmark	5,393	10,984	9,201	4,439	5,370
France	38,809	51,121	45,237	25,069	32,353
Germany	226,578	477,765	190,796	74,414	91,961
Great Britain (former UK)	139,306	204,468	214,518	137,374	14,667
England	112,252	156,171	174,452	NA	NA
Scotland	16,131	32,854	29,849	NA	NA
Wales	3,209	2,589	2,052	NA	NA
Northern Ireland	7,714	8,970	7,469	NA	NA
Not specified	—	3,884	696	NA	NA
Greece	8,973	47,608	85,969	92,369	38,377
Ireland	19,789	48,362	32,966	11,490	31,969
Italy	57,661	185,491	214,111	129,368	67,254
Netherlands	14,860	52,277	30,606	10,492	12,238
Norway–Sweden	20,765	44,632	32,600	10,472	15,182
Norway	10,665	22,935	15,484	3,941	4,164
Sweden	10,100	21,697	17,116	6,531	11,018
Poland	7,571	9,985	53,539	37,234	83,252
Portugal	7,423	19,588	76,065	101,710	40,431
Romania	1,076	1,039	2,531	12,393	30,857
Spain	2,898	7,894	44,659	39,141	8,849
Switzerland	10,547	17,675	18,453	8,235	57,677
U.S.S.R.	548	671	2,465	38,961	20,433
Yugoslavia	1,576	8,225	20,381	30,540	18,762
Other Europe	3,447	14,706	10,908	9,287	15,532
Asia	32,360	153,249	427,642	1,588,178	2,738,157
China	16,709	9,657	34,764	124,326	346,747
India	1,761	1,973	27,189	164,134	250,786
Israel	—	25,476	29,602	37,713	44,273
Japan	1,555	46,250	39,988	49,775	47,085
Turkey	798	3,519	10,142	13,399	23,233
Other Asia	11,537	66,374	285,957	1,198,831	2,026,033
America	354,804	996,944	1,716,374	1,982,529	3,615,225
Canada & Newfoundland	171,718	377,952	413,310	169,939	156,938
Mexico	60,589	299,811	453,937	640,294	1,655,843
Caribbean	49,725	123,091	470,213	741,126	872,057
Central America	21,665	44,751	101,330	134,640	468,088
South America	21,831	91,628	257,954	295,741	461,847
Other America	29,276	59,711	19,630	789	458
Africa	7,367	14,092	28,954	80,779	176,893
Australia & New Zealand	13,805	11,506	19,562	23,788	20,169
Pacific Islands (U.S. adm.)	5,437	1,470	1,769	1,806	21,041
Other	142	12,491	3,884	15,866	1,032

1991	1992	1993	1994	1995	TOTAL
1,827,167	973,977	904,292	804,416	720,461	62,224,327
146,671	153,260	165,711	166,279	132,914	37,865,858
4,455	3,934	2,914	2,123	2,190	4,358,398
701	957	776	621	694	214,305
629	769	762	639	588	373,799
3,978	4,492	3,959	3,592	3,178	806,786
10,887	12,875	9,965	8,940	7,896	7,134,028
16,768	21,924	20,422	17,666	14,207	5,069,181
NA	NA	NA	NA	NA	3,084,066
NA	NA	NA	NA	NA	812,608
NA	NA	NA	NA	NA	94,244
NA	NA	NA	NA	NA	36,914
NA	NA	NA	NA	NA	798,321
2,929	2,168	2,460	2,539	2,404	716,404
4,608	12,035	13,396	16,525	4,851	4,775,338
30,316	11,962	3,899	2,664	2,594	5,424,543
1,303	1,687	1,542	1,359	1,284	381,407
1,796	2,296	2,253	1,804	1,607	2,155,710
554	790	713	515	465	1,291,039
1,242	1,506	1,540	1,289	1,142	828,812
17,106	24,491	27,288	27,597	13,570	716,388
4,576	2,774	2,075	2,163	2,611	515,480
6,786	4,907	4,517	2,932	4,565	228,548
2,663	2,041	1,791	1,756	1,664	283,479
1,003	1,303	1,263	1,183	1,119	414,138
31,557	37,069	59,949	64,502	54,133	3,653,635
2,802	2,741	2,781	3,183	7,828	155,606
1,183	1,961	2,907	3,732	4,874	201,589
342,157	344,802	345,425	282,449	259,984	7,588,835
23,995	29,554	57,775	58,867	41,112	1,125,679
42,707	34,841	38,653	33,173	33,060	638,150
5,116	5,938	5,216	3,982	3,188	160,504
5,600	11,735	7,673	6,974	5,556	499,782
3,466	3,203	3,487	3,880	4,806	431,169
261,273	259,531	232,621	175,573	172,262	4,733,531
1,297,580	445,194	361,476	325,173	282,270	15,779,035
19,931	21,541	23,898	22,243	18,117	4,401,315
947,923	214,128	126,642	111,415	90,045	5,378,882
138,591	95,945	98,185	103,750	96,021	3,235,669
110,820	57,849	58,666	40,256	32,020	1,119,239
80,308	55,725	54,077	47,505	46,063	1,533,981
7	6	8	4	4	109,949
33,542	24,707	25,532	24,864	39,818	482,608
—	—	—	—	—	143,362
—	—	—	—	—	42,668
7,217	6,014	6,148	5,651	5,475	317,986

Table A.2   Provisions of the Major United States Immigration Laws
and Programs

1819	The federal government requires numeration of immigrants.
1864	Congress passes a law facilitating the importation of contract laborers.
1875	Congress passes the first federal restriction of immigration, prohibiting the importation of prostitutes and alien convicts.
1882	The Chinese Exclusion Act curbs the immigration of the Chinese.
1882	Congress excludes convicts, lunatics, idiots, and people likely to become public charges, and places a head tax on immigrants.
1885	The contract labor laws end.
1891	The federal government assumes the supervision of immigration and the next year opens Ellis Island.
1903	Congress expands the list of excluded immigrants to include polygamists, anarchists, and other radicals.
1907	Congress raises the head tax on immigrants and adds to the excluded list people with physical or mental defects that might affect their ability to earn a living, those with tuberculosis, and children unaccompanied by their parents.
1907	The United States and Japan make the Gentlemen's Agreement restricting immigration from Japan.
1917	Congress codifies previously excluded classes and includes a literacy test banning those over sixteen who cannot read some language. People escaping from religious persecution are exempt from the literacy test. The law also bans virtually all immigration from Asia.
1921	Congress sets a limit on European immigration of approximately 358,000. National quotas are instituted and based on a formula allowing each nation 3 percent of the foreign-born population of that nationality who lived here in 1910.
1924	Congress enacts the Johnson-Reed Act, setting the annual quota of each nationality at 2 percent of the number of foreign-born of that nationality resident in the United States according to the 1890 census. This quota is replaced in 1927 with the national origins provision, basing each nationality's quota on its proportion of the population according to the 1920 census. Proportions are based on a figure of 153,714 annually from Europe.
1924	The Oriental Exclusion Act bans immigration from Asia.

1930   President Herbert Hoover directs consuls to enforce strictly the provisions of the immigration acts barring "those likely to become a public charge."

1942   The United States and Mexico agree to the *bracero* program permitting temporary foreign laborers to work in the United States.

1943   Congress repeals the ban on Chinese immigration.

1945   Congress passes the War Brides Act facilitating the entry of alien wives, husbands, and children of members of the U.S. armed forces.

1948   Congress enacts the Displaced Persons Act allowing the entrance of 205,000 displaced persons in addition to those admitted under the annual quotas.

1950   Congress amends the Displaced Persons Act and adds to the numbers that may be admitted under its provisions.

1952   Congress passes the McCarran-Walter Immigration and Naturalization Act, which
—eliminates race as a bar to immigration and naturalization;
—reaffirms the national origins system but gives every nation a quota;
—provides for a more thorough screening of immigrants;
—establishes preferences for those with relatives in America or those with skills.

1953   Congress enacts the Refugee Relief Act authorizing the admission of special nonquota refugees.

1957   Congress passes the Refugee Escape Act liberalizing the McCarran-Walter Act and allowing more nonquota immigrants to enter.

1960   Congress passes the World Refugee Year Law permitting the entrance of additional refugees.

1962   Congress enacts the Migration and Refugee Assistance Act facilitating the admission of refugees.

1964   The United States and Mexico terminate the *bracero* program.

1965   Congress passes the Immigration Act of 1965, which
—abolishes the national origins system;
—establishes a limit of 170,000 from outside the Western Hemisphere and a limit of 20,000 from any one country;
—admits immigrants on a first-come, first-qualified basis;

—establishes preferences for close relatives as well as refugees and those with occupational skills needed in the United States;

—places a ceiling of 120,000 on immigration from the Western Hemisphere.

1976   Congress extends the 20,000 limit per country to the Western Hemisphere and establishes a modified preference system for the hemisphere.

1978   Congress establishes a single worldwide ceiling of 290,000 for the admission of immigrants and a uniform preference system.

1978   Congress creates a Select Commission on Immigration and Refugee Policy to study and evaluate existing immigration policy.

1980   Congress passes the Refugee Act of 1980, which

—increases the total annual immigration to 320,000;

—increases the number of refugees from 17,400 to 50,000 annually;

—defines "refugee" to include people from any part of the world, not just the Middle East or communist countries;

—creates the office of U.S. Coordinator for Refugee Affairs.

1986   Congress passes the Immigration Reform and Control Act, which

—prohibits employers from knowingly employing undocumented aliens;

—grants an amnesty to those who came illegally to the United States before 1982 and makes it possible for them to become resident aliens and U.S. citizens;

—provides for the admission of temporary farm workers.

1990   Congress passes the Immigration Act of 1990, which

—increases immigration (excluding refugees) to 700,000 until 1995 when it becomes 675,000. The limit can be exceeded;

—increases employment visas to 140,000 from 54,000;

—creates a new category for "diversity visas." Beginning in 1995 it provides for 55,000 visas annually.

1992   Congress passes the Chinese Student Protection Act, which permits Chinese students in the United States from June 1989 to April 1990 to adjust their status to become immigrants.

1996   Congress passes a new welfare law that limits some federal benefits for immigrants.

1996   Congress passes the Illegal Immigration Reform and Immigrant Responsibility Act, which

—authorizes new border fences and increases size of INS;

—tightens restrictions on illegal immigrants to make it easier to deport them;

—tightens procedures for asylum seekers;

—pilot programs for verification of immigration status for those seeking employment;

—makes sponsors of new immigrants more responsible for their welfare.

SOURCES: Edward P. Hutchison, *Legislative History of American Immigration Policy, 1798–1965* (Philadelphia: University of Pennsylvania Press, 1981); U.S. Congress, Senate, Committee on the Judiciary, *U.S. Immigration Law and Policy: 1952–1979*, report prepared by the Congressional Research Service, 96th Congress, 1st sess.; *Congressional Quarterly* (1980, 1986); and annual reports of INS for the 1990s.

Index

Bailyn, Bernard, 12
Bakke, Alan, 194
Bakke case, 194
Balance. *See* Population-Environment balance
Balkan peoples, 53, 86
Baltic countries, 19, 49, 99
Baltimore, Maryland, xi, 20, 33, 43, 54, 79–80, 122, 153, 175, 177, 193
Baltimore, Lord. *See* Calvert, George
Bangladesh, 198
Bangladeshis, 116, 198
Bank of America, 157, 165–166
Bank of Boston, 167
Barbadians, 121
Barnett Bank of Southern Florida, 146
Barrios, 137–138
Bartók, Béla, 91–92
Basque language, 71
Basque studies, 71, 190
Basques, 51–52, 54, 58, 71
Batista, Fulgencio, 145
Becerra, Xavier, 140
Belfast, Ireland, 3–4
Belgium, 89
Bell, Thomas, 59
Bellevue County, Washington, 107
Bellevue Hospital, 40
Bellow, Saul, 164
Bengali language, 198
Bengali newspapers, 113
Bengalis, 113
Beobachter (periodical), 71
Bergdoll, Erwin R., 180
Bergdoll, Grover Cleveland, 180
Bergen County, New Jersey, 106, 107
Berger, Victor, 156
Berkovich, Boris S., 162
Berlin, Germany, 49
Bernstein, Leonard, 164
Beverly Hills, California, 117
Bibb County, Alabama, 36
Bigotry, 50, 76–81, 83–86, 90–95, 98, 114–115, 120, 135, 138–139, 143–144, 158–

159, 161, 163, 170–171, 173, 178, 186, 191–192, 194–197, 202; *see also* Anti-Catholicism; Anti-Semitism; Discrimination; Nativism; Prejudice; Racism; Religious persecution; Xenophobia
Bikaben (newspaper), 71
Bilingual Education Act (1967), 126
Bilingualism, 126, 179–180, 182–185, 194, 203–204
Bismarck, Otto von, 23
Black Hand, 169
Black nationalist movement, 192
Black-Polish Conference (1968), 194
Blacks, 52, 62, 98, 111–112, 118–123, 176–178, 192–195, 201, 203–204; *see also* African Americans
Blackwell's Island (New York City), 40
Blaine, James G., 77
Board of Governors of the Federal Reserve System, 162
Boarding houses, 31
Boat people, 113, 115, 195–196
Boca Raton, Florida, 107
Bodegas, 144
Bohemian language, 81
Bohemians, 81
Boise, Idaho, 52, 71
Bolivar Street (Chicago), 70
Bolletino del Nevada (periodical), 71
Border patrol, 127–130, 134, 202
Borough Park (Brooklyn, New York), 177
Boston, Massachusetts, 2, 21–22, 30, 33, 37, 39–40, 42, 44, 54, 62–63, 77, 81, 107, 116, 122, 143, 151–152, 154, 159
Boston Red Sox, 176
Boston School Committee, 77
Boston's Brahmins, 154
Boulder, Colorado, 113
Bowers, Henry, 77
Boxer, Barbara, 162
Bracero Program, The (Craig), 131
Braceros, 125, 131–134, 138
Brademas, John, 167
Brahmins. *See* Boston's Brahmins